D1477128

The King of Ketu

'iyá ni wurá, babá ni digi.' *
Yoruba proverb

* mother is gold, father is glass

Other books in English by Antonio Olinto

The Water House
Theories and other poems

The King of Ketu

Antonio Olinto

Translated by Richard Chappell

REX COLLINGS
LONDON · 1987

First published in the United Kingdom by
Rex Collings Ltd
38 Kings Street, London WC2E 8JS

© Antonio Olinto 1987

Olinto, Antonio
The King of Ketu
I. Title II. Orei de Keto, *English*
869.3 (F) PQ9697.049
ISBN 0-86036-213-2

Printed and bound in Great Britain by
The Camelot Press, Southampton

Dedication

This book is Zora's
and the two of us dedicate it
to our friends Jorge Amado and Zélia Gattai Amado,
to Carybé and Nancy,
to Antonio Celestino,
Jorge, Carybé and Antonio being of
Oshosi, who is also called Odé –
to Pierre Verger, the Fatumbi,
to the oluoh, Agenor Miranda, priest of Ifá,
to Stella of Oshosi, Yialorisha of the Ile Opo Afonja,
in whom many of the traditions of Ketu
will merge.

KETU MARKET

Ojo Awo, day of the secret, day of Ifá and Eshu

I sing of the market woman as she sits on her wooden stool, setting out yams on a board with a basket of potatoes on the ground and green leaves in a corner while the scent of peppers from the next stall was mingling with the sun, I sing of her at the moment when she gathers her painted mat up, and once she had one with a colourful peacock but had learnt that it would bring her ill-luck, today's mat bears a lioness, not the male but the female instead, I sing of her on that dawning day as the adiré-seller is hanging out her bluish-indigo cloths at the entrance to the side-street and the calabash woman trudges past with her son strapped to her back, children run screaming by and a man dressed in green rides a bike through the middle of the stalls while from afar the woman hears a voice which says loudly: 'ku-joko', that's the greeting given to anyone sitting down, other 'ku-jokos' rise up from different sides as market day springs to life and a stark naked little boy stops in front of her, I sing of her at that encounter as she recalls her son and the days when she bore him on her back, without him her body is lighter, the son who was to be Alaketu or the king of Ketu, yet how could he have died so tiny when he was not even ill?, she had woken and started to clean up the stall and he had died amid the morning surrounded by shouting and bargaining, close by a man had been haggling, and a stallholder was bawling, a whole audience had followed it all with great mirth but as she put her hand on the little boy's chest she had felt it was cold and her cry had for a moment paralysed the market, I sing of her with that recollection in which she feels herself to be once more the mother of the king of Ketu, I sing of her at the start of her tale in Ketu, with the stalls stretching out across the market place and the calabash woman saying:

'Here comes that little one who steals your cassavas.'

She looked up and saw the man who would from time to time

come out with a potato stuffed away, he was in dark trousers and a torn shirt, the woman decided to throw a cloth over the cassavas and yams, the man stopped and sat down on her small stool:

'How's Abioná getting on?'

She looked at him without answering, her name was Abionan but there were people who said Abioná, the former smiled, she was called Abionan because she had been born on the road, she had been born out of doors as her mother had often told her, out on the road between Ketu and Opo Meta, mother had been warned by the babalao of Ifá not to go out a lot that week because he had sensed that the baby was about to be born, but gone out she had, she had pains half way along the road and sat down on the ground, other women had run up and carried her over by a tree, it was an old baobab without many leaves, mother opened her legs as she looked up at the sky where, as she would explain, two big white clouds, two clouds were passing by like elephants, as she watched the clouds she felt those pains growing, the women were pulling out the baby, an acid smell seemed to come from everything and when she raised her head she saw a body so tiny that it seemed not to be a person, shrunken with the umbilical cord dangling loose, one of the women shouted 'it's a girl', then mother rested back against the baobab, night was approaching, a babalao who lived nearby came to see the baby and said that it was born to rule, everyone knew that mother and father belonged to royal families of Ketu, and that from those families kings were drawn, from girlhood she had known that she would be the mother of an Alaketu, a king of Ketu, the mother had so often related the birth to her that she had treasured the words with which mother had described each instant of that beginning of life, one day she had wanted to know the exact spot so mother had taken her along the road from Ketu to Opo Meta, that was before she had become a market woman and a stallholder and she had stopped at the very spot and had the idea of imagining herself being born, recapturing what she as a baby must have felt on being born, arms in the air, body running in blood, the navel, the crying, the other women wiping off the blood and drying her, only the baobab had disappointed her for she had imagined it with more leaves, afterwards whenever she passed she would halt at the exact spot where she had been born, and when between the first and second market days she had to walk from Ketu to Opo Meta, she became used to seeing that stretch of road as her holy place, she had even

2

thought of buying it, which she would do in the future when she'd had another son, the king of Ketu, and put the money together for it, now Abionan looks at the man who was smiling, he had not yet taken a yam or a cassava from the stall and she turned to her neighbour to say:

'Just look, Yatundé, that little one likes me.'

'Not a bit of it. He just wants to take another cassava. There you go minding your own business not meddling in anyone else's life and along he comes and sits down on your stool without so much as a by your leave.'

The man quickly got up:

'Heavens, what hospitality. I'll go and have a chat in another stall.'

'Go on, then, go.'

The women all around laughed, this time the man left without cassavas and Abionan noticed a tall customer approaching with three marks on either cheek, he wanted two good-sized yams and argued the price, Abionan took her time and then agreed to a part of the discount that he seemed to be demanding, suddenly it was the busiest time of the day and the market surged up in one single clamour, you could hardly hear what was being said across the way, the sun was falling upon the hide and matting awnings, small children ran after each other and tussled and shouted and now and again bumped into a stallholder who would give the nearest child a shove:

'Get out of here, omokunrin.'

The sound of the Yoruba words crossed the air and Yatundé started getting a meal ready for her son, lit a fire underneath the trivet, warmed up a piece of meat, a customer was now coming up who Abionan knew, he only spoke French, it seemed that he had been an official in Porto Novo, but another customer popped up, then a third and a fourth and for quite a while she did nothing but serve customers, both men and women, some would say that Ketu women knew how to shop very well, they would obtain the lowest prices, argue the most agressively, Abionan loved to get into a war over prices but she would soon grow tired and lose interest, only when the other woman insulted her would she step forward and get angry, she had once spent two hours quarrelling over prices, people had gathered round to see the two women in the crisp, fast dialogue, today Abionan put her hands on her hips in the midst of an argu-

3

ment and refrained from pursuing it, the prices were holding steady too, there was a rate for everything, there had been at least one attempt to control prices, but no one controlled the stalls at a time when cassava was short and prices were going up, the smell of food became stronger, Abionan decided to go over to the cooked yam and smoked meat stall and she asked:

'Yatundé, look after my things, I'll be back in a moment.'

She went off to the right, saw the onion stall, after that the maize stall then the stall for flour and the one for engraved calabashes, small, large, long and round, it was a huge stall where many men worked, opposite was one for small calabashes that belonged to Francisca Pereira who was said to be a relative of old Mariana of the Water House, the Brazilian who had become a friend of Abionan's, she would make long stays at Mariana's house, both before and after Mariana's son, the president of Zorei, had been killed, Abionan, who felt sure that she would be the mother of a king, liked Mariana, the mother of a president, beyond that was the soap stall and the one for medicinal herbs, nearby was the tailor who took fittings and sewed out there in the market, a little farther on came the stalls for obis and orobos and for palm-oil, passing over to the lane there were the stalls for smoked meat, pork and lamb, cooked dishes, dried fish then across on to the motor road where there was a lot of traffic and it was dangerous for children there stood the stalls for ginger and palm-wine, cigarettes, bicycle parts, ornaments and earthenware pots and in addition there were medicine stalls run by the old nago women, pots and pans, tinware, coconut oil, bread, clothing and footwear, at the extreme left you could see the spot where the buyers and sellers who came in lorries met, Abionan stopped by the cooked yam and smoked meat stalls, after her son's death she had become known for talking little, she pointed to a piece of yam and the stallholder complained:

'Can't you speak, woman?'

She apologised, she was far away and thinking of other things, she was quite happy to talk but then a quarrel broke out over at the palm-wine stall and the stallholder remarked:

'Every market day this happens, they ought to ban palm-wine in the market.'

'That won't do any good, they'll only go and drink across the way, then come back and quarrel amongst us here.'

She bought a piece of meat and then came out eating yam and

4

meat, where would her husband be at that time?, she had not seen Ademola for weeks, she would never look for him and, since her son's death, she had not wanted to see him for months, one day he had come to the market, something he didn't usually do, and talked to her, he was wearing a pink and yellow robe very much in the old style, he looked fine and though she had never been interested in a man as a man, her mother would say that it was a family tradition that women should think only of producing two or three children and care for them, a man was of no importance. Ademola had looked fine that day, the first time he had come she had after a long conversation remarked in almost a whisper:

'Of the five royal families of Ketu, you belong to one, I to another. A son of ours could be king of Ketu, the Alaketu.'

He had laughed:

'That counts for nothing nowadays, Ketu's part of Dahomey now, or Benin, the king of Ketu doesn't rule like in the old days, he's a little king with merely a title.'

How could anyone really think that the king of Ketu had lost his importance?, Abionan tried to convince him and Ademola had ended by saying:

'If we're going to have a son together, I'll accept any idea.'

Where would he be today?, perhaps in Ketu, because he travelled little, she recalled the early days of their marriage, Abionan had recently arrived back from the Water House, coming full of thoughts about government and kings, about transforming Ketu into a once more decisive place in the region, and as mother of the king of Ketu she would also be able to rule and change things, Ademola's reaction was something to be countered and she had since learnt about King Sa who had built the city walls, in Ketu there were still descendents of the historians of the kingdom who knew the history of each king by heart, Abionan had heard the story of King Sa who had been a great sovereign and had changed Ketu, he had even been helped by two giants, Ajibodu and Oluwodu, supernatural characters sent by the gods to elevate the power of Ketu, Fatogum, the babalao, used to tell stories of the orishas to Abionan who would listen to them in silence, when she thought of the people of Abomey who had battled against Ketu she felt angry but now Ademola was saying that they were all one country today, yesterday Dahomey, today Benin, and that there was no reason for conflict between Ketu and Abomey, in the first weeks after their marriage they had talked a lot about such matters and it was hard for Ademola to realise that Abionan was wholly preoccupied with the idea of having a royal son, that she debated and reasoned with this one end in view and that when she had made up her mind to follow her mother's path and sell in four markets of Ketu all around, walking by night from one to the next, it was a final decision of one who wanted to lead the normal life of the district, selling the products of the earth and seeing the people of whom her son would one day be king, even after her son's death this aim had not changed just as if he had never died, having a son was easy anyway and the thought that the little boy's death had been caused deliberately never left her, she had still to avenge it and she gave a start when Yatundé grabbed her arm:

'I've made two sales for you, they wanted to take the yams anyway.'

'Thank you.'

She sat down on the stool, pulled out her skirt and tucked a good part of it between her legs, that her son had been killed she had no doubt, the little boy had spent the night at the house of their uncle Olaitan who himself scoffed at kingship, boasted of being a man who never worked and whiled his life away drinking beer in the living room, he was the brother of the father who was the side of the family in which she had no faith, that family did nothing at all except snoop on the business of everyone around and talk, obstruct and scheme but would Olaitan really have gone as far to kill a child merely because its mother wanted to make it king?, perhaps the uncle considered himself a claimant to the throne and so wished to avoid having a future rival?, in the evening the little boy had eaten at Olaitan's house and she recalled the uncle having given her son lots of food and sweets. After the death in the market and the still body in the bustling morning, Abionan had left her stall for several weeks, she had gone to Porto Novo, Whydah and visited old Mariana and spent long periods talking to her, they were not conversations like everyday, often they went hours without saying anything, the two women, one older and the other one younger, just looking out at the beach in the distance and the cemetery on the sand with the wind blowing up and coming through the house, there were photographs of President Sebastian Silva on the wall, and Abionan at one point inquired of the other woman whether an uncle would kill a nephew for a throne.

Mariana remained quiet for some minutes, her eyes on the cemetery in the sand, before saying:

'It's possible, yes. Lots of people kill for a job like that. The other day I was reading a book which talked about an Englishman who killed two nephews, he and the brother were fighting over the throne of England, he felt that the brother's sons were a danger and so he killed the little boys.'

After a pause:

'That was a long time ago, but today people still kill for a position of power, every day the papers have news of a death here, a death there, a president perhaps, or a minister, or else someone important is kidnapped – things are still done to get a place at the top.'

'But for a little boy who couldn't even walk it's a bit much.'

Old Mariana had fallen silent, the sound of the waves reached up to the room, those days at the Water House had been a convalescence, Abionan had come back to Ketu determined to push ahead with her plan of having a royal son and she approached the other uncle, her mother's brother, Obafemi, who was called the kingmaker and lived near the Alaketu, he knew a thing or two and had followed the deals made between the members of the five families in the choosing of two kings. Obafemi had said little but seemed to support and approve the woman's idea, at one point he had said:

'It's your dream of course, but it's a legitimate dream, after all you and your husband are from royal families.'

She started to say something and the other went on:

'What I don't understand is why you aren't fighting for your husband Ademola to be the king, when the throne falls vacant of course. Ademola is the right age but you'll have to wait a long while for your son to reach it.'

'He's not equal to it, a king has to learn to be a king from childhood.'

In the market now the time was nearing when business slackened off and gave people an urge to have a sleep, Abionan shut her eyes and dozed off for a few minutes, there were afternoons when she felt herself to be a part of the surrounding stalls, the market got into her nose and her skin, it was as if her whole body had welled out over the boards and the cassavas and drained off across the ground, she would then manage to recover and reconquer her faded body, absorb it back in again, master her arms and her legs, her hands and her fingers, train her eyes on ordinary objects and recognise each one as either a cloth, a leaf, a log, a yam, a trivet, a ceiling, a stone, a calabash, a cassava, or a mat, and from time to time she would like to go round the market and sit down by the holy tree which was called Ake's, she would have a nap there on the afternoons when there was no work too, she recalled having heard the story of the tree and how the inhabitants of Abeokuta, on the other side of the frontier in Nigeria, had made a pilgrimage to Ketu to pay homage to the tree and had taken cuttings from it which they had planted in the middle of the market at Abeokuta which Abionan had known in her childhood days, old Mariana said that Abeokuta was a holy city, her grandmother Ainá had been born there and Mariana would speak about her with respect, the old woman would tell of many very old things, about her days in Brazil, the place she came from, the journey with her mother, her grandfather and brothers, the period when she had lived in Bahia where Ainá sold in a market which Mariana held to be the same as Ketu's, afterwards came the sea voyage, the calm, the deaths, the arrival at Lagos, it was all a story that made Abionan forget her own life and her right hand now clutching her face as she thought, she would recall Fatogum lifting his arms and opening wide his eyes at the point where she recounted the Dahomeans' invasion of Abeokuta which had defended itself for days on end and drove out the men and women who formed their army, there were women fighting with more bravery than the men, then the Dahomeans from Abomey had destroyed Ketu and Abionan imagined the city without people, the houses without roofs, the lands deserted, and the gods abandoned, it had been necessary for Queen Ida to take charge of the reconstruction and in the now still market Abionan vows to herself that she will have a son to be king and make Ketu even more important, Yatundé's voice distracts her from her thoughts:

'Your husband was in the market this morning.'

'Here at my stall?'

'No. Over the other side where the lorries wait for the people who bring in the maize.'

'Did you see him yourself or was it someone else?'

'I did. I was going to visit my aunt who has a stall nearby when I saw Ademolá having a talk with the lorry men.'

She looked at Yatundé, for years they had worked side by side, they talked cheerfully, at times brightly, something would click between them and then they would break out in loud voices and make remarks about whatever came into their heads, then Abionan started thinking of the following, why on earth did people need to talk at such speed without really paying any attention to what the others were saying, just listening to the sound of voices, both their own and a lot of other people's too, Yatundé got the meal for her son and herself there on the spot and sold her peppers to a lengthy patter which was comical to hear and made everyone laugh, but now she was serious:

'The lorry men bought up the maize from the farmers before the stallholders could.'

'Why?' ·

'I was told that they want to create a shortage of maize in the market so that they can go and sell it in their stores at a much higher price.'

Abionan had heard that story before, at least no one was doing it with cassavas, yams or sweet potatoes yet, Yatundé seemed to read her thoughts as she said:

'They'll soon be doing the same with my peppers.'

Abionan prayed quietly to Eshu, she thought of Eshu-Elegba at Dangbo, she had been in Dangbo several times when she had been to Porto Novo and on her visits to old Mariana, Eshu had powers that no one could conceive of and it was necessary to make offerings to Eshu, she thought too of the 'iya kekere' of the market, the godmother who had a special altar and remembered the founder of Ketu market, for under the protection of Eshu and the godmother the market would survive, the stallholders would manage to defeat the threat from the lorries and it was of course necessary to make offerings to Oshosi and go to Ojubó-Odé, the Hunter's place of worship, and pray to the Hunter to protect the market and all within it, the plants, the roots and the beasts. Fatogum was in the way of telling tales of the orishas, he had one day talked of the Hunter and of the old kingdom of Ketu screened off by the bush, today there were no trees like in those days, the Hunter would leave his house and go off into the green depths, he would hunt animals with sharp fangs and once he had looked and seen that the wild animals had vanished into a small thicket beyond the river. He grabbed a branch of a tree, tore a creeper off another and made the sort of simple bow which he enjoyed making. A straight stick with a sharpened tip served as an arrow. The Hunter forded the river and ran along the path through the midst of the bush. Whenever he did this, more people from the villages left their houses and took to the trackways he had cleared. New villages arose farther away, yam was planted, hunting done in different country. Once, when the path had come to an end, he saw Oshun bathing. It was the loveliest thing to have appeared in Oshosi's life. He stayed there quite still, contemplating the water running off her arms. The animals were wild boar, they were now a long way off and the Hunter never thought of chasing after them. He was quite ashamed of his dirty state. He stank of a wild beast. He had bloodstains on his clothing, bits of leaves in his hair and animal hairs showed on his arrowhead. He followed the river downstream and went to bathe where he would not disturb Oshun or soil the water. He threw off the hides which clothed him, dived in near the edge and rubbed his hair. He wanted to be quite clean to go back to see Oshun. But he did not see 'he goddess for she had already left the river. For days and days the Hunter would return to the same spot until one day he went upstream and found Oshun beneath a waterfall. Oshosi was now dirty again with blood and leaves but Oshun liked him the way he was. They stood and looked at each other facing the waterfall and decided to live together:

'I didn't know that. Is it part of the story of Oshosi?'

At that Fatogum had smiled in his way and chuckled a little wrily:

'That was told me by another babalao. But I do make up tales too.'

'You make them up as well? That's all wrong.'

'I've always made them up. But when I cast for Ifá I don't, then I only tell the truth but ever since childhood, I have been making up stories about all the gods.'

'Didn't Oshun later on marry Shango?'

He chuckled again:

'Oshun is a goddess but she is a woman too.'

Abionan grew angry, for no man understood anything but she did like Fatogum and she also respected the fact that he was a very good seer, honest, concerned about people and wanting to be right in his forecasts, but the rest, Olaitan, Ademola, her father, none of them were worth a thing, only Fatogum and the son who was to come and be the king of Ketu were ones to rise above other men, perhaps

10

there were two other women, they talked a lot to start with and mentioned the names of people they knew, they talked of markets and towns, of births and deaths, then suddenly Abionan fell asleep and was to wake up only with the sun beating down on the wall, mother had been already all set to leave:

'Drink this goat's milk and let's get moving.'

They had walked on the whole of the next day, passed through Ipinle, and had their meal at Itajebu, mother hardly spoke at all, there were little birds that seemed to be following them, the child tripped on a stone and they had to stop as their weariness was getting too much, then late in the evening they reached a town which mother explained was called Sakete, she didn't see any dances or drums but the market was there, the lights shone in the night and they went to sleep late because mother couldn't trace the house of the relatives whom she knew lived in the place and they had to go round several streets until, in a complex of rooms like those in Ketu, there was a space for the mat and for sleep, this time there was no conversation but a dog was barking nearby and the child slept with the barking seemingly running right through her body.

The next day mother had been in no haste to resume the journey. They wandered round a lot of streets, ate bean cakes, dried fish and maize and when mother tugged her by the hand she thought that it was to make her step it out, but they went slowly, the roadway was now full and different from the others, with people in different clothes, she heard words she didn't know and mother explained:

'That's the language of the Fons.'

She saw girls with their breasts loose, women with tattooes on their tummies and breasts and sometimes on their legs, she noticed that mother seemed to have changed, her gaze was set and when they stopped to sit down by the roadside, people continued to go by, mother called to a man standing nearby and asked with that same gaze:

'What's that smell?'

'Smell?'

'Can't you smell it?'

'No.'

She seemed worried:

'Well I can. It's a different smell.'

The man had raised his nose, then after a moment's pause asked:

'Won't it be the salt-tang?'

Abionan didn't know that expression, nor did mother seem to, the man explained:

'That's the smell of the sea.'

'Is it near?'

He did a sum:

'One kilometre.'

Mother leant against a tree:

'Can we see it from here yet?'

'No. Not from here. Only if you climb to that hilltop.'

Aduke and Abionan had stood and looked at the hill, suddenly the child grew afraid, she sensed a fear such as she had never known before, she wanted to speak and she was afraid to speak, she looked at mother and observed that she too was afraid, minutes passed without a word, the traffic along the road seemed to be increasing and only much later did mother take her to a house where they found themselves a place to sleep, they slept without eating, all night long there was that smell, it came in from every side, it got into people's skin and the girl dreamt of the road, of that smell, and of dried fish, as she was looking at a hill and wanting to see the sea, but she could see nothing, she awoke in the middle of the night and smelt the smell, the following morning mother took Abionan's hand and in silence they retraced their route back to Sakete, they travelled quickly, mother didn't want to halt, she looked again for the road and they went on past Itajebu, it was late at night when they reached Pobe, they could scarcely see any lamps in the silent market they slept right there in the square and there was no longer the smell of the sea in their sleep.

Abionan was often to hear the word okan which meant sea or ocean, afterwards Fatogum would recite to the child, now nearly a girl, some lines by Ifá, the god of prophesy, the 'voice of the babalao' was solemn and his face serious, he uttered the words as if they dwelt in his breast and needed to come forth:

Iwaju okun

Okun ni won-on se

Eyin okun

Okun ni won-on se.

The face of the sea

is sea.

The back of the sea

is sea.

Fatogum explained without changing his tone that there were sacrifices and offerings which Ifá demanded should be made before the sea, on the beach or upon a hill, and once the people of Ido needed a king and went to ask the sea for one, the sea is the sea, those in the presence of the sea gain courage and strength and the sea has neither face nor bottom, no one sees the end of the sea and Abionan was sad that mother would not see the sea, after that journey it was hard to raise the subject and it was only much later when close to death that the sea would encroach upon Aduke as she lay on the beach in front of the Water House, Abionan felt guilty about seeing the sea which mother could not see, the first time she had stayed and stared for hours, she wanted to grasp every detail of waves and boats and the horizon, she had watched the gulls so as to find out why they were the birds of the sea, she had breathed the smell and was once again the child with mother leaning against the tree, the smell was now wafting in on the breeze and with the breeze it seemed to free her body of a burden, she had gone over to watch the activity of the fishermen from close to and gathered some shells from the ground, cleaning the bigger ones which she took to mother and the latter had heard the beginning of the sentence:

'Mother, I was on the beach. . .'

She had immediately interrupted what her daughter was going to say, never before had she been so gruff, almost furious:

'I don't want to know.'

'Mother, the sea. . .'

'I don't want to know.'

Abionan had been afraid to go on, mother was looking at the foot of an iroko, the tree rose powerfully upwards and she wanted to give her the shells but didn't know how, she dropped them on the ground by mother who looked at them for a long while, then stretched out her right hand and ran her fingers over the biggest shell, Abionan left her making that gesture fearing that mother would see that she had seen her, she had earlier thought that what was forbidden for mother might be forbidden for the daughter too, and she had consulted Ifá, wouldn't mother and daughter follow the same destiny?, Fatogum cast the cowries which were also from the sea, read her fortune and replied not, what was forbidden for the mother was not forbidden for the daughter but it would be necessary for her to place an offering before a river or a waterfall, Abionan prepared the constituents of the offering with the greatest of care, a handful of maize,

19

a sliced calabash, a palm leaf, a hen cut in two and nine obis all set down on the bank of a stream of water so that she felt free to see the sea and see the sea she did.

In the midst of the talk of the market women, evening is drawing in, Abionan now stops recalling her mother, to proceed with her plan it was necessary to visit Fatogum several times, perhaps he could see her today before setting out on the road to Opo Meta, Solange was now talking about organising a group of women to defend the market, to make a protest against the lorries, to discuss it all with the Alaketu and take the matter up with the government in Cotonou, Omitola concluded:

'What you want is a union.'

'All right then. We can't go on like this.'

Abionan pronounced:

'Why think of Cotonou? Everything can be settled through the Alaketu right here. There's absolutely no need to go to such lengths'.

Tomori interjected:

'There you go again with that idea that the king of Ketu will settle everything.'

But he really could resolve it, thought Abionan, but she didn't pursue the argument just then, the king of Ketu needed to win greater authority and she had to see Fatogum before leaving Ketu, maybe he would tell another made-up story or talk about Orunmila, the god of prophesy, she was mixed up over the names of Ifá and Orunmila, after all which one was the god?, Fatogum would explain with great patience that the two were one and the same person but that Orunmila might be the god and Ifá the name given to his power of prophesy, what was for sure was that Orunmila had no bones and was therefore weak requiring to be supported by Eshu who assisted him in everything, once he had spoken about the wife of death.

'Is death married?'

'Of course.'

'Why?'

'Everything in the world can be married to its opposite.'

Abionan thought and just before he went on:

'So death's a man?'

Fatogum informed her of the name of death's wife, it was Ojontarigi, and it had happened that Orunmila decided upon conquering the wife of death. He set out on the road thinking how best to abduct her. Death was married with a single wife, Ojontarigi and a lot of people were puzzled that death was monogamous, why shouldn't he have three or four wives just like everyone else?, Ifá told Orunmila that to please Ojontarigi, he would have to make a sacrifice. He explained quite clearly what needed to be bought and where the offerings should be placed. Orunmila followed Ifá's words to the letter. So that, when he arrived at death's house, he had little difficulty persuading Ojontarigi to go out with him and be his own. After that sacrifice there was not a single thing he was unable to achieve. Death learnt what had come about. He was in no doubt and took up a cudgel and went to kill Orunmila. When he arrived at Orunmila's house where he and Ojontarigi were together, death came upon Eshu who seemed to be sitting there quite by chance unless he was in fact minding the entrance. Eshu saw death coming and said:

'My greetings, death, dressed in your red apparel.'

Death stopped a minute to talk to Eshu, the latter wished to know the purpose of his visit.

'I've come to kill Orunmila who has abducted my wife. I'm going to kill him today, here and now.'

'Why the hurry? Let's sit down together and have something to eat.'

Eshu gave death something to drink and eat and he remained there eating and drinking quite contentedly. Once he had had his fill of all that there was, death took up his cudgel and rose, Eshu inquired:

'Where're you going?'

'I'm going into Orunmila's house.'

Then Eshu inquired very calmly:

'Would it be right to kill someone whose food we've just eaten? As you know all that food and that drink was Orunmila's. You can't kill him after having eaten his food.'

Death was put in a great dilemma, he was looking first to one side and then the other, he realised that there was neither a way out nor an answer to the words of Eshu who seemed very quietly to be awaiting a decision, death finally said:

'Do you know something? Tell Orunmila he can keep the wife.'

After the story, Fatogum had been smiling with his head half bent, studying the reaction of Abionan who said:

'There're several things wrong with that story.'

21

'What are they?'

'First, it's now Ifá who reads the future to Orunmila. They are one whole but they are two. So who after all is the prophet?'

Fatogum thought the question funny but said that the matter was quite clear and in no way mixed up, he went on to explain:

'Ifá is the system of prophecy while Orunmila is the individual who makes the prophecy. For anyone who doesn't understand how the system works it might all appear very complicated. In Ibadan, where I heard that story of Orunmila abducting death's wife, I met many people who couldn't distinguish Ifá from Orunmila. Even in Ketu there are people who don't see any difference between the two. What everyone wants is to know the future and few people bother themselves to find out the finer points of prophecy.'

Abionan listened attentively, then picked upon the story of Orunmila and death to say that she felt that it was after all right that death was a man, where was there anyone who thought that death was a woman?' Fatogum's voice had a serene note:

'Woman or man, it's all the same thing in life and death.'

Abionan had gone on talking:

'I don't like it that death lets his wife go so readily like that. He should at least have demanded his wife back.'

In the market now, Omitola is retelling the death of a cooked yam seller, it had happened two nights before, and the body had been taken to Ilara, today was not a day for witches and egunguns had not appeared in the market, as a child Abionan had been scared of the egunguns with their colourful clothes and their masks, she knew that they were the dead coming past for a second time, the dead moving around the stalls talking to people, or if they didn't talk making noises that seemed like words, when Abionan had married Ademola the two had followed through the whole tradition for on the morning after their wedding she had gone to the market to stock up for her husband's first meal and everyone knew what she was doing, the older stallholders were teasing her and made witty comments, Abionan had always lived in markets and been always sure that one day she like her mother would have a stall of her own, following the true path and selling at four different markets, it was the best way to put her son in touch with the people of the country right from early on and when she decided to take the necessary steps to have her own stall, she had spoken to the chief and had discussed it at home, the uncles were divided, Olaitan against, Obafemi in favour, her mother's elder sisters had backed the idea and one went as far as to say:

'The best thing for a female to do is work in the market.'

'And when you have a son it'll be better still,' added Obafemi.

The one who had settled the matter had been Fatogum, he had cast the holy chain with the eight pieces of metal, all that he could see in the pattern and positions of the chain was that Abionan might even be punished if she didn't go and work in the market, later at old Mariana's the girl had recounted what took place, the latter's comment had been curt and succinct:

'Market is freedom.'

As a child she had come to know markets in Nigeria and in Togo, she had started helping out her mother selling in them, now she made up her mind to spend some months visiting the markets of Whydah, Agua, Cotonou and Porto Novo and she had gone on as far as Abomey in spite of the anger she felt over Abomey having in the past conquered and destroyed Ketu, in Porto Novo she learnt to deal in various wares, first in little carvings of ibejes, twins, then she had been on a pepper stall, she had seen markets big and small, elaborate and plain, with roofs of matting and roofs of zinc or amaianthus, some were much dirtier than others, she got to know markets in Dangbo, Azonwirisse, Itakon, Ajara, Yoko, Affame, Igana, Alepe, Tantanoukon, Pobe, Aba, Holybol, she crossed the river and went as far as Zagnanado, and went over the border to see Nigerian markets, Atanka, Mekoh, Ilara, Atta, she had known many from her childhood when she would spend the whole day playing about in the market, chasing the drunks, seeing women arguing, there was a spell during which she had lived next to an enormous palm-wine stall, she learnt to spot the different types of drunks, there were those who talked to themselves, there were those who fought, there were the silent ones and they drank without stopping and just stared at things, these Abionan found the saddest, there were those who wouldn't leave women alone, there was one who would strip his clothes off and go about naked, the women would jeer at him and the children shout, the smell of the palm-wine followed Abionan wherever she went, and it was in the market that she saw the Alaketu for the first time, she thought him imposing, he was the king, the king of Ketu, it is possible that already as a child frequenting the market she had thought of being mother to a king, then there were the drunks who played with children, there was one who never stopped grinning but only after a calabash of palm-wine, but then he would turn serious and not look at anyone and then he'd drink and start grinning again, smiling more and more so that he was soon looking round, confident and cheerful, there were those who lived sleeping, drinking and sleeping, there were those who stole things from the stalls, there were those who didn't want to pay for their drink, – these were taken off to jail or were kept away from the market, – there were those who arrived in a rowdy mob talking at the tops of their voices, pointing at people and dragging at each other's clothing, there were those who stumbled and fell over backwards, sideways and forwards, there was one who spoke incomprehensible words, he seemed to be giving orders to invisible people and there was another who always said the same thing, he would arrive, start drinking and after a good amount of palm-wine would say 'we are coming to the end, it'll be my end and your end, the end of all animals, birds and fishes, there's not a thing to be done to avoid the end', he would go on like that for an enormous time, then he would repeat the words, it was only the end that seemed to stand out from everything he was saying, on the busier market days people would gather around the man, but on slacker days hardly anyone stopped to listen to what he was saying, Abionan had discovered where he lived and one afternoon she decided to follow him, and saw the house, his wife, two children and an old old man sitting in the doorway, at home he would not utter a word, or didn't seem to, it was the children with their navels sticking out like hook noses, who yelled, there were those who stayed in groups talking quietly all day long, they didn't get excited, they looked disapprovingly at the rowdies and the troublemakers, there were those who dressed in long Yoruba robes of red, yellow, white and green material, there were those who came in trousers and shirt, and those who turned up in shorts only, there were those who would buy large calabashes and just pass the palm-wine around their friends, there were those who you could see had no money and waited in hope of being treated to a drink, there were those who didn't drink but seemed to enjoy the excitement finding it all quite funny and one day Abionan tried the palm-wine, thought it ghastly and was amazed that so many people drank the stuff and there were also women who came along, bought their calabash full and went off to drink at home.

She had always played in the market from childhood, Tomori now asks:

house to bring them to the party. Then the widow is summoned and the elder says to her:

'If you have had no intercourse with another man since your husband's death, come forward and toss warm water over your husband's head.'

If the woman has kept faithful she throws warm water over the skull which is then washed with a soap and sponge. If she has found herself a new man or has had intercourse, even if on only one occasion, the woman has to flee before the ceremonies have even commenced, never to return. If she does return, she can be poisoned by anyone in the family. If though guilty, she still decides to splash warm water over the dead man's head and someone has learnt her guilt or later finds out she can be condemned to death by the family.

After hearing this story, Fatogum spent some minutes in silence, gazing at the man's organ that marked the spot for offerings to Eshu and in the end remarked:

'The gods of one nation demand different things from the gods of another.'

And then he had spoke of his days of training in Ibadan, Ifá and Oyo, he recalled the cult of the earth at Abeokuta, and said:

'The earth is a gift of Olodumare and Odudua. In ancient times it was all water and swamp. Olodumare sent Odudua off with a vessel shaped like a winkle-shell full of sand, Odudua selected sixteen assistants and took a large bird, there are some who say it was a hen but it might have been a sort of bird that people don't know of. Odudua tossed the sand upon the water, the bird began to sprinkle the sand about covering the water until there was room for men to live. That was how Odudua created the earth. Without earth you cannot live, you cannot walk and upon the earth people live and die. There are other tales that tell of a lizard testing the earth to see whether it was sand. There's also what is retold in Ifá, that it was Obatalá who on the orders of Olodumare came along with sand and pieces of metal to create the earth, and then Obatala was appointed governor of the earth. Orunmila who can see into the future and knows what is going to happen, was acting as Obatala's assistant.

Abionan had from then on come to look upon hens and any sort of bird in a different way, after all they had helped Odudua and Obatala with the creation of the world. Fatogum had gone on to recall his life in Ibadan, Ifé and Oyo, he would never forget the things he saw and heard, he had spent twelve years' apprenticeship in fortune-telling, for the first one he was a sort of clerk to all babalao services in Ibadan, he would listen to everything they said, learn the prayers off by heart, get the meals ready, do the housework, act as receptionist, be present at all the castings of cowries, and of the chain with the pieces of metal attached, the holy chain called the opele, tend Eshu's image, which was used independently of the male organ which represented that god also, he learnt the verses that were spoken to the penis of Eshu, at the festivals at Oyo the people sang songs concerning all the prayers made to Eshu and there was a cheerful note in all references to Eshu, the act of reproduction and the desire for fertility, like in these:

We are singing in homage to Eshu
He used his penis to make a bridge
The penis split in half
The travellers tumbled into the river.

In dance Eshu was also different from the other gods who danced slowly and with more or less gentle movements, Eshu would stamp his feet on the floor more violently, Fatogum had learnt to understand Eshu, to feel him almost as a friend, but an independent friend who, being linked with Ifá and prophecies, is also linked to changes, from time to time Fatogum got into great confusion when a casting of lots produced an incomprehensible result, he would then think that it must be one of Eshu's pranks, he had said as he talked to Abionan that Eshu also ruled the market and selling and buying, you only needed to look at the many ancient carvings of Eshu showing him with strings of cowries and coins wound about his body, Eshu was present in any financial transaction so how could he be a quiet and well-behaved god?

He had had a long apprenticeship, his master, who was called Fatima, was in the way of saying:

'Treasure everything in your head, all the knowledge that you keep picking up keep safe in your head, treasure the two hundred and fifty six odus and the interpretations of all the combinations in your head, and be clear about the differences between casting the chain (opele), casting cowries, casting obis and using the yellow powder and never forget that the reply depends always upon the question.'

He had learnt too that the question depends upon the one who makes the consultation, there are difficult questions, there are people who open up readily, and you seem to be able to see right

'The worst are the flatterers. There is not a ruler who can escape them. If he is very vain, he is lost. Simply from being my father's daughter, I cannot go to Zorei without being surrounded by flatterers. They say everything. That I'm pretty, that I'm like my father. They want to know whether I'm going to stand for election, whether I want to become something, whether I've good contacts in Paris, whether the French like me, whether I havé backing in this or that region of Zorei, that I deserve everything and that I have only to make one move for thousands of people to follow me. It is one endless act of flattery.'

Fatonde, who had been on the corner of the veranda and not said a word till then, interjected:

'But that could all be true.'

Young Mariana had thought that funny.

'Fatonde's an optimist. It might indeed be all true, but it's the way they talk that reeks of flattery. They speak and look at you with that toadish eye or put their hand on you or seize your arm so that you can't get away.'

When the son had been born, Abionan would go out with him on her back thinking what Ketu would be like when he was king, she would recall the conversations with the two Marianas, the advice of Fatogum and the words of Fatonde and she felt beset by dangers, anything could happen, which did in fact end up happening but would her son's death have been caused by her uncle?, Olaitan had vanished after the child had died and had sent a message saying that he had left on a journey to Togo, he had some money to collect there but it was the detail about the money that made the woman distrust him, after all the uncle was not duty bound to explain the finer points of his business to her, so what reason did he have?, he was of royal lineage to be sure, he might have wanted to be the next Alaketu, but could her son, now still hanging on her back, have been a rival to him, or couldn't he?, Abionan would think of obeying young Mariana's advice, her eyes open at the end of that night, the two women alone on the veranda and the friend's voice slightly lowering its tone:

'His struggle begins now.'

'Struggle?'

'To make your son king of Ketu you need from now on to please all the members of royal families but to please them without flattery and get to know them, find out what they like, what they do, what they say, what they desire in life.'

She had continued:

'Besides that, Abionan, you'll have to know the problems of Ketu, how the power of the Alaketu can be incorporated into the country within the division of power in Benin, what possibilities there are for the old kings to retain their authority in a modern state, so that then you can proceed to bring up your son with those ideas in his head and make it come natural to him to see the problems and seek to solve them from young.

Finally she had even said:

'If I could, I'd come and help you.'

'Why not?'

'My life will be more in Zorei than in Benin.'

'We can visit each other and continue to talk things over.'

Mariana had laughed and agreed. The next day she had gone back to her studies in France, old Mariana had gone to see her off at Cotonou airport, the granddaughter hadn't wanted her to, why leave the Water House?, getting tired like that?, but the old woman got into the car on time and watched the plane take off, Abionan went on from the airport to Whydah, for she had wanted to see the local market, old Mariana was a sort of queen of the district, everyone knew her, from there she went to Porto Novo, bought some wooden figures of twins, they were very small ones, and caught a lorry which was going to Ketu, she passed through towns which had been long known to her, Sekete, Pobe and Aba, she was thinking of Ketu as the most important place in the world, the Hunter had stayed there, kings had lived there, they had fought there and battles lost there, but the city had survived, the best market of all the ones she knew was there and when she arrived back it was with great joy that she went round the houses, went in to see her mother and told her things about the two Marianas and Fatonde, then she went into Fatogum's house who seemed to understand the words of young Mariana that Abionan had passed on to him but he thought that nothing had begun just the day before but everything had begun earlier still or had already begun earlier than earlier still, even the name that the baby had received contained a bit of his future and great care was necessary over choosing names, the mark of the name follows one even after death, it is the name which remains outside the body and when the latter has disappeared only

34

the name testifies to its former existence, the presence of the gods shows itself in names, Ifá goes on the beginning as Fá, families of hunters or wishing to honour hunters will have Ode in the name, be it Odeyale or Odetola, those of Ogun will be Ogundipe or Ogunmola, and yet can put water, omi, or baby, omo, in a name, or mountain, oke, or Oshun, the goddess of the river, or joy which is ayo, for the name will remain as an indestructible reality, and if a man is going to be king his name must anticipate what he will be, everything is foreseen but there are errors of foresight, gaps which cannot be glimpsed and in those gaps something unexpected can arise, the child who is going to be king can lose his reign before becoming anyone and at times Fatogum could see the future with such vividness that he was astonished but he could also see the possibilities of that future dying as a future, dying before becoming the present for the lines which run in the future can become overstretched and what you see can destroy the whole structure, the paths start from each person and are predictable paths, at the meeting of several paths conflict appears and there lay in the replies to the consultations nothing but conflict, Fatogum was used to perceiving conflicts before they revealed themselves, a conflict of man with woman, of man with man, or woman with woman, of one side of the market with the other, of one street with the other, of one town with the other, conflicts with reasons and conflicts seemingly without reasons, only if there was a deep reason, hidden and going back over many lives, one which arose between one person and another and caused an explosion, would death follow from the conflict and there foresight would end, looking into the future Fatogum would see death as a point along the road, both his and that of everyone who was with him in Ketu, but there would be Ketu beyond him and beyond the others, going into those houses, sleeping in those rooms, and he would wonder whether he would have fulfilled his mission of fortune-telling and assisting properly when he talked at greater length with Abionan, the babalao spoke as if the future weighed upon his shoulders, he would lean forward a little and stare at the floor, he said that no one could change the future, or at least that it was impossible to change it wholly, not even the gods had achieved that, what could be done was to take precautions so that the event did not do too much harm or offer timely sacrifices which make us so much one with the events that they seem to be always in our favour or ourselves always in their favour, and then everything goes into the future, not just what happens to people, but also objects, places, birds, insects, creatures of the earth, plants, because all these forms blend together in the future, but by the same token if it was not possible for a person to change the future, what was the point of his, Fatogum's, work, as he listened to problems and saw fear in the eyes of others?, but maybe you could change it just enough for a change of course, when a forecast spoke of the death of somebody, the babalao would fall silent, dropping his hands on the floor, and as he could not tell lies, he would in as few words as possible refer to the death that Ifá foresaw, then he would cast again to confirm it and find out the details of what was going to happen and death would bring the future into the past and the past would come back to defend those alive today, Abionan would frown as she endeavoured to understand everything Fatogum was saying, she had always been afraid of egunguns and ancestors, she liked the living and the future living, not the dead, or rather she liked only the closest of the dead who were living with her, her son and her mother, she took them with her from one market to the other, it was as if they were inside her, in her breast or her belly and Abionan could bring them out when she wished.

Fatogum looked at the woman and said that he might be making a trip to Pobe to see Fatonde.

'There're things he knows which he learnt from the great Fatumbi, that he can teach me.'

'You know everything.'

He laughed,

'I don't know everything, no. For example, I always go wrong with rain. They say it's such an easy thing to know if rain's on the way that even Europeans forecast rain with those machines that they have. A babalao ought to know more about rain.'

Abionan recalled having seen Fatogum forecast that there would not be rain for some time, the drought had already dragged on for months, so now they wanted him to make rain but he replied that he didn't know how, only a rain-maker could get it to rain and there turned up one who had come from Oshogbo, he filled a big pot with water, boiled it in public with everyone all around and danced and sang round and round the pot, mixed mysterious potions into the water but it didn't rain, the whole city was looking at a cloud passing by, it passed and disappeared, men and women went back to Fatogum and suggested a ceremony of egunguns, the ancestors could also help rain to come at least it had come in Ede-Ekiti when masked egunguns had gone out on the streets and chose trees in the middle of the town where they sang, danced and retold ancient tales of the loftier powers that ancestors had, it had rained the next day, Fatogum was not too convinced because a major god was lacking at the ceremony, an Ifá, one who had the power of truth, now in Ketu he talks of egunguns because he can't think of any other way of making rain, the local egunguns were down-to-earth folk and they didn't possess the know-how of making rain, Fatogum was later to explain to Abionan that lots of people know how to find out whether rain is on the way, there are men and women who feel the ache in their backs or the joints of their hands every time it's going to rain within the next ten hours, the hard part is to attract the rain when the weather is dry, then only a good sacrifice to the orishas would do the trick, and from time to time Fatogum would talk about animals and plants:

'Living creatures live with us on earth, they're our companions. Even wild animals form part of our life. The snake saw a rainbow in the sky or the rainbow saw the snake. The chameleon is so friendly that it runs over us when we're asleep. We sacrifice creatures to the orishas because offering a life produces peace among the gods and purification among men. We also kill creatures to eat. And we eat plants which have life too. There are sacred plants like the iroko tree. And there are herbs that cure evils. One of those plants near us here banishes evil thoughts and envy towards others. Envy kills, but a plant can kill envy.'

Abionan said:

'Perhaps I'll go and visit old Mariana in a month's time. I'll pass through Pobe and have a talk with Fatonde.'

'He also knows plants like no one else does.'

'There's no one to beat you at that.'

Fatogum had agreed up to a point, yes, plants he did know, he knew those that could cure illnesses, he had cured many by now, but there might always be roots and leaves whose value he still needed to know, for example the Ifé district had trees that didn't exist in Ketu, in Ketu he had seen plants that were unknown in Oyo, sometimes he would spend days in the bush, trying a leaf, pulling up a root, testing a twig, one taste would remind him of another or set him thinking about plants whose application he knew, he would always return happy from those sallies into the bush and would with a smile bring back leaves and roots to stew or bake, he wanted to find out how they'd turn out after being baked or stewed and Abionan learnt from him which herb you should chew or swallow when you had a tummy ache or when you felt sluggish, with no clear thoughts, as she toed and froed between the markets she would always take some plants to chew, the obi was nice too, she always took a few tucked up in a cloth, now she suddenly feels it is growing late and she would have to get ready before starting her walk to Opo Meta so she got up:

'Until four days' time.'

The lamps in the market began to appear, everywhere little lights, it was the time when Abionan would gaze at the lighted stalls and packing-cases with the women squatting, she liked hearing the conversations which would bounce across from one lighted space to another and speaking as little as possible, she didn't always manage to understand every word and the indistinct sounds brought about a great serenity within her as if there were a conversation within a conversation, a meaning beyond the everyday words which meant cassava, pepper, calabash, potato or bean, Abionan would hear mat and think of something else although she also was on the mat she carried from market to market, with the green and red lioness's face, whether the language the woman was talking was Fon, Ewe or French it seemed all the same just as if languages were of no importance, so she would forget that the sounds must, and did, have a meaning and would remain sitting just like now when she had come back from Fatogum's and the night entered her body with its noises, smells and its lamps strewn around the market place, she recalled her mother at her stall and thought about the women who had sold on that spot when she was small or even before she was born, or in the days of king Sa, or on the eve of the invasion by the soldiers of Abomey, or when Oshosi walked the earth and came bringing game to be sold in the market, she thought of Eshu stopping before each stall, she again saw the old, old woman whom she had met as a little child and as she ate and drank bits of food, drips would stay lodged in her wrinkles and she thought they were rivers down which a fluid was flowing, and imagined her at her stall for a hundred years, old Mariana had also spoken of her market experience, she would tell of her grandmother in Brazil and her stall in a big market in Bahia:

'Afterwards my grandmother Ainá sold lots of obis and lots of orobos in Lagos, she used to use packing-cases for a counter and

'It might have really been her.' Abionan couldn't remember who had said it.

'It could have be. Who knows what might exist in the world without our knowing it?'

In Opo Meta Abionan now imagined that it must now be past midnight and a vast weariness gripped her body, she lay down on the mat, closed her eyes and felt the breeze blowing slightly, the image of the baobab remained inside her eyes, she slept and dreamt long dreams, long stories with people going in and out, Ademola was wanting her to go on a journey, the yard of their complex was too full, then visitors arrived, at a certain point Abionan awoke to hear people talking loudly together not far from her stall, she closed her eyes once more and saw inside them again, the forms of people going and coming, there were billowing robes, a journey where?, her husband tugging at her, he seemed in a hurry, then everything dissolved and she found herself by the sea, talking to a man whose physiognomy was scarcely visible, she re-awoke and in the sky made out a beginning of daylight, she had to get up to see to the purchase of the yams and cassavas, she slept again and in the same instant dreamt she had a son with big, wide-open eyes, sitting on the mat, the market was Ketu and it was sunny, and Abionan wanted to pick up the child, then she woke up for good, and the noise of people talking and walking past had grown, she got up and went to make her purchases.

The man was waiting for her.

'You're late. What was the matter?'

'I overslept.'

She looked at the yams and sorted the ones out that seemed better, the man asked:

'What's the news from Ketu?'

The woman continued sorting out the yams, then moved on to the sweet potatoes.

'Nothing new. The tax collector's wife gave him a thrashing.'

'And he took it?'

'He hadn't much choice: she's terribly strong and he's like a dwarf.'

'So why did they marry each other?'

'Heaven only knows.'

Abionan scrutinised the cassavas more minutely.

'The lorries are moving into competition with the market and buying from the country folk direct so as to sell in the stores at a higher price.'

The man seemed to be thinking the matter over.

'But who's going to buy dearer if it's cheaper in the market?'

'If they buy everything up, the market won't have anything to sell, so anyone who wants anything will have to pay more at the store.'

Abionan placed the yams, sweet potatoes and cassavas in her big basket, estimated the value of what she had selected, took a cloth pouch out from under her skirt and counted out the money.

'Sweet potatoes are going up,' announced the man.

'We'll argue over that when they do.'

She put the basket on her head and walked slowly through men and women selling fruit, vegetables and peppers, gaily-coloured robes could be seen moving about, red predominantly, other women were following in the same direction with baskets and calabashes, screams and shouts crossed paths in mid-air, one man dressed in a yellow robe was leading a small ox leashed by its horns, Abionan went into the market and put her basket down, Yatundé was talking:

'It's going to be hard going today. I could hardly find any peppers.'

It was necessary to pay homage to Eshu, so Abionan left her yams at the stall, took a tin of oil and went over to where the little mound of earth like a male organ was situated, sat down before it and poured a little oil out on to the ground, Fatogum had told her that a small coin, a little oil or even water would be enough to please Eshu, after looking at the oil gleaming in the sunlight, she put down two coins as well, stayed sitting there for some minutes looking at the organ and as she got up she saw more people coming along, when it was a case of making a sacrifice or an offering, Abionan would give two things instead of one, one in her own name and the other in the name of the son who was to be born, as long as Adeniran had existed she had set out the two coins or two bean cakes or two obis with greater joy but now the offering was a pledge, but a pledge made with no solace, it could be that Olaitan or a evil god was trailing every step she was making and seeking to harm her, she had heard tell of women who had fallen sick and this prevented them from having children, anything could happen and on reaching the stall again she ran into Uncle Obafemi whom she hadn't seen for ages.

'May you not die this morning.'

The Yoruba greeting made her smile before setting down her basket, she replied:

'May you not die while you are seated.'

'How did the buying go?'

The man looked at the cassavas, held up the biggest one and studied it closely, Abionan was smiling:

'I always buy well.'

The man greeted Yatundé:

'May you not die while you are selling in the market.'

Abionan attended to several customers, two men and a woman, she took some time arguing the prices and the uncle remarked:

'You know how to sell too.'

'I learnt from my mother.'

The sun began to blaze down on the right-hand side of the stall, a small boy ran past through the middle of the water which was draining away down the left-hand side, a customer in a dark blue turban seemed to be quarreling with Yatundé, a hen leapt out of the coop which held it and a group of women, men and children tried to grab it, Abionan wanted to know:

'What's my uncle doing in Opo Meta?'

'I've come to collect a payment that's due.'

The other went on serving customers, in a respite:

'Have you got it now?'

'I'll collect it this afternoon.'

The man picked up a stone from the ground and started playing with it.

'But I've also got some business with you too.'

The woman halted, yam in hand, waiting.

'Do you remember the house I bought in Cotonou?'

It was a green house, three doors and one window.

'Well, I'm going to open a shop there. The city has expanded on that side and now the house is near the shops.'

Abionan sat down on a stone:

'Good idea.'

'It is, isn't it?' agreed the man.

The group chasing the hen came back, a tall, thin boy raised it aloft in triumph.

'I think you can help me in that shop.'

Two customers came along, one of them picked up a sweet potato, weighed it in his hand, picked up another, the two talked prices, this time Abionan hurried the sale along, she hardly bothered to argue over the price and sat down again, the uncle was amused:

'I can see I'm getting in your way, you came down too quickly.'

Yatundé's son cried.

'I've been thinking,' the man continued 'you could mind the shop as a partner.'

'Partner?'

'Yes, join as a partner so as to live in Cotonou and manage things.'

'What will the shop sell?'

'Drapery, haberdashery, sewing threads, brooches and ornaments perhaps, and even souvenirs and things like that.'

She fell silent and thought.

An uproar arose at one extremity of the market, children screamed, a customer took refuge in Abionan's stall and she looked up to see a group of egunguns, in front came two men with poles in hand, they beat them on the ground, the older folk got out of the way so as not to touch the egunguns, only the children yelled and played, it was the ceremony in tribute to the forefathers, the egunguns being the souls of the dead which had come back to haunt the places they had roamed in their lifetimes, the first egungun was wearing a wooden mask, the carved protruding lips looked like a woman's sex set lengthwise, the nose had been carved with two lumps, one on each side, beneath the wooden eyes there appeared the real eyes of whoever was wearing the mask, on the forehead a bow turned downwards, around the face a series of strokes converging on the eyes, nose and mouth, the wood had a dark tint, the egungun's body was covered with long bands of cloth of every colour, red and green bands mainly, they seemed to emerge straight out of the mask and on its wooden lips, nose and eyes Abionan now pinned her attention, the egungun stopped at the stall, Abionan stood by in respect, the egunguns behind halted too and the woman who had hidden near Abionan cowered on the ground and kept still, the mask was now more obvious and it seemed to be saying something, Abionan wondered whether it had been made by the woodcarver of Idigny who would spend the day with her each time there was a market there, only Victor Ajayi possessed that strong line, that knack of carving wood and giving a violent look to the face which emerged from it, the egungun moved forward and then up came the second one whose mask seemed bigger, with small lips, a squat nose, the eyes seemingly downcast, the brightly coloured bands with more shades of blue, the third egungun who had an elongated mask, the open mouth revealed rows of wooden teeth, the eyes gaping, his dress consisted not just of bands but of a golden material draped haphazardly, the fourth egungun moved past quickly and went and stopped at Yatundé's stall, the children ran up by the egunguns and were driven off by the men with the poles in their hands, that whole side of the market was now absorbed by the egunguns passing, mother used to say that the dead came back to visit the places they had loved when alive, they would again set their feet on the market or a square and see again the people who had been around them, life was continuing along the other side, and we needed the life which is here no longer, the goings and comings and the dead and the living, as a small child Abionan had been afraid of the egunguns, today a little of that fear lay still within her and she thought of mother's death, the woman who had sheltered in the stall came out and thanked her, Abionan looked at her uncle again:

'What do you think of my proposal?'

To accept it would mean leaving Ketu and the uncle seemed to read her thoughts for he said:

'You'll be able to stay in Ketu over the weekends. After all the distance is not great. Ademolá could even spend part of the week in Cotonou.'

He felt he had to put forward further arguments:

'A steady secure business, and in a house, is better than trading in the market.'

A customer appeared whom Abionan knew by sight, she chose the best yams, named a price, Abionan disputed it and the two started an argument that went on for five minutes, now it was the time of day when Opo Meta market was liveliest, suddenly instead of one customer there were six, Yatundé was talking loud, a palm-oil seller was arguing with a neighbour, it had the appearance of a quarrel, a man passed close by tugging a ram leashed by its horns, another appeared on a bicycle but had to stop because he couldn't make any headway, he dismounted and continued on foot and when the flow of business seemed to ease, Abionan sat down to attend to a customer, the uncle had remained quiet all the while and the woman replied:

'You go and collect your payment. I'll think over what you proposed. When you've got it, I'll tell you what I think.'

He nodded his head in agreement, kept looking at the stalls all around, a jam of people seemed to block the traffic nearby and Abionan restacked the potatoes on a wider shelf, the uncle asked:

'When's a new Adeniran coming along?'

She raised her eyes to him:

'Soon.'

The man smiled.

'There's no one else like you.'

She smiled too:

'We'll need your help when he grows up and the time comes.'

The man ran his right hand over his head:

'By then I shall be very old.'

She looked carefully at him:

'I don't think so. You'll be still a lad, and with more experience.'

'How many years would you give me?'

'It makes no odds. You'll live past ninety.'

'Obatala willing, nothing's impossible, but the second Adeniran has to be born as quickly as possible.'

He said this again with a smile.

'You can rest assured of that. He'll be here in nine month's time.'

'Has he already started?'

'Not yet, but he will do soon.'

He got up still laughing and, waved goodbye before moving off, the sun was getting hotter, Yatundé wanted to know what it was that the man found so funny.

'Nothing at all, nothing. He just wants me to go and live in Cotonou.'

'What for, for heaven's sake?'

'To look after a shop of his.'

The two remained silent and, when Yatundé did speak she thought it a good idea, after all Cotonou was a big city, it had everything, a cinema, a beach, dances and parties, big buildings, cars and bikes in the streets, it must be fine to live there but Abionan couldn't agree:

'I prefer Ketu.'

'Did you tell him that?'

'Not yet, I'll think about it this afternoon.'

There was a few minutes' peace, perhaps the onset of hunger, nevertheless she did want to give it more thought, it would perhaps be to her advantage to accept the offer, the second son could be born in Ketu, when he was to be born she could catch a lorry in Cotonou and be in Ketu a few hours later, the boy's upbringing would take place both in the one city and the other and from when small he would be in touch with Ketu and its people, with the uncles and cousins and with the other royal families but, on the other hand, he would also get to know Cotonou and the important people in the capital, he would frequent Porto Novo as well and become friendly with the ancient families there, he could also go to Mariana's house at Agua from time to time and it might well be a good idea to bring the boy up in several different settings, Cotonou would be an increasingly important city, it was there that decisions which changed the country were made, and it was also necessary that the power of the obas, the kings of the communities, like the king of Ketu, be maintained, and that could be done in Cotonou, Abionan remained seated thinking of the pros because she already knew the cons, the prime objection was that nobody should abandon Ketu voluntarily which was the finest place in the world, the place where her son would be king and where things had a meaning.

Then again in Cotonou he would only be a short way from Mariana and the Water House, yet whenever he wanted to leave Ketu and pay visits to Agua, he would not have the slightest difficulty, the main thing was not to make Cotonou the centre of his life, now she really was hungry so she stood up and went out, she stopped at a food stall and saw pieces of lamb in a pan and vegetables on a plate, she ate seated on a half wobbly stool, she ate and watched a group of little girls playing close by, her uncle's invitation was a temptation, Cotonou was growing bigger and bigger and had big houses, tall buildings, French shops with different wares but she could in no way think of leaving Ketu, the layout of Opo Meta market was neat, the rows of stalls stood out more clearly here, there were also decorations that lent colour to the whole ensemble – unless perhaps it was only its proximity to Ketu that made the woman like that mixture of folk selling and buying – she returned to her stall at a gentle pace, she stopped in front of the palm-wines, men sitting talking in loud voices, nothing could beat the liveliness of the markets, a shop was very like a prison, you would be awaiting customers, stuck indoors, and when she reached the spot where Omitola was selling she decided to stop a while, the latter was shouting at a boy who had toppled one of the shelves in her stall, Omitola looked at Abionan and said:

'What a face you've got, woman. What's wrong?'

Abionan laughed at the question:

'Does it show in my face then.'

'It all shows. You've got something on your mind.'

'I certainly have.'

And she talked about the invitation and of the conviction that she would have to turn it down, but deep down a doubt remained that it would be better to accept.

'But your conviction is correct indeed. Who's going to swap a market for a shop?'

Abionan said that she'd maybe make more in a shop but the other didn't believe her, then they talked about the morning, how business had gone, the passing of the egunguns, the journey they'd be making that night to Idigny and when Abionan got back to her place she found Yatundé sleeping against the beam from which a sheepskin was hanging, a bit of metal lay on top of the paper which contained mounds of peppers, seeing the metal, Abionan remembered that it was the day of Ogun, the god of metal, if Fatogum were here, she would have gone and consulted him on the uncle's offer but she was able to guess what his reply would be for she was quite convinced he would agree with her, staying on in Ketu would be better, once she had asked if his name was a mixture of Ifá and Ogun, the man had smiled and said something to the effect that everyone has a name proper to them, like her name, Abionan, which was just as it should be, yes, Fatogum would be in favour of Ketu and against Cotonou, the woman thought it odd to have received the uncle's invitation on a day of Ogun, the god of iron and steel, of war and machines, of quarrels and agreements, nothing could be done without Ogun's backing because he cleared the paths and went ahead and then what the woman heard was Fatogum's voice:

'Ogun goes ahead and clears the path for the other orishas to pass, when proclaimed king of Iré, Ogun didn't like being king and preferred hunting, war and adventure. He is also the master of riches and money. That's why we say "Ogun, on'ilé owó".'

And Fatogum had said the entire Yoruba saying that Ogun was

the possessor of money, the master of the house of the rich, and the master of innumerable mansions in heaven – but also the master of the art, the crafts and metalwork, Ogun had seven names but Abionan could not remember them all and Fatogum would say them one by one, Ogun Alará, Ogun Oniré, Ogun Elemoná, the names echoed over in her head with the á and é making music, she recalled a ceremony for Ogum that she had seen in Nigeria during the long journey that she had made with mother, she was still a child then or had she started not to be a child, she would have been what?, eleven?, twelve years old?, it had been a dance with well-defined clear movements, very staccato drum-beats and it was on this day of Ogun that she would have to choose, but the choice had already been made beforehand and who knew whether every choice is already made long before it becomes necessary, every thing that we do in life forces us to a particular choice when the time comes, and their great journey around the Yoruba cities had begun one morning in January when mother had said to her:

'You're coming with me.'

Everyone had been against it, the uncles, the aunts, the grandfather and uncle George, he had shouted with the forthrightness of an old, old man:

'It's crazy enough for you to go, but crazier still to take the girl.'

There had been days of arguments until one night Abionan had heard Olaitan remark:

'She wants to visit the cities far from the sea only because she can't see the sea.'

The little girl was left in thought but another night she had heard mother say:

'We'll leave tomorrow.'

It had been a journey on foot, it had taken more than six months to judge by what mother had since related and for Abionan it had been an enormous period, she forgot almost entirely about home, only the market place in the middle of Ketu and the general look of the city were not forgotten and on the morning of leaving, Olaitan had asked:

'What about money?'

'I'm taking enough which is everything I've managed to save. If I run short, I shall sell in the markets or on a corner.'

They had set out before sunrise, but there was already a brightness beating down on the walls, everyone in Ketu seemed to be asleep, only hens and kids were astir on the road, mother was carrying a basket on her head and she looked as if she was going to market. Abionan knew that inside it were pieces of smoked meat, tins of gari, clothes and various bits of stuff, two mats were laid across the top of the basket and the little girl carried a bundle of clothing, now they had left the city and the mound of Eshu where mother made an offering, the road was still deserted, the girl looked behind and saw the rooftops, with smoke rising to the sky with its pink clouds, soon afterwards a group of women appeared, all dressed the same, they would be relatives or friends and they were on the way to market, the road began to fill and mother and girl walked at a calm steady pace, then the country began to change, higher hills rose up and some of the trees were different, at one point mother stopped close by a stream and asked:

'Do you want to rest?'

'Me, oh no.'

She recalled having looked around, not a single house could be seen, she spotted a red lizard which darted past over the stones in the road and it vanished down the other side, soon another one appeared, a darker one, and made the reverse journey disappearing close to the girl, it was as if they were playing at swapping places, she thought it was funny, but mother was now getting up to go, Abionan followed behind carrying her bundle and they walked on another two hours, before mother thought it was time to eat, which they did slowly chewing every piece of meat, they had found a cluster of stones and stopped and rested there for some while after their meal, when they arrived in Ilara that afternoon, mother said:

'This city's in Nigeria.'

'So we're in Nigeria?'

'Yes, we are.'

She had looked to see whether it was different but found the same type of bush and the houses resembled the ones in Ketu, she had thought that one country would be unlike the next but mother had explained:

'All round here is Yoruba land, it's the same on either side.'

Ilara's market was like Ketu's and mother told her:

'I have sold many things from that stall on the right.'

Seeing the little girl's amazement, she went on:

'It was long before you were born. At that time I decided to go round Opo Meta, Idigny, Iro Kogny and Ilara, to see what it was like. Afterwards I went back to going round the markets from Ketu.'

Mother greeted an old, old woman:

'May you not die while you are selling.'

The old woman rubbed her eyes and smiled with a toothless mouth:

'Well, if it's not my old friend from Ketu.'

They got talking, Abionan went over to look at the other stalls,' there was one with dead creatures, rats, snakes, a monkey skull and great big snails where she spent ages staring at every creature, then she got tired and went to gaze at a stall selling blue materials, from the smell she sensed that she was near the palm-wines, and when she came back mother was saying farewell, then they crossed the market and went into a house on the other side, where mother seemed to know everyone, that was where they slept on that and other nights, the mother and girl would go off to the market early in the morning, where they had started running a pepper stall, one day two men were arguing over prices, and speaking a language between themselves which was unknown to the little girl.

'English' said mother.

'What an ever so hard language. It's not like anything else at all.'

'It's the language they speak here. Like French which they speak in Porto Novo and Cotonou.'

In the days that followed Abionan was to hear lots of English and came to be used to the sounds of the new language, one Sunday mother dressed the girl up in clean clothes and said they had to move on, they set out before noon, struck a road which the girl thought was narrow and this time they travelled on for many days, so very many that she couldn't count them all, when they stopped at the end of each afternoon, they would sleep at houses where the people let them put their mats down but twice they had slept right by the roadside where Abionan had fallen asleep quite unafraid until they reached a broad river, with waters flowing fast, there were men in a canoe whom mother asked:

'What river's this?'

'The Ogun river.' said the tallest of them.

'This is it then.'

Mother stood looking and Abionan did too, the tall man wanted to know where they were going.

'To Abeokuta. Is it far?'

The man pulled a wry face:

'Pretty far.'

'How can you get there?'

'By canoe.'

He paused and helped haul the boat up the bank.

'It'll be hard to find anyone going from here all the way to Abeokuta with a canoe. The best thing's to sail farther downstream in one canoe, then catch another and then another and with three canoes you should manage it.'

The man would be leaving the next morning and he'd be able to take the woman and the girl and so they slept under a tree listening to the river running by, it was cold at daybreak and when Abionan woke up she saw a lantern alight on the boat, then she went back to sleep.

When they got into the canoe, Abionan had the feeling that it was a bit unsteady but she calmly sat down amidships with mother astern, put her right hand over the side and dipped it in the water, it was nice to feel the water running through her fingers, there were boughs and leaves in the current and she snatched out a big leaf, she looked at it to see what it was like and then she tossed it back into the river, on the banks there were great trees and from time to time a house, branches hung down into the stream and some even reached into the water, the sun burst through the boughs, and at a bend in the river she saw a group of children bathing, both boys and girls, they were shouting and flinging water at each other, Abionan nearly fell out when the canoe yawed and she spotted a great big stone which seemed to hold up the river which had to make a bend around it, suddenly the man steered the canoe into the left bank and said:

'This is where I'm stopping.'

He helped the mother and girl out and Abionan still felt the list of the boat when she was ashore, the tall man explained:

'You can take this road in front of the house and a quarter of an hour from here you'll come to another house where my friend Emanuel lives. Tell him that it was me, Omolokum, who sent you along. Emanuel goes a lot farther downstream quite regularly and can take you.'

Mother thanked him and dragged Abionan along by the hand, they got on to the road which ran through the middle of the bush, the ground was damp and different from Ketu, her feet got bogged down in tracts of mud, and the little girl almost slipped over, then the house loomed suddenly up, she came out from among the trees and came upon it when it was only four metres away, a dog barked and there appeared inside a man wearing just long trousers.

'Mr Emanuel?'

'The very same.'

'May you not die while walking up to me.'

He answered the greeting with another, the woman said she wished to go to Abeokuta, the man stared hard at her, as if not understanding but in the end replied:

'Only if you can hold on for a few days. I have to go to Abeokuta with my mother who's ill but only when she's a little better.'

They went to see the man's mother who was in a corner of the room, lying on a mat that smelt of something musty, she hardly spoke but just looked at the pair of them with big eyes, the man spoke:

'She's been like that for some three weeks now. In Abeokuta she'll be staying with my elder brother who has a big house and can look after her. She won't get any better here in this damp.'

Abionan's mother took patient care of the woman and made her a broth, she kept looking at them with wide open eyes and not saying anything, the little girl felt she had stayed ages in that house, but mother told her it had only been for two weeks and in that spell Abionan learnt to deal with the river and to understand it, to know what it wanted, and sometimes she would hear its voice, the river would be speaking to her or was it Ogun speaking?, after all the river was Ogun and he could speak to people, except that Ogun was metal, so why should his name be given to a river?, but later mother had told her that Ogun and Ogun were two different things, another day she went out alone in the canoe, she had learnt to handle it for she had watched Emanuel, what he did and how he did it, mother took no notice at all, because she was too taken up with caring for the sick woman, Abionan would every now and then go into the room and see those two big eyes and she would get scared and go back to the river, she played around catching fish, and saw the things that the river carried past, tree-trunks, sods of earth, branches covered with leaves and even a branch with a nest on top, the waters carried everything along, and one afternoon she saw a dead ox being swept along by the current, she followed it until it was lost to view around the bend farther on ahead and began to pick out the different flies that flew over the river, at times they seemed to be standing still, she saw snakes as well and one was so beautiful, as soon as she saw it the little girl ran away and the snake went off in the other direction too, then she laughed and said to herself that each had been scared away by the other, then there were also the canoes that sailed up and down the Ogun river, the little girl would watch them for a long while, some big ones which held five people or more and were flat in the middle and rising higher towards the stern, where there were two men with poles and paddles, in the middle were the women and children and now and again an open umbrella, they would go faster downstream, but upstream was hard going, she saw bananas, pots, packages, bundles and mangoes, and on occasions the paddler at the stern would call out hallo to the girl, or a child would wave its hand with a smile, the women went along with set faces looking straight ahead and would not look aside, then there were long canoes full of pitchers and parcels, one day she saw some kids in one of them, they were bound and held fast by two men and she thought the boat would capsize when it reached the bend but on it went, on some mornings the river was especially busy, two or three canoes were sailing up and down all at once and one after the other with people of all sorts dressed in print material, gaily coloured umbrellas with bands of every colour around the centre spike, or people with almost nothing on, men just in their shorts, and naked boys, the river seemed like a city street but at other times it was deserted for several hours and no one went by, the little girl would keep waiting for one canoe at least to come and would amuse herself listening to the calls of the grey parrots that frolicked in the trees around, and she would see eagles flying higher in the sky, monkeys springing from bough to bough behind the house and she liked the tiny birds too, the blue swallows that seemed to be chattering in the lower branches that fell almost into the river, Emanuel had said that there were crocodiles too in the Ogun river, not right at that spot but further away and she would imagine a crocodile emerging from the water and coming into the house, going right to the room where the old woman with the big eyes lay, one afternoon she saw canoes full of sand going past on the river, she learnt to distinguish what sort of loads they were carrying, sometimes it would be firewood, other times the blue materials that mother called adire and lots of baskets, there were canoes with sails, cloths which were dark coloured or dirty with earth which mother had explained were used to catch the wind which moved the canoe along, others had decks which looked like little houses, at nightfall it was still light enough to pick out the river and she saw an old woman smoking a pipe and looking out in front where the clouds seemed to be still reddened and the girl had entirely settled into her riverside life when, one night, Emanuel announced that his mother seemed better, so they would be able to sail downriver bound for Abeokuta.

On the following morning the man and the girl's mother took the old woman out to the canoe, set her down firmly amidships, wrapped up in shawls and with a mat underneath, Abionan soon pinned her eyes to every change of scenery and after the bend, a huge bare trunk rose up, looming from the water as if it had been born from it and palm trees shaking in the wind, she saw trees that were so tall that you couldn't quite see what was on the topmost branches, houses with thatched roofs, maize plantations, then squat bushes which Emanuel explained were cocoa, now and again a yellow fruit would appear which stood out amid the green, and at one time she thought the river would cease to exist because she looked and could see only land and trees ahead, and only when she was getting close to what seemed like the end of the river did there appear a narrower bend where the current swelled, but then the river became calm again and the canoe sailed quietly onwards, the waters changed colour, they had been dark, then they had turned to yellow, then reddish and now they became dark again, on some reaches she could not see any banks at the sides, only leaves, suddenly the trees thinned out and a house appeared and it was just as abruptly that they arrived at Abeokuta, the trees vanished and the banks stood clearly out, with people washing clothes, children playing, and lots of houses, Emanuel had no need to announce that the voyage was over.

'My brother lives near that rock over there.' And he pointed into the distance.

They took the old woman out of the canoe and set her down on some coarse grass, she sat with her big eyes moving round from one thing to another, the man went off and when he returned he said:

'I've fixed up a lorry to take my mother. My address is over there,' and he said something about Olumo rock, 'Everyone knows me, you've only to ask.'

As he picked the old woman up in his arms, he added:

'You can easily find somewhere to sleep.'

Abionan's mother thanked him and the pair remained there gazing at the houses, dirty fishing nets were spread out by the riverside and mother took hold of the little girl by the hand and off they set on foot, they soon came to a big market with adirés everywhere, the patterns on the material were pretty, and sometimes they had inscriptions in Yoruba, mother exclaimed:

'If only I could buy them and take them to sell in Ketu.'

The girl saw no problem, just buy them and take them, mother disagreed:

'That's out of the question. Only on a lorry or the back of an animal. Don't you realise the distance we've come?'

Beyond the adiré stalls there were others, more everyday ones with fruit and meals, meals which mother and daughter ate, then they sat for a while in a kind of alleyway between two stalls watching the bustle, Abionan noticed that they spoke more English there than in Ilara and the sounds of the voices were different even when they spoke Yoruba, she saw a group of neatly dressed little girls playing in front of a house and that was where mother and daughter slept by the time the lights began to illuminate the market, the girl clearly heard many voices of the night, she woke without waking and sensed people passing nearby, in the morning she felt rested and buoyant and ran over to the area outside the stalls, so that mother had to shout to her:

'Come back, girl.'

She came back smiling and mother went out with her, they talked to people in the market, Abionan took note of everything and didn't follow what mother was doing, she was finally taken to a house by the river where mother went in and the girl stood looking at boats and baskets, mother came back with a smile:

'Let's stay and sleep here.'

The little girl gazed at the house, it had a thatched roof, and the walls were high, that night she slept hearing the nocturnal sounds, people?, animals?, in the morning she went out with mother to somewhere near the market where a lot of talking was done, three days later mother was selling obis and orobos on a busy corner, Abionan spent the days sitting thereabouts or playing nearby, she got to know boys and girls whose tongue seemed strange to her at first, then she got used to talking like they did, they played at everything, ran about and mother would every now and then decide to rest indoors and the girl would go to the water's edge, it was diffe-

and wine, then they went to stay the night in a pretty village where there were chickens everywhere, indoors even, on perches all along the street, a bonfire in the middle of a small square that lit up faces and clothes, the girl threw bits of firewood on to the bonfire and watched the sparks rising skywards like stars, it was hard to get to sleep, the two of them had put down their mats in a corner of the square and lay down to sleep in the open air, the girl spent hours looking at the remains of the fire, she was closing her eyes but soon opened them again to see the embers glowing in the dark, next day Aduke went off to look for a house for them both to stay at and found one not far from the market, it was a different shape, long with stalls down each side which also ran down the side turnings and the landlady argued the price for over an hour, there was a festive atmosphere about the city, people in the doorways talking in loud voices saying things and cracking jokes, the house where they were staying had more than ten children of various ages and it would be difficult to know who was who, the people seemed to get around much faster in Ijebu-Odé than anywhere else that the girl had been before, or perhaps it was because a big festival was approaching for that was all everyone was talking of, the pronounciation of their words was different and the girl took days to pick it all up, at first Aduke didn't want to work, the two of them would go off round the city as soon as they awoke and stand in the market watching all the activity, then eat at some stall or other and mother would get talking a lot with the women who wore tall headties on their heads and walked with swinging hips which attracted people's attention, one day she saw one of them running after a man, it looked as if she was going to hit him, everyone was laughing, and she noticed that there was a lot of laughter in the market and on the streets, mother began to smile more often too, and one afternoon Abionan heard the word 'sea', she looked round quickly to see who it was, an old woman in a dark-blue skirt was relating how she was saved in an accident, the fishing canoe in which she had been, it was by a city called Warri, was nearly capsizing when her grandson had leapt into the sea and grabbed one of the sides of the boat, Aduke listened to the story in silence, the girl recalled the first trip she had made with mother to near the sea and she wondered what would have happened if the two of them had climbed the hilltop from where you could see the sea but she couldn't directly remember the trip back, for mother had moved so fast that Albionan couldn't quite keep up, in Ijebu-Odé she came to know the girl Elizabeth, she thought the name was lovely and Elizabeth said:

'It's the name of the queen.'

'What queen?'

'The queen of England.'

In Ketu no one talked about England, only France, would there be a queen in France as well?, mother replied not, Abionan became Elizabeth's best friend and the girls would go out to the market together, they played the whole afternoon long and once the latter wanted to know:

'Don't you go to school?'

'I did in Ketu. But not while travelling.'

Abionan found out that the festivities were to mark the coronation of the new king of Ijebu-Odé, and she learnt that the king was called Awujale just as the one of Ketu was called Alaketu, the king was out of the city awaiting the proper day to return to be installed as the chief, Aduke asked everyone what the ceremony would be like, a giant of a market woman, the girl reckoned she was nearly two metres tall and beside her mother was like a dwarf, had explained in a voice that seemed higher pitched because of the woman's size:

'He's coming on foot from where he is now, he'll cross the Ye river and stop at each small village he comes to along the way. Whenever he arrives at a place sacrifices are made to placate the orishas. When he enters Imushin, the king there is waiting to meet him. Then more sacrifices. Animals of all sizes are slaughtered. He'll stop at Ilese. The next day he'll come over the river Owa and enter Ijebu-Odé.'

Aduke had made up her mind to go and wait for the king at the river Owa where there were people clinging to both banks, vividly coloured robes stood out in the clear morning and Abionan was standing close by when the king set foot on the bank, many people threw themselves to the ground as a mark of respect and the king walked calmly up the road with the people following him, then he entered the city and there were small boys on the rooftops, the stalls were closed without stallholders, women were wearing clean skirts, the king stopped on a corner where Abionan saw a sheep tethered, soon a man appeared with a knife and other men held the sheep down, the girl felt it as the knife slit the creature's throat, blood

80

started to pour out and the king walked on until he halted at another corner and there another animal was killed, many were the animals sacrificed all along the king's route and suddenly the throng following him all rushed upon a house, Aduke and Abionan recoiled in alarm, they climbed a hummock at a street corner as a group of men started pounding on the walls of the house with pieces of wood and metal, men and women tugged down the door on the left, and others thrust at the windows in the middle, there was also a door on the right which was shut but was soon opened by a blow from an axe brandished by a soldier, the uproar kept growing for some minutes till it became the only reality in the street, the king was present throughout, without a gesture or a word, other men had already climbed on to the roof and had set about hurling down scraps of roofing, then the mud of the walls yielded and the demolishers seemed to be gripped by renewed enthusiasm and when one of the windows was wrenched out and flung to the ground, an old woman nearby ran off in fear, small children screamed amidst the general tumult of demolition, and the rear wall caved in for good though the front one still held out, the left-hand door also fell in, clods of mud were spattered over the street and within a few minutes there was a house no longer, everyone cheered and shouted at the final collapse of the last wall, little boys ran out holding bits of window, men bore one of the doors aloft in triumph, Aduke was afraid and pulled the little girl by the hand and all the while the king just looked on, Abionan thought that they were all against the king, why destroy a house that seemed to be so good?, then the king left the space in front of the house and continued his walk through the city, the coronation ceremony was trapped in silence, you wouldn't have believed that only shortly before the people had torn a house to the ground, the big market woman whom Aduke asked what the battle against the house was for, was amused at the latter's ignorance:

'Don't you know? It's the end of the old and the start of the new.'

For the rest of the day the men drank lots of palm-wine, the strange acid smell of the drink seemed to abound everywhere, and when she started to eat her piece of smoked meat the girl thought it was full of palm-wine so strong was the smell, Elizabeth wanted to know:

'Did you like the festival?'

'Ever so much. I like seeing the house destroyed even more.'

There were drums beating on every street corner, in front of the spot where the king had been crowned men and women were dancing and a great crowd still remained gathered, mother and daughter found a drunk in the room where they slept, the two mats were rolled up by the door and it was a good deal later that the theft occurred, they were in the street and Aduke was holding a cloth pouch that held some of her money in her right hand, the rest was tucked away in another pouch under her skirt, when a man ripped the pouch off her and said with an ugly look:

'Keep quiet. Don't say anything to anyone.'

They had set off walking, she could see he was really drunk, at first Aduke thought of shouting out, the little girl wanted to speak but lost her voice but mother quickly regained her senses and motioned to her daughter:

'Let's follow behind him.'

The man stopped at a palm-wine stall, ordered a calabash, paid for it with part of Aduke's money and drank it straight down, almost without stopping, he made only one brief pause before getting to the end, another man shouted:

'That's some drinking.'

A second calabash was consumed minutes later, then the man couldn't take any more and someone asked where he lived:

'Over the river.'

They wanted to take him.

'I can go by myself.'

He staggered away, bumped into the yellow wall of a house on the corner, the mother and daughter followed behind, then he suddenly spun round, saw them both and wagged a finger at them:

'Don't say a thing to anyone.'

The words could hardly be distinguished, Abionan wanted to go back but mother gripped her firmly, the man continued on his way, they were now out on the road, people passed by talking and the man stopped, Aduke dragged the daughter back behind a tree, the man looked both ways, saw the shade of a bush, went over to it and lay down.

The woman approached with the girl and sat down nearby, she made the girl sit down as well and watched the man, Abionan was wanting to know what move mother was going to make, but she was afraid to ask, they remained there a long time and anyone passing on the road might have thought it was a family scene, the man asleep, the mother keeping a look out and the little girl quiet,

Abionan had the feeling that they stayed there all day long, the sun changed its position, the man began to snore, and only after an enormous time did Aduke slip her hand under his arm where the pouch was, calmly remove it from him, get up, call to Abionan and the pair mingled into the others on the road.

When they came back into the city, there was even more dancing, the day was drawing to its close, and something of a shadow was now settling down upon the house, so mother said:

'Let's have a bit to eat and then sleep.'

They halted at an acará stall, and the girl looked down the street:

'What if he comes back?'

Mother was clear about that:

'He won't come back.'

They could not get to sleep quickly because there was a bonfire in front of their house and lots of people were still shouting and laughing at the tops of their voices, Aduke remained quiet and Elizabeth appeared:

'Where have you been, Abioná?'

She was another one to call her Abioná, before she could answer Elizabeth explained:

'I've looked everywhere for you to take you to see the men in masks.'

'What, egunguns?'

'No. They are just funny men in masks, they make mischief and say funny things.'

She was still afraid and thought any man who turned up would be the drunk, they went to sleep late, the cries of the city seemed to come in from afar and she dreamt about people in masks robbing the pouch in which mother kept her money, the festival continued on to the next morning, when they went to see the king's palace which was surrounded by merry people, the little girl ran after red lizards, the big ones that shook their heads at people, while Aduke went into a temple of Obatala, the market seemed to be full again, every stallholder back at her stall and the traffic grew with every moment, by just before midday you could hardly pass between one stall and the next, when the two of them sat down behind a wall, mother announced:

'We're setting off tomorrow.'

They ate in silence for some minutes before Abionan said:

'Is that because of the man?'

'No, it's time we continue our journey. There's no chance of working here either in the market or in the street.'

'Where are we going to?'

'Ibadan.'

Abionan went to tell Elizabeth who opened her eyes wide:

'Ibadan? That's the biggest city in the world.'

'Have you ever been there?'

'No, but my father goes there every month.'

They had left in the morning, the girl was by now used to walking along roads full of people, snatches of conversation could be heard, but this time mother grew rapidly tired and they sat down for an hour under a big tree, then they went to eat on the bank of a stream which bounded over the stones and an old woman appeared who took her blouse off, her breasts dropped down like two leather thongs, she went into the water and washed her arms, neck, breasts and face, and dried herself with a towel that she took out of her bundle, then she found a place to eat and a man on a bicycle shouted from the road:

'Eku-je, may you not die while you're eating.'

The old woman mumbled her acknowledgement, Aduke decided to sleep a while and the girl stayed awake, only in the afternoon had they set off, they had walked a good way further before the sun disappeared behind the bush, Abionan wondered whether they would sleep there on the spot but they found a house at a bend in the road, mother asked permission for the two of them to rest in the entrance by the door but they stayed a lot longer watching the night draw in and listening to the noises of animals and insects, Abionan soon fell asleep and on the morrow they took to the road once more, only on the third day did they come to rising ground from where they could see houses and yet more houses spreading up and down a succession of hills, lots of smoke mounting into the sky and a hum seemed to rise up from the whole, streets with lots of cars and countless people appeared both near and far, to begin with mother and daughter were disorientated and didn't know which way to turn, it was the biggest city the girl had ever seen and as it was growing dark Aduke decided not to enter the confusion of the streets that night, they slept at the place where they had caught their first sight of the hills covered with houses, the noise of people passing continued till early morning and Abionan felt that her life was changing, it was a powerful feeling, and one she didn't wholly comprehend, sensing simply that suddenly the world was different.

And into that different world mother and daughter penetrated the next day, first they descended a steep street full of small children and houses, the hillside ran down to a road carrying a great deal of traffic, driving past were motor cars and small buses with women seated on benches, they had difficulty in getting across to the other side and they kept on walking till after midday and still they were in the city, then they went through lots of markets, they ate and everybody seemed jolly, in the afternoon Aduke sat down near by an old woman who was selling obis and orobos laid out on top of a packing-case, she got into conversation with her and inquired about the markets, the old woman informed her:

'The one who knows best about markets and knows all the markets in Ibadan is that man over there.'

And she pointed to a stout man, without a wisp of hair on a head that gleamed like a piece of painted metal, the little girl thought he was a strange figure, big lips twisted forwards which made him look like a toad, the old woman informed her further:

'His name is Obatala.'

'Do you suppose I can go over and ask him about the markets around here?'

'Go over and he'll talk to you.'

Aduke went to see the man and greeted him:

'May you not die while you are seated there.'

He looked up:

'Where do you come from, woman with that funny accent of yours?'

'Ketu, sir.'

They talked of this and that before she mentioned markets.

'Markets?' repeated the man with a smile, 'There are many markets in Ibadan. Do you know how many?'

'No.'

'There are 26 large markets in Ibadan.'

And he gazed at the woman's astonishment.

'26?'

'Yes.'

'Which is the best one?'

'They're all the best.'

He continued to grin.

'If I wanted to work in one of them, what would you advise?'

'That depends. If you're selling cattle – but it's only men who sell cattle – the market's the one at Sanngo. That's just straight on up. It's worth going.'

'But which is the biggest?'

'The biggest and oldest is Iba market, or Oja-Iba, there are also people who call it Oja'ba.'

'That's where I want to sell.'

'Leave going there until early tomorrow.'

They talked on, then the woman pulled her daughter away who continued to stare at the man's gleaming head in fascination, the hubbub of the city was rising, tooting cars passed by, the traffic was congested and mother and daughter kept close to a gari stall, at night car headlights lent an unexpected beauty to everything.

In the morning they went to see the cattle market, and there were some with very big horns, even bigger than the ones at Abeokuta, men were shouting all around the place and talking a language that mother and daughter didn't understand, mud lay on the ground and they stayed there for nearly an hour amazed at all the activity, then Aduke asked the way to Oja-Iba and they set off on foot through the midst of bicycles and women with high calabashes, and one of them passed in front of Abionan with several layers of materials on top of her head, at times it was hard to move even two steps forward, people going and people coming intermingled, nearly all the women had children strapped on their backs, then suddenly they came into what seemed to be a street lined on either side with stalls and saw a board up which read 'Oja-Iba – Ibadan', big baskets and calabashes of every dimension containing meal and potatoes, sacks of produce stacked up in the corners, enormous yams on the ground, a man in a long striped robe was slicing pieces of yam and setting them out by a stool and mother and daughter saw chicken coops stretching for more than a hundred metres, then came robes, skirts, materials, hats, meals, goats and, a row of stalls with monkey skulls and other dead animals on display, another row exhibiting herbs and plants, there were those for medicines, those for pottery, stalls selling tables and chairs and from time to time the land would rise as if to form a hill and the stalls would rise with it, ditches of water ran down, remains of vegetables and tomatoes were trodden underfoot by passers-by, a smell of vegetables followed mother and daughter who had by now reached a higher point from where they could see lines of stalls running off in different directions, walls of wood and mud alternated and Aduke decided to have a word with a young stallholder who was laying out yellow and blue adires on a packing case, the topic was the market, how to obtain a permit to trade?, who to speak to?, and the latter wanted to know:

'What do you sell?'

'Food.'

'Then the best is Mokola market.'

'Why?'

'There you have everything in the food line, rice, bananas, vegtables, fruit, palm-oil, the lot.'

'But I like this one here.'

'Yes, it's nice here.'

They talked on, Aduke asked whether the girl slept in the stall there on the spot.

'No, a taxi comes at night to pick up me and my things as well. I come back early in the morning.'

After a while it was settled that Aduke and Abionan could sleep there for a few days, they agreed a price and at night after the girl had caught her taxi, the market became even more beautiful, lights lit up on many of the stalls and there were stallholders working and talking with people moving among them just as in the daytime, they spent a week sleeping there until Aduke obtained a licence to sell peppers, she learnt where to get her supplies, then they moved on to another section of the market where there had commenced a period which the little girl was never to forget, with people stopping to buy, the conversations and the arguments, they would sleep underneath the pepper stand, some nights they would not lie down till very late, there were conversations that seemed to be unending and someone would ask:

'What's Ketu like?'

'Much smaller than Ibadan.'

'And the market?'

'It's fine.'

Then came the details of the round of the four markets, one in each place and about the women who went from market to market, a plump young woman opened her eyes wide in astonishment and said:

'I'd get very tired having to go on foot from one market to the next every night.'

Abionan noticed that mother was smiling more easily now and

she would let the girl go around the market on her own, in a few days she came to know all the goings-on, the quirks and smells of each area of the market and she liked the stalls with the dead animals, one day she picked up a monkey skull, there were still bits of skin stuck on the bone but it didn't scare her now any more, as always the palm-wine spot held a great attraction for her for she never tired of being amazed by the way in which men took to drinking bouts and the recollection of the drunken thief in Ijebu-Ode only heightened her fascination, she had got into the habit of following drunks to see what they would do, she got to know two girls, Oladeji and Louise who went around with her, and the three of them ran about amongst the market women, they screamed when a drunk staggered or bumped into a basket of potatoes or tomatoes, one of them once fell over a shelful of oranges and the fruit went rolling across the ground and the stallholder yelled in anger, all the stallholders around hurled abuse at the drunk who got up seemingly quite unaware of what was going on and Abionan arrived at her mother's side holding an orange.

'Where did you get that from, child?'

'A drunk scattered oranges all over the place on the other side, this one was left over.'

'Left over indeed, what do you mean? Go and return what isn't yours.'

Abionan did so, Oladeji had no mother and lived with an uncle who also worked in the market, he sold goats and her friend related how uncle was the sacrificer of lambs at a temple of Shango near Oja-Iba, the sacrifices formed part of the girl's early childhood and she had been present, she said, when over two hundred lambs had been killed by her uncle who would splash the animal's blood over the stones and the people, and sometimes she would come out with a bit of blood on her breast and back, Louise did have a mother who was a decorated calabash seller, some of them coloured, and brothers, five or six, a whole range of little boys, from the youngest at two years old right up to the eldest at eleven, the eldest one would pull Abionan's hair and she would chase after him and throw him on the ground and she became famous for her strength.

'Do you fight boys back in Ketu as well?' Louise wanted to know.

'No. I never fought there.'

Ibàdan was a party, Abionan had things to do the whole day long, she went around the market, talked with other girls, followed the drunks, ate where and when she could, crossed the streets on the fringes and entered unknown parts of the city, she saw notices and posters, went into indoor restaurants to see what they were like, one day she smelt a different smell from one of them, she asked what it was and found out it was a Lebanese one, she got to know the drapers' shops with their ornate doors through which people went to make their purchases, she heard loudspeakers with music blaring all day long and they made people happy to hear it, Abionan and Oladeji would dance to the sound of the music, and the people gathered to watch, Louise was more timid, she just stood looking on, sometimes cars with music on inside passed by, men with well-to-do clothes would come into the market and seemed to give the impression that they were above everybody, not even the king of Ijebu-Ode had looked as haughty as that, the girls jeered at the men and ran off, mother seemed to be getting happier all the time, selling her peppers with relish and made friends with all the neighbouring stallholders and she went out for walks with them, they would go out to eat together and the girl would go with them, but she really preferred to go walking through the midst of the stalls, one day Abionan, Oladeji and Louise went out of the market and through some strange streets, Louise asked:

'Will we find the way back?'

'Just ask other people on the way. They'll show us.'

They would stop whenever a fine or unusual house appeared, they came across a man with a serious face talking about religion saying that everyone must repent their sins, Abionan wondered whether she had sinned, and the man's voice was impressive, and rose above the noise of the motor cars:

'Who repents not of their sins will find death in life and be dead long before dying.'

It all seemed rather nice, although Abionan barely understood the words when she heard them put together like that, there were also traders who cried their wares:

'A potato peeler which cuts by itself, a marvellous peeler, you don't even need to lay hands on it.'

The girls stared closely, but you did need to put your hands on the peeler of course, otherwise it wouldn't peel a thing, they went into a protestant church, a whole mass of pews, Abionan missed the saints that they had in the catholic churches, she saw girls in European dress, very short skirts and gaudily coloured scarves round their necks in a cafe where they sold dark-looking drinks.

'Palm-wine?' Abionan wanted to know.

'No, silly. That's Coca-Cola.'

She was called silly again when she asked what that great big building was, was it the king's palace?

'That's the university,' explained Oladeji.

And she went on to say that in there they studied important subjects, way above those in the children's schools, at the university everyone was older, there wasn't a single child studying there, Abionan looked at the house for a long time and thought it was beautiful, on the way back they went a different way which was busier, and several times they had to ask which direction it was to Oja-Iba, when the girl reached mother's stall, night had already fallen and the girl tried to keep away from her but Aduke summoned her:

'Where have you been all this time?'

'I went out for a walk with the other girls. We went as far as the university and came back by a road we didn't know.'

'Come and eat because it's late now.'

She couldn't say how many weeks they had stayed in Ibadan, but certainly it was ten, or more than three months, and the city became familiar to her, she could get easily to any part and mother found herself asking the girl to help her find this or that quarter, she came to know the hills upon which the city lived, she visited nearly all the markets and liked the one at Dugbe, it seemed bigger than Iba, she had also been at the one at Oje which was big too, twice she ate at the one at Mokola, that was where there was most food to be seen and she spent a day at Apata-Ganga which emptied out in the afternoon, and turned into an ideal spot for a small child to play in, then she crossed over to the one at Aranyan which was small and got to know Agugu, Sabo, Labo, Elekuro and when she visited Oja'gbo with mother and the latter asked why it had that name, an old man said:

'Oja'gbo is the market of the bush, in olden times it was right in the bush, but today it is within the city.'

She had gone back to Oja'gbo several times, and it was where there were entertainments around the stalls, the girl heard about magicians, men who performed magic and answered questions,

90

groups of drummers enlivened Oja'gbo at all times of day and Abionan had stopped to watch the women dancing, the sound of the drums could be heard from far away and she saw weddings, the couples would cross the market, she would be present at funeral trains and will listen to groups of musicians, religious preachers would meet there every day, mother thought of moving to Oja'gbo but Iba market afforded better conditions and she had already become used to it, the little girl began to get the feel of every stall, everything became transformed from one part of the market to the rest, the way of picking up the goods on sale would be different, the women who dealt in materials spoke words that others wouldn't use, they seemed to know more words than the other traders, and the calabash sellers could tell a good tale too, she eventually discovered that Oladeji adored stories, she would talk about her grandfather who had been lord of the land, Abionan asked whether he was the owner and Oladeji said he wasn't, the lord of the land was whom you sought permission from to plant and harvest a crop, nothing could be planted without him saying it was all right, the orishas would assist and the yield would be great and she told of many strange things about the return of the dead and the lord of the land possessed rare powers, Abionan inquired:

'If the lord isn't the owner of the land, who is then?'

'Anyone. It doesn't really matter who the owner is. The lord is the one who knows when to do the planting and whether the planter will be lucky or not.'

She talked about her grandfather and how he would crouch down at the spot where something was going to be planted, one time that she recalled it had been maize, and after stooping down, he had taken a handful of soil, smeared it on his hands and sniffed it, grandfather would also pray for the return of the family dead to watch over the plantation and Oladeji would stay awake at night to see the dead return, the lord of the land would invoke them at great length speaking in an even placid voice, the wind would descend upon the field and in that wind the dead would seem to be descending, the girl said that she could feel the dead passing close by and brushing against her arm, one night amid the drum-beats of the ceremony of summoning up the dead, she had had an irresistible urge to dance and she had danced on the earth for an enormous length of time, grandfather had accompanied her with gestures and chants and she was never again to forget the delight she took in dancing.

Abionan had also danced one afternoon, the musicians of Oja'gbo played pieces that she thought were really lovely, she would go dancing off between two stalls, they quickly drew apart to watch her, and, following custom, stuck money on the sweat of the girl's forehead, other small children and women danced with her, and mother, who was at another stall, was called across to watch what was happening, she stood there in silence and when the daughter wearied and stopped she caught hold of her hand and, without a word, took her back to Iba market, on later days she would look at her daughter from time to time as if studying her and would at length say:

'I think you'll have to learn to dance to the orishas.'

The girl just stared at mother and wondered why learn to if for you can dance without even thinking, Aduke must have read her thoughts for she said:

'Everything we do has to be done properly and you can only do it properly by learning.'

Then she saw fit to add:

'When we are back in Ketu you shall learn.'

She felt homesick for Ketu, for those familiar houses and the market place and its lively market, although Ibadan was lively too.

'When are we going back then?'

She knew that they were going first to Ifé and Oshagbo, mother explained:

'We'll come back this way again afterwards and then we'll see.'

They had resumed the journey on a day when Iba market seemed busier and livelier than ever and Oladeji asked:

'Will uncle let me come with you?'

'Ask him.'

He did. The road to Ifé was bordered by small markets, sometimes with a settlement around them and sometimes with neither homes nor streets, just stalls, but even there there would be customers and lorries that stopped, there were cars too, and the girls would run on ahead, they found it all tremendous fun, they discovered great-crowned mango trees, they went into the bush to see what was there, Abionan's mother called after them and they went and slept the night at a settlement of some ten houses in a row, babies cried in a room lit by two lanterns and one of the houses had a grave in front of it, Aduke laid out the three mats alongside a wall painted blue and Abionan and Oladeji soon went off to sleep, a dog barked the whole night long, the next morning the girls examined the grave and Aduke said that it must be of the father of the small children who were playing on top of it, they rolled off the grave on to the ground and the air on the road was cold, in the afternoon Aduke announced to the girls that she was tired:

'We're going to sleep here tonight.'

'What, here?' asked Abionan eyeing the poor stalls of a market which was the smallest she'd ever seen.'

'It's a lovely spot.' explained mother.

Indeed it was. The girls climbed a tall tree and from up there they could see far along the road, with mountains covered with squat trees, to the left grazing land could be seen, full of goats or some similar creatures, Oladeji before sleeping told some family tales:

'Do you know my little sister?'

The other nodded.

'Well that sister's my grandmother who's come back. Didn't you notice what her name was?'

'No.'

'It's Yabo which means "mummy's back". My grandmother died and my mother got sad. A year later, when sister was born, my mother saw that she was just like her mother. So mummy knew that granny was back with us.'

Abionan had started thinking about that. When she had a child, would it be someone in the family coming back?, but she soon stopped trying to imagine who would come back in her son because a great big lizard ran past along the road, the girls ran behind and as they ran they saw a city loom up, it was Ifé.

Mother went with the girls all the way down what seemed to be the main street, and talked with other women, then she took the girls to a large house at the front of which was a shop where men were working pieces of hide, on the first day they went to see the stone that Aduke said it was important to see, then a man in a long Yoruba robe turned up:

'That's the obelisk of Oranyan.'

Mother hadn't wanted any explanations, she'd much rather stay alone with the girls, after the man had gone, the woman turned to Abionan:

'That's where the founders of Ketu set out from.'

It was then that the girl felt curious to take a closer look at the city which mother said was the origin of everything, in the house where

93

they went to sleep the night there was a dwarf hunchbacked boy who grinned at both of them, at first Abionan and Oladeji went quiet, half in fear, but the dwarf grinned so much that he soon seemed really nice, it was as if his hunchback and size didn't exist and they discovered that he made things out of clay, the next day they saw the dwarf, who was called Adimu, pick up a handful of clay in the back of the house and work it up into the shape of a pot which he then took to an oven, Abionan, who had never seen anything like it, was spellbound, then Adimu made the face of a man with lines on each cheek, and Oladeji wanted to know who it was:

'It's the king of Ifé who's over there in the museum.'

Abionan looked at the king's face and she thought it was very handsome:

'Where does the king live?'

Adimu laughed in his way:

'That one's dead now. He was the first king of Ifé, the founder. The present one's quite different. He's fat.'

Aduke took the girls to a market, it was a small one, the palm-wine stall took up a vast area and the next day the two went round the city on their own, they stopped when there was something nice to see, the long stone was funny for it looked like a dried tree-trunk, another day Adimu came with them and he knew all the places, he showed them houses and shops and walked quickly in spite of being hunchbacked, when the three got tired, they sat down on a stone and the girls talked about Ibadan, the dwarf got quite enthusiastic:

'That's where I wanted to live. I was going to sell my pots and my heads in the market.'

Abionan was surprised at his wish for something that she knew so well, the dwarf went on:

'Are the markets nice in Ibadan?'

Each girl wanted to explain for herself what the markets were like and Abionan talked about Iba where mother sold, then about Oja'gbo where she had danced and Oladeji said the cattle market was the nicest, cattle of all sizes, Adimu looked now at one girl and now at the other and admitted:

'One day I'm going to run away from home and go to Ibadan.'

'Do you have to run away?'

'Yes, I do. My mother thinks I'm too weak and unable to fend for myself.'

Abionan looked at Adimu's sharply hunchbacked back, she

thought he looked quite capable of looking after himself and the three went all round the city, sometimes he missed his clay and then he would stay behind at home and make pots, heads and figures, he studied every detail of his work and observed:

'This one looks like the owner of the hide shop.'

The girls giggled, there were heads looking like people from round the neighbourhood and like Adimu's uncle, there were other men in the house and Oladeji asked:

'Which of them's your father?'

'None of them. My father departed the world a long time ago. I was never to know what he was like.'

The men in masks at Ifé had nicer robes than the ones in Ketu and Ibadan with brightly coloured ribbons and as they crossed the street patterned cloths fell from their bodies with a certain style, Adimu, who was twelve, had a very great respect for the men in masks and once said:

'My uncle explained to me that everything that happens has a reason. I'm a dwarf and hunchback for a very serious reason, my mother thinks it's so that I can do everything better than others, so that was why I started making things out of clay.'

He paused:

'No one in Ifé does it better than I do.'

Oladeji broke in:

'In Ibadan there're lots of people making pots and figures. Some of them might be better at it than you.'

'So they might. But if I go there I'm going to be better than they are.'

He added that the masked men were our dead forefathers.

'The dead always return.'

Abionan had remembered Oladeji's sister and looked at her, now and again the three would eat on and on, laying bets against each other as to who would be able to go on eating even more, Aduke warned her daughter not to eat so much and Adimu would make everyone laugh when he rolled about on the floor, his hunchback helped to make his movements become comical and one afternoon they spent hours watching the men at the hide shop sewing cushions and carpets, Adimu said afterwards:

'I had thought of working in leather but didn't like the feel of leather in my hands. Clay's better, you take hold of it and you feel it softening into the form you want.'

95

Aduke had now felt it was time for them to continue the journey to Oshogbo, this time it was Abionan who asked their dwarf companion:

'Will your mother let you come with us?'

She did. As they would be coming through Ifé on the way back, it could be quite easy to bring him back, but the boy's mother, a tall black woman, with a long face and hard eyes, had declared:

'But only as far as Oshogbo and then straight back to Ifé. And he's not going to Ibadan, oh no. It's still too soon. He'll only come with me, and that when he's fifteen.'

Adimu somersaulted with joy and delight, Aduke set out with the three of them along the road which was still empty at that early hour, she wanted to reach Oshogbo the same day, the distance was not great and they walked all morning, the three children sometimes lagged behind or else went on ahead and an old man talked to Aduke along the way:

'If you go through Ilesha it'll take longer. But this way you'll get to Oshogbo tonight.'

Abionan would always stop when she saw a river or a stream, they ate at a market where there were abaras and salt meat and Adimu wanted to catch an almost black hen which fluttered off into the bush, the girls went after it but once inside all they found were branches and leaves and the hen had vanished, they were frightened of encountering other types of creature so they came running back and mother was already on the road waiting for them, they arrived at Oshogbo while it was still light and Abionan liked the look of the city, with its zinc roofs and smoke in the air.

Aduke had left most of her belongings behind in Ibadan for all they needed were mats, this time it was hard finding a house where they could sleep and in the end they spoke to a short, very fat man who took in the mother and children provided they paid one week down in advance, it was near the palace of the king of Oshogbo and the fat man pointed to the palace and said:

'There's where the Ataoja lives. That's why I charge more.'

The location was pleasant and busy, then in the morning the three children began to explore the shops, markets and streets and 'Abionan liked the layout of everything, the streets stretched out along higher ground with the houses on either side, standing lower down so that to enter one you had to walk down into it from the street, around noon an old man showed them a man in light coloured robes who was coming out of the king's palace and said:

'That's the Ataoja.'

Abionan gazed at the king's face which seemed to be far away and thinking of something else, she saw him disappear into another house nearby and in the afternoon mother announced:

'We're going to visit the Shrine of Oshun.'

Abionan knew that Oshun was the goddess of rivers, of fresh water and of beauty, Adimu didn't know anything about this, he'd only heard of Shango but Oladeji knew everything about the orishas, they walked for half an hour before reaching the spot where the Shrine of Oshun stood.

Behind a wall stood the building, with designs on it, it seemed to be sheltered by some trees, mother spoke:

'That's the grove of Oshun.'

They went into the shrine where there were people sitting on the floor, the wind shook the leaves and they stayed inside for ever such a long while, then they kept to a track which opened out by the river, Abionan heard mother say that it was the river Oshun and it was just as lovely as the river Ogun, the waters came round a bend and there were plants growing straight up from the middle of the river, the children dipped their hands in the water and Adimu sat down on the bank and began to knead a bit of clay, he made a man with a drum, the girls stuck their hands in the clay too and began to make things, Abionan thought up a cow but it came out too small, it seemed more like a goat or a dog, Oladeji tried making a house, the river had a still and regular sound, birds flew from branch to branch and Aduke sat on a stump and looked at the waters, she stayed like that for over an hour and Abionan would glance at her from time to time, she couldn't remember having seen her like that before, the clay from the riverbank swelled in the hands of Adimu who had already moulded three men, then a canoe went by and the three children dropped what they were doing so that their eyes could follow the progress of the canoe which had a man in it trailing a long stick in the river, Aduke rose and called the children, she went back to the shrine and looked carefully all around while the clay figures were left propped against a slender tree.

Night fell on the way back and Oshogbo was full of lamps like those in Ketu, the children gathered near a shop where they sold beer, there was a radio turned up high and Abionan was now beginning to understand a little English though she spoke Yoruba the whole time, phrases in English would sometimes appear in a dream and there was one that would recur, it was a man talking to her all the time with her not understanding, the dream would end without her managing to find out what the man with his cross voice wanted.

The following morning they went back to the Shrine of Oshun, the figures had dried out but the clay was coming to pieces, Adimu shaped some more and he was ages playing around with different shapes and objects, the two girls climbed a tree which bent over the river and from there they tossed the little fruits of the tree into the river, then they came down again and walked the length of the riverside, Adimu washed his hands in the river, set his figures up on a stone and then went off to see Oladeji and Abionan, they came across a fisherman, sitting calmly, the man looked up and then Abionan said:

'May you not die while you're fishing.'

The man acknowledged her and the children stayed to see whether he'd catch anything, it took a while but at last a small fish appeared on the line which the man lifted up, Adimu asked whether there were a lot of fish there, the man explained:

'Didn't you know that it was on this spot that Oshun made a pact with the king of Oshogbo? She promised to supply lots of fish for the population and they will never forget Oshun but always come here to leave offerings for her.

They talked on, then Aduke called the children for it was time to eat, which they did as they sat on a rather wet stump covered with slime, they ate with their hands and watched the sun beating down on the river, women who had just been at the Shrine of Oshun also came down to the bank and took their food out of packages, there was a great silence about everything and after their meal Aduke took the children to the shrine, they lay down on the floor, and there they stayed, Abionan thought it funny to go to sleep when it wasn't night but eventually she slept or drowsed off, on the way back the road was full of people and a man with a small drum under his arm was dancing and singing, kicking up the roadside dust.

None of the children had any idea what was to come when Aduke one afternoon announced to them all that they were to be received by the Ataoja the very next day, the king of Oshogbo had made an appointment for her to visit him and she could bring the children too, Abionan went to sleep thinking about all that and had a dream that the king was telling her off, the next day mother dressed the girl in a new frock bought in Oshogbo, combed Oladeji's hair and inspected Adimu's robe, at the time of the audience, the four went through the doors of the palace and inside there was a very large hall, the king was sitting with some people beside him, the woman stepped forward and greeted him and the Ataoja smiled:

'So, well now, woman, do you come from Ketu?'

'Yes, I do, sir.'

'And are these your children?'

'No, only this one. The other girl's from Ibadan. The boy's from Ifé.'

There was a pause as the Ataoja looked at each child in turn.

'And what is the purpose of your trip?'

'I wanted to see the Yoruba cities. And I wanted my daughter to see something of the world.'

The king observed:

'Fine. You pronounce words a bit differently, but enough to be understood.'

'I've been learning along the way. But there's a difference at every place.'

The king invited the visitors to a meal, rice appeared which Abionan put into her mouth but almost spat it out because of the pepper in it, though as everyone else was eating without appearing to notice anything unusual she persevered, she liked pepper but not that much, the conversation in the hall broadened, they talked about travelling and the Ataoja said that Lagos was a pleasant city, another man thought that Lagos was too big and the girl wondered whether it could really be bigger than Ibadan, yet a third declared that he had liked Porto Novo but no one seemed to know Ketu, an old man remarked that the best city of all was Ejigbo because of the festival of Obatala then the Ataoja summed matters up:

'But the best city to live in is Oshogbo.'

Mother rose and thanked the king for his kindness, the three children went out with her and in the street on the way back they started discussing all they had seen, Abionan asked:

'What did you think of the king?'

Adimu turned up his nose:

'He's just like anyone else. There's nothing particularly special about him.'

Oladeji thought that the king's face was imposing and Abionan complained about the excess of pepper, Adimu said that he was used to even more pepper than that and then in the afternoon men with drums appeared, who played into the night, children gathered around, over a hundred boys and girls, who accompanied the beating, they talked, made comments and sleep came only with difficulty to Abionan who could see a patch of sky through the open window of the house, the mat started to prickle her back and the next morning they went again to the Shrine of Oshun, and the children dipped their faces into the water of the river, it was a perfect day and the sun came through the branches of the trees, well-dressed folk came to visit the shrine and, other children turned up, one of them, a girl, who seemed to be eight years old, stared at Adimu's hunched back, so that Adimu asked:

'Never seen a hunchback before?'

He seemed annoyed but smiled, the girl ran off in alarm, he went back to making his clay figures and tried to recapture the face of the Ataoja, he sought the girls' opinions and Abionan studied the clay face:

'It's quite like it.'

Oladeji didn't know:

'I can't remember his face any more. I only know that it was impressive.'

They came back along the road playing, and Aduke seemed to be happier than usual, she spoke animatedly with other women, and there were more festivities at night, the sound of drums came from further afield and Aduke was ages talking to the short fat man, the next day she said:

'It's time to think about the journey back.'

She stayed another two days and took the children to the Shrine of Oshun for one last time, Adimu's figures were now set out in a row on a stone, no one had tampered with them and this time Aduke spent ages inside the temple and then she remarked to her daughter: 'I'd be really happy if there were somewhere like that in Ketu.'

When they set off back to Ifá, the woman turned round on the brow of the road and looked back at the city once more, Adimu's mother wanted to know how everything had been, whether her son had behaved properly, the boys and girls heard Abionan, Oladeji and Adimu tell all about the visit to the Ataoja with the details of the palace and snatches of the conversation, about the Shrine of Oshun, the river and the clay figures, five days later Aduke and the two girls were back in Ibadan where mother went to her place at the stall, for the first few days she seemed tired and went out little, when she required a further stock of peppers it was Abionan who would obtain them, do the business and bring them back, mother stayed behind and leant back against a wooden post at her pitch, once she had replied to a question from her daughter like this:

'I'm resting to get ready for the journey back.'

'Are we going to Ketu?'

'Yes, we are.'

'When?'

'We're going round two more places, Ejegbo and Oyo. Then straight to Ketu.'

Abionan had got talking to Oladeji about the cities, Ejigbo was near there and Oyo a little further off, but her friend knew nothing of Ketu, she thought it must be on the other side of the world and when the day of parting came, the girls walked through Iba market once more and it seemed busier than ever and with so many people that they could hardly get through, Oladeji promised she'd come and visit her in Ketu and when it came to leaving mother and daughter took very long to get out of the city, for they walked for quite some while but were still in Ibadan whose hills they watched disappear, the road was full of cattle being taken to market, they saw sacks of merchandise, loads of obis and orobos, lorries with bananas and people, mother and daughter were loaded up with bundles and mats and things that Aduke had decided to buy, they did not walk very quickly and mother would stop every so often, the day was hot and Abionan was sweating, they crossed streams and saw bridges, they ate in a long market which was merely a row of stalls all along the road and Abionan was surprised to see a man selling tyres of various sizes, for cars, motorbikes and bicycles, nearby there were children playing with old tyres, Ejigbo was a small place and as soon as they arrived, Aduke asked a fruit seller:

'When's the festival on?'

'Next week.'

Abionan had sensed that there was something in the air, and looked up to see clouds, so was it going to rain?, until now the journey had met with no rain and they had been able to walk on the roads at their leisure but what if it were to rain?, she heard her mother talking about rain as if following the thoughts of the girl who was at every instant looking around, she was missing Oladeji, travelling without her friend and without Adimu became more wearisome, then the fruit seller said to mother loudly:

'Rain will come only when the festival's over.'

'Why?'

The stallholder looked at the other one in apparent surprise at someone not knowing that:

'Well, that's because the festival is held to summon up the rain.'

They had found a place to sleep in a long house that had more than ten windows opening on to the street, they put down their mats and the city seemed to be filling up all the time, people were arriving, generally dressed in white, many were sleeping right there in the street, and Aduke and the girl spent the next day in the market, it was small but nice, less colourful and not as busy as Iba but it had more food and fruits on display, the acarás had pepper in them but not too much and there was a stillness that Ibadan didn't have, as if people were talking in lower voices, in Ibadan the world seemed to be full of noises, people's voices and the roar of cars, ones heard from a long way off which seemed to be continued by cries close to, endless conversations between one stall and the next and customers who spoke non-stop, only when in Ejigbo did Abionan realise how noisy Ibadan had really been, she had grown used to that mixture of sounds all day long and now found it most odd that despite the preparations for the festival and the joyful arrival of such a lot of people, the world seemed quiet amid all the men and women who came into the house where they were staying, Abionan spent two days without hardly stirring from the spot where she had sat down and mother would say:

'Let's go to the market.'

She had replied that she didn't want to, she was quite all right where she was, nor did she go and meet other children, now and again she thought she had seen Oladeji or Adimu, but looked harder and discovered that they were someone else, actually there was a hunchbacked boy in Ejigo who came up to her also, but he had an ugly face, quite different from the Ifá boy, but on the third day she did go out with mother to see every nook of the market, they heard of the festival devoted to Oshagyian, the great orisha and patron of the city who helped its people overcome their difficulties and mother said that Oshagyian was Obatala when young and so related

102

to the same Obatala that Abionan knew in Ketu, nearly everybody in Ejigbo went about in white, on the eve of the festival she saw lots of men carrying long poles, they walked down the streets as if wanting to vaunt their strength, the little girl was scared at first, she saw strong men with nasty faces waving their poles in the air, mother said it was an act and they weren't really going to fight, Abionan got used to the idea that the two parts of the city were going to pretend that they were at war with one other and from early on the first day of the festival, mother and she were in the main street of Ejigbo, the two armies were facing each other, the men on one side attacked then the other, vigorously brandishing their poles, the blows they made against the sky produced a noise which Abionan listened to raptly, the combatants on the other side counter-attacked and for quite some time too, now the others pressed down on the ones here and made them retreat, now this side would appear to have been enraged and would force the others to run, from time to time there came a respite when the two groups started exchanging insults, shouting abuse, calling names and the row was becoming almost unbearable but the little girl found it all very comic, it was in one of those respites that Aduke took her daughter by the hand and went to show her the king who was seated, dressed entirely in white not far from the warfare, looking at the action quite serenely, he turned to one side and said something to another serious-looking man, the stallholder whom Aduke had been speaking to earlier appeared close by and asked:

'What do you think of it?'

'It's a lovely festival.'

The stallholder looked at Abionan:

'Was the little girl frightened?'

'Just at the start.'

The two sides then resumed the onslaughts, and the whole day long it was one great chase around and about and behind the houses while at the same time as they were fighting, another group of priests was chanting an orikhi in praise of Oshagyian, the girl realised that they were praying for peace and prosperity for the region and from time to time a priest would go right across the street, brushing aside the men who were pretending to be fighting and stamp his feet on the ground, at the end of the afternoon all the priests came out in procession, mother and girl walked along behind them, and three of the ones dressed in white went into a wood, picked up vessels covered also in light cloths, beneath which the shape of the vessels could be seen, and came walking back without rushing, at that point the battle ceased and the men bearing poles escorted the priests up to the door of the king's palace.

It was here that Abionan had thought the festival was nicer because the king came forward to meet the priests and danced before them with firm steps and his feet shuffling on the ground, the dust rose for a moment and mother and daughter kept very close to the king as he led the procession into the palace, afterwards the women and children went back to the market and everyone seemed to be talking all at once, mother bought two dishes of food, the noise increased and Abionan greatly relished the handfuls of rice she was putting into her mouth, night suddenly drew in, the voices went loudly on, a dog was running past, little boys were picking up bits of wood smaller than the fighting poles and fought amongst themselves, women yelled out and it was late when mother and daughter entered the house where they were staying, for more than half an hour Abionan had gazed out of the open window, there were stars in the sky but not a hint of rain, when she shut her eyes she was to have the sensation of opening them straight away again and saw then that it was day, the sun was streaming into the room and beating down on the ground, and the women of the house were preparing for another day of festivities, men holding poles were still playing in the street and they looked like children, Aduke took the little girl to the same place as where they had seen the vessels covered with white cloth, the king was there already, seated near a young lady in long, entirely white, robes, he had a crown on his head, and now and again gently smiled.

The crowd was growing at every moment and Abionan managed to keep close to the first line of people, behind the king stood the Shrine of Oshagyian, wood and other bits and pieces were gathered together in front of the shrine and everything was set alight, the flames leapt up and the dark smoke which came off the bonfire changed direction in the wind and men came forward from among the crowd, Abionan watched to see what they were going to do but they just walked through the cloud of smoke and stopped in the path in which the smoke was drifting and then went back to their places, the women also went up to the fire and put their faces into the middle of the smoke, Aduke got up and imitated the others and when it was the girl's turn, the smoke seemed thick, on the way back she saw women and men arriving with huge calabashes on their heads and they went up to the shrine and set them carefully down on the ground, in them was food of various sorts, other women were carrying large carved wooden spoons and mother told Abionan that the king and the important people of the city were going to eat that food inside the shrine, the two of them would also join in a general celebration where there would be food for all and the girl stopped gazing at the shrine and the king, because lots of children had taken to running around, there seemed to be more merriment than the day before and mother started talking to an old woman with a long nose, the latter wanted to know whether she was going to stay on in Ejigbo:

'No. I've come just to have a look.'

'So, you're back off to Ketu?'

'Yes. That's where all my family are.'

She also said that she had had an urge to see some different markets and the old woman retorted:

'All markets are the same.'

Abionan had wanted to intervene to say that every market is quite different, but mother had already begun to answer:

'Well, that may be so, but each of them has a lot of special things, for instance, its fruits, its materials, and its own way of going on. In Abeokutá the adires are simply gorgeous.'

The old woman butted in:

'So are the ones here.'

Aduke paused before going on:

'Even the ways of cooking and eating are sometimes different.'

Mother and daughter ate with the old woman, they had white food, rice cakes, the white of the cooked maize amazed the little girl and the three ate with their hands and gazed at the shrine's entrance, out of which the king came, drying his hands on a very white towel and he sat down again on his throne, the bonfire died down to nothing and the following day Aduke stared hard at the sky and remarked to her daughter:

'It's going to start raining heavily.'

Abionan had also turned her eyes to the clouds that were travelling over the sky as mother continued:

'It's time we got back.'

'But what if the rain catches us along the way?'

'We can't avoid that.'

The old woman set them at rest however and said that it would only rain hard in a month's time, then mother got everything ready, rolled up the adires and her other belongings in heavy plastic sheets that she had bought in the market and thought they ought to start out very early.

'I want to be in Oyo today.'

They were. They walked faster than they had ever done before, the girl complained of being ever so tired, mostly because of the weight of the things she was laden with and Aduke replied:

'How will you become a market woman if you can't even get used to carrying things a short way?'

'Is this what you call a short way?'

Abionan thought Oyo was a beautiful city. They walked through the market, went to the Shrine of Shango and on the way the girl ran into a group of egunguns the like of which she had never seen before, instead of masks they were wearing sheets full of holes at the front and with wide horizontal stripes, all round the material it was yellow, the bottom was green, their arms were covered with bits of stuff of various colours, the material was black and white striped and on the tops of their heads were red, green, yellow and pink cloths, the egunguns seemed gayer than the ones in Ketu and near the shrine she saw men playing long drums with wires from one extremity to the other and fastened to an elegant thong of leather which fell from the men's shoulders, they were playing loudly and now and again someone would stick a coin on one of their sweating foreheads and then they would all play the drums even harder, she did not know whether it was the king's palace or the shrine of the orisha, the house was long and had stilts shaped like people, wooden heads that supported the weight of the whole house, in the market they ate almost without stopping and went to sleep the night close to the palace or shrine, the following morning they went round the whole city and saw houses and shops, mother spoke to women and men who worked in the market, where they sold lovely brightly-coloured leather goods and from time to time they heard drums playing, Oyo seemed to be full of the sound of drums, men with broad faces would burst out in hearty laughter and in the end Abionan did visit the Shrine of Shango and learnt that the king of Oyo who was called Alafin was not in the city, he had gone on a journey to Lagos and would be away many weeks, mother and daughter sat down on the ground before the wooden figures that represented Shango and when they left, the sun was scorching, atabal players were accompanying the excited dance which a group of women were performing beneath a very leafy tree and everyone seemed happy, the city had long houses, and Abionan went to see the men working in leather, coloured pouffes, they worked and talked, one said one thing and another would reply, but there were periods of silence, each concentrating on the bit of leather he held in his hands and no one paid any attention to her, she thought Oyo seemed smaller than Ibadan but she liked the streets where there was room for a child to shout and play, the first night she ran as far as the end of the main square and looked at the houses with their lights on and children sitting on the floor, two old men went past chatting and then she had a great urge to scream so she screamed and when she came back mother wanted to know:

'Was that your scream?'

'Yes.'

The woman had seemed about to ask another question but didn't, the little girl had run under the tree where the women had been dancing, perspiration was running down her face and she felt a great contentment within herself, Fatogum was to say much later with Abionan listening attentively:

'Oyo is sister to Ketu.'

'Sister?'

'Indeed so. From Ifé two groups of people went forth to found cities. One came to where Ketu now stands. The other went to Oyo.'

The next morning Abionan had noticed that mother was all the time gazing at the sky, she wondered whether she was afraid the rain would come at any moment, the clouds passed over rapidly and the girl thought about the journey back:

'Is Ketu far from here?'

It was. The woman went into detail and said that now the distance would be greater than all they had covered from Ketu to the Ogun river.

'Will we go down the Ogun river again?'

They would. But just to cross it, explained mother. They spent a few more days making preparations for the journey and bought two large umbrellas, one dark red, the other looking rather like a rainbow, with stripes of every colour, Aduke thought that the plastic sheeting could be further reinforced and she now seemed to be in a hurry, Abionan too was seized by a great homesickness for Ketu, she could see once again the house where they lived, the market place and the market and it was in Oyo market that they had said goodbye to the journey and all that it meant, Aduke had appeared to be afraid that Ketu might have vanished while the two had been away, and that night she had drawn her daughter up close to her and begun to speak in a hushed voice, a lamp shining a few metres away:

'This journey was for you and for me as well. Since childhood I have dreamt of going out into the world, finding out about other markets, seeing the place where they make adires, visiting the Shrine of Oshun at Oshigbo, diving into the hurly-burly of Ibadan. Now I'm tired. Seeing new things is a fine thing but tiring too. The journey back'll be long and it might rain and both of us get wet but it has been all worthwhile in spite of tiredness and the theft we had in Ijebu-Ode. I shall always remember this journey. And I'll be making more when my tiredness is over.'

Abionan was sleepy and, she heard only half of what mother was saying but she learnt that they would be leaving next morning and leave they did.

The sky had been cloudy and at first mother and daughter stepped it out and stopped only to eat, the road seemed always the same and unchanging, and the girl was afraid that they would come back to the place they had left, they crossed a desolate stretch with hardly any houses in sight and they slept on the bank of a stream with their mats laid out on the grass, they woke before daybreak and walked on all morning without stopping, in the afternoon they reached the Ogum river, the river's dark waters moved quietly by and made Abionan recall Emanuel's house with the sick old woman and her eyes open wide, canoes sailing by and the grey parrots in the branches of trees, this time they needed a canoe to cross the river and the boatman was waiting, he charged to take people from one side to the other and mother kept worrying about the rain:

'Do you think it'll rain today?'

The man sniffed the air:

'Not for the time being. It'll be another week yet.'

They had hit the rain before reaching Ilara. Hard, heavy spots, mother and daughter stayed an entire afternoon under a tree, the plastic sheets protected the bundles, mats, adires and clothing and they opened up the two umbrellas as Aduke said:

'Keep quiet. Don't talk when it's raining.'

The patter of rain on the earth soon became something quite natural and Abionan was thinking about the rest of the journey, when it cleared up, mother decided:

'We'd better make the most of it. Back to the road. Let's see if a house turns up.'

One did. Aduke paid to sleep in the living room, the rain set in again and the girl began to feel cold:

'Is it going to rain all the way to Ketu?'

'We'll get there before the worst of the rains.'

It hadn't rained the next day and the pair covered a good stretch in a minimum of time, they crossed streams whose waters were overflowing, but crossed them carefully, lifting up their skirts and taking their packages over one at a time, at Ilara they met the old, old woman who was Aduke's friend and the latter screwed up her face:

'What a lengthy journey. Are you only returning now?'

'Yes.'

She added that, provided it didn't rain, they would continue on their way to Ketu the following morning, Aduke and the old woman spent the night talking, they hardly stopped, from time to time Abionan could while half-asleep overhear the sound of their voices, in the morning they found that it wasn't raining so they set out for the road with the luggage which for Abionan was getting heavier all the time, mother had walked on without speaking, stepping it out with eyes looking ahead till they had reached Ketu almost at nightfall, the family had gathered round to make their comments, and argue and listen, Abionan slept in mother's arms, the next day she had run off to the market place, gone into the market, seen the holy tree once again and followed the king of Ketu who had been coming out to make a visit, now in the market at Opo Meta she recalls that journey so vividly and now she can again see the Ogun river, glimpses of Ibadan and Ifé, the Shrine of Oshun, which had mother liked most?, Abionan feels sure that it would be Oshogbo with the streets higher than the houses, the Shrine of Oshun and the visit to see the king, now she knows that the king had received them because mother was of the royal family of Ketu and she doesn't notice when the uncle turns up to find out her answer:

'Have you made your decision yet?'

The woman looked at him in silence and uncle went on:

'I hope you have come to the conclusion that managing a shop in

Cotonou is the best thing that can happen in your life.'

She still didn't know what to say but began:

'I have thought it over. . . .'

She stopped for she was not being wholly frank:

'I mean, I wasn't thinking the whole while about your offer, I was reminiscing about the journey I made round the cities of Nigeria.'

Uncle smiled:

'I well recall that journey. Everyone in the family was against it except myself.'

'Quite. I thought back over nearly every moment of the journey, the places where we stopped, the markets where my mother sold, the rivers and the festivals, the king of Oshogbo, and all of it.'

Uncle frowned:

'And so?'

'Amidst my recollections I thought about your offer, I thought about it and my first feeling was confirmed.'

'Which was?'

Abionan smiled:

'My first feeling? That I'd be happier in the markets of Ketu, Opo Meta, Idigny and Iro Kogny.'

Uncle stared at her for a few moments:

'I think you're making a mistake.'

'Maybe.'

The man continued:

'A great mistake.'

She hung her head and thought about what he had said:

'Please try and understand me. I was highly honoured at your proposition for it's not every day that you're invited to become a partner in something good, but I would be unhappy there.'

She lifted her eyes back to him who was smiling rather sadly:

'I'm the loser but that's by the way. You're who knows what's best for yourself.'

Abionan asked:

'Did you get your money?'

'Yes, I did.'

Yatundé came up, saw that the matter was serious and backed away, Abionan said:

'Come on in. I've already given uncle my answer.'

The other did not ask what it was, but the man persisted:

'If you change your mind before next week, there'll still be time.'

He bade farewell, Abionan and Yatundé watched him as he moved rapidly between the stalls, her friend wanted to know:

'Was he really upset?'

'Quite a lot.'

The market was reaching its lull, when even the little boys who charged naked from one stall to another had become quiet, the sun had disappeared behind the trees and Abionan felt weariness in her body, she took a deep breath and then Yatunde asked whether she had any regrets.

'No regrets. I'm just tired.'

Nearby a dog barked.

'When afternoon comes I'm always tired.'

The other agreed:

'Me too.'

'Then, when it's time to take to the road and walk on to the next market, I brighten up.'

More customers kept turning up and an old woman in a green-and-white robe took nearly everything that Abionan had, then she bought some peppers from Yatundé and then a man dressed in European clothes with a red tie, and a young girl who seemed to be newly-wed, so that Abionan in the end went over to visit Solange, she passed other stalls and remembered that Oladeji had since been several times to visit her in Ketu, the girl in Ibadan had kept up her childhood friendship and on one of these visits she had stayed a month going round the markets with Abionan, young Mariana had also done that and Oladeji now had a very fine stall in Iba market and sold brightly coloured materials from India and England, adires from Abeokutá, silks, and lengths of cotton, it was a peaceful pleasant trade, the girl had become quite pretty and she went about surrounded by admirers but didn't want to get married, she still told stories and uncle still lived with her, this was how Oladeji had explained the arrangement:

'Now it's not I who lives with him but he who lives with me. He's grown old, all he likes is drinking beer, I do the housekeeping and he adores me.'

'What about you?'

'His presence gives me a great deal of security. We talk a lot, sometimes all night long, his opinions are always sound, and when he talks he's never thinking about himself.'

They recalled the journey they had made together to Ifé and

Oshogbo then Abionan remembered mother whose death she did not like remembering, Oladeji had said on the first visit she had paid to Ketu:

'Do you remember Adimu?'

Abionan smiled:

'How could I not do?'

'Well, he's living in Ibadan now. Together with his mother. He's a great friend of mine. He comes to see me at my stall and sits there talking for ages.'

'What does he do?'

'Pottery and sculpture, just the same as he did when a child.'

'Has he got any bigger? Is he taller now?'

'A little bit, but he's still tiny and hunchbacked, almost exactly as he was. And he still keeps smiling.'

She had learnt that Adimu had established a reputation as an artist, for people would come from Lagos and abroad to buy the earthenware heads made by the man whose name had now featured in newspapers and magazines, Oladeji talked about him a lot, and Abionan concluded:

'I think he likes you.'

'He certainly does. At times he stares at me for ages on end, gazing full of admiration until he makes me feel quite embarrassed.'

She paused:

'I like him very much too. No one is better at understanding people, taking, or giving advice or consolation.'

Abionan had learnt too that Adimu had promised Oladeji that he would one day make a journey to Ketu to see his friend from childhood days again but now as she ends yet another market day at Opo Meta, she shrugs off her childhood memories, because the important thing, she thinks, is to conceive a new son, she feels that the time is coming, the next time she is in Ketu something will have to be done, then she hears Yatundé announce:

'It's getting late.'

From the other stalls there was the movement of other women packing up their things, gathering in their mats and Abionan got up, stared the shelves away at the back, propped the stools up against the shelves, shook out her mat and rolled it up, picked up the big calabash and thought of the decision she had made on her uncle's offer, she couldn't have done otherwise, how could she leave

112

Ketu?, yet always at the back of her mind was the idea that Yatundé had put in one word:

'Regrets' 'Any regrets?'

She had of course no regrets, but whenever she had to choose, and the choice had been made, the trace of it would always linger, an idea that perhaps the opposite decision might have been nearer the mark, she would then start thinking of what she stood to lose by her choice and as she was putting her things on her head, Abionan again saw uncle's face, the uncle whom she would be needing in the future, but how could she struggle for her son to become king of Ketu if her own business was moved elsewhere?, a shop in Cotonou would mean betaking herself to another setting and another centre, and with it would go her cares and her thoughts, her activity and her achievements and how could the second Adeniran rise up amid Cotonou's modern buildings, traffic and shops?

The women gathered together beyond the market while Abionan and Yatundé ate slowly, each from her own plate of rice and meat, then they drank water, the lanterns of Opo Meta began to illuminate the passers-by and that night's journey would be quicker for the distance from Opo Meta to Idigny was a great deal shorter than from Ketu to Opo Meta and even Omitola, who would quickly tire, strode on ahead this time, Solange appeared and joined them, but Tomori was forced to return to Ketu as family problems had cropped up, and so the four women proceeded, at first in silence, but then after fifteen minutes of walking, Solange said:

'You've been keeping very quiet today. I was watching you from a distance, what was up?'

'I had to think of a reply for my uncle.'

'I've already heard about that. He wanted you to go and work in Cotonou.'

There was a commotion up ahead, it was a nanny goat broken lose with its owner after it, the women went up to get a closer look and lots of people were laughing because the man simply couldn't quite catch the animal and was swearing, then the goat knocked an old woman flying, along with her load and everything else and Abionan, Yatundé, Omitola and Solange went up to help, questions were asked:

'Are you badly hurt?'

The old woman got herself up, thanked the others who had

quickly grabbed her things for her, the goat was re-captured, the man came up to apologize but the old woman complained:

'You'll have to pay if you've broken anything of mine.'

But everything in the calabash was intact and the woman resumed their march, the night grew warmer, Abionan felt perspiration moving down her face and suggested:

'Shall we have a bathe at the bend in the creek?'

Omitola declined but yes, she would wait for them, Yatundé also said that she wouldn't but Solange agreed to and when they reached the spot, the four women set their calabashes down on the ground and Abionan at once threw off all her clothes, Solange did likewise and the pair of them went into the stream, Solange found the water cold but Abionan like it while Omitola and Yatundé talked in undertones so that you could scarcely hear what they were saying, the brook gently babbled and there was a stone in the middle where Abionan sat down and dipped her right hand in the water, she felt as though all doubts were at once disappearing and that everything was now quite plain, the water was washing her memories, making them clean and clear and coherent, now she was certain she'd done the right thing so then she started to rub down her arms and her neck and her breasts, then plunged her head in the flow once again, she saw that Solange had left the water and was looking for her towel to dry herself with, the night had filled with stars, the wind was stirring the leaves and Abionan felt a desire to remain longer in the water but she could not hold up the journey of the others so she came out on to the bank and found herself a wide piece of cloth on which she dried herself, her figure scarcely showed through the shadows as she thought that the next day she would be with Victor Ajayi, Idigny was always the quietest of the four markets and now she remembers Adeniran playing on the ground in that township with his arms stretched out in front.

IDIGNY MARKET

Ojo Jacuta, day of Shango, god of thunder

I sing of the childless woman as she comes into Idigny with its houses hardly visible and the market with just the odd lantern picking out traces of figures, I sing of her at the moment when she takes her load from her head and sets it all down on the ground, I sing of her in the first minutes of silence which she spends in Idigny as she looks out to the small church beyond, rude and tiny with a floor of bare earth, so often had she been inside and the saint on the altar was for her to have a beauty quite out of this world, I sing of her at that instant when she knows she has been welcomed and sheltered by the town's silent shadow and with a weary motion lays out her mat adorned with the lioness and as she sits puts a comb through her hair that's still wet and feels the sense of release that the bathe in the brook has given her, I sing of her on this arrival at the third stall of her round with its shelves still empty and unquenchable at the prospects and certainties of movement and the forms of yams and cassavas almost visible in advance of the morning to come and the voices to fill those now silent spaces, the stools are strung up down a gap, beneath the darkness quite useless, and the scrap of hide awning in the breeze dangling loose, gently flapping, while her companions stirred on their pitches to the sounds of objects being dragged out or stacked up, I sing of her in the act of lying down and closing her eyes for the sleep she was wishing would come straight away, her skirt standing out against the lighter ground of the mat and her left arm like a pillow, I sing of her when and while she is sleeping with the day of Shango drawing yet nearer and the noise of the market slowly rising apace, I sing of her as she opens her eyes and seeing Victor Ajayi's face in front of her, with a smile in his question:

'Have you slept well?'

She had. She felt light, the man helped her up and then she saw the supplier of yams, potatoes and cassavas, a very old European hat was on his head, he was pushing his barrow up and he stopped for Abionan to make her choice, at this start of day not a word was to be heard, only hands moving forward and back, lifting and weighing, feeling and touching, the rough surface of the cassavas was such a familiar touch and the potatoes seemed to be bigger than those at Opo Meta, when the woman thought she had sorted out a sufficient amount, she wanted to know what she owed and the supplier answered solemnly:

'The price hasn't yet gone up from last week.'

'We'll settle up later then.'

She was left to stack up the yams, the sun was blazing down on the front of the stall, the crying of a child came from the hidden extremity of the small street which bent round and so hid the spot where Solange and Omitola were, two women began to argue on the other side and Abionan looked up at Victor Ajayi:

'Are you coming with me?'

The man rose without a word, let her go on in front and the two passed close to Solange's stall who said with a smile:

'Hey, Victor. May you not die while you are walking this morning.'

The man replied without halting, Abionan quickened her pace, thatched houses appeared and a group of children were having lessons in the open air, the teacher had meticulously plaited hair, there was a girl's laugh that kept on and on and Abionan all of a sudden stopped, she was by the spot where the male organ symbolising Eshu stood dewy-wet.

Abionan sat down on the ground, set a piece of yam and another of sweet potato and yet another of cassava before the organ, she stopped in thought for a moment, it was in Idigny that her thoughts were clearest for she would remember Adeniran lying on the grass not far from Eshu waving his arms and legs about as babies do, he was howling and making noises with his mouth but he wasn't crying, the woman would fix her eyes on her son and on the organ and she would think about when he would be king, there was one occasion when she stopped there thinking so long that Victor Ajayi, who had that morning been away making a delivery out of town, seemed to have got alarmed and wanted to know what had happened, the woman had smiled and said that all was well, she had merely forgotten about her life, today her son no longer existed, Abionan hung her head and closed her eyes, from the distance came the clamour of the children having their lessons, with her closed eyes sounds appeared as if they were images, streaks moving over from one side to the other, scratches marking off the gloom within, a louder noise seemed to be coming from the market and, Abionan got up, Victor wanted to see which way she was going to go, she went off towards the church, small with its unpainted walls, and the woman went in, stepping on to the bare earth floor, the altar loomed white and vivid, and Victor explained:

'Father Tom's in Ketu. He isn't back till this afternoon.'

She motioned that she understood, went out of the church and reached the stall in time to deal with a customer, Victor sat down on a stool and watched while a little boy ran past naked, the rumpus of the market increased, arguments at the tops of voices suddenly rose on the air without Abionan being able to tell where they came from and the woman felt happy for no reason at all, perhaps because it was the day of Shango, the lord of thunder and the master of storms and she would always make an offering to Shango on his day, Fatogum used to say that Shango represented the wrath of god, anger, but was God angry?, wondered the woman, but how could you not be angry at man's idiocy?, the babalao had started by saying that he actually considered that anger could drive people forward, anger ends up by being positive because it can make people progress, a god of anger had therefore to be an important one, he had once recounted to Abionan the story of a man who had lived, or rather recovered, only through anger.

'Out of anger?'

'Quite so. He was dead. It was a friend of mine, Ambroise. He was dead, or very nearly so. As he lay dying, he knew that the woman whom he liked was becoming subservient to an uncle whom he detested, she could even have gone and married the uncle. He found out that the latter was already mocking him, telling everyone that he was going to keep the nephew's wife and the nephew's house, and the nephew's cassavas, so thereupon the nephew went wild and got up out of bed, everyone was astonished, after all the man was pretty well dead, it was something in his lungs or else he hardly had any lungs left, and the complaint was further complicated by another one, a cancer somewhere or other yet nevertheless, the man got up, recovered and lived on till the uncle died a few years later. And just when the uncle died, he did too.'

Fatogum paused before concluding:

117

'I think that he then had no more reason to live.'

But Shango was the god of justice too, Abionan always cherished old Mariana's saying that there were men who breathed fire from their mouths, perhaps fire was connected with justice, the protestant vicar at Ketu had disagreed, fire was a sign of purification, the lightning and thunder in the rainy months scared Abionan who would keep praying to Shango to prevent a flash of lightning striking her down, she had heard tales of men and women who had been killed by lightning in mid-market, would every death be then an act of justice?, Abionan looked up to the sky in spite of herself, clouds were quietly passing by, but it was not the season of heavy rains so anger would take on a different aspect on a day like that, she thought of the anger she felt at her uncle and at the near certainty that he had contributed to the death of her son and that anger had also helped the woman with her struggle, Victor Ajayi seemed to have followed her thoughts because he asked:

'An unkind thought?'

She didn't respond, she thought on about what she needed to discuss with the priest and she would go back to the church later.

The church at Idigny made Abionan think of young Mariana who had spent ten Yoruba weeks accompanying her friend on her rounds of the four markets, Mariana liked the church, nearly every time she had been at Idigny she would stay inside for a time and once she had said:

'Whenever I come in here I recall the church of Notre Dame in Paris.'

'Why, are they alike?'

'Quite the contrary. One's the opposite of the other. And that's why I recall it.'

Abionan wanted to know:

'What's Paris like?'

Mariana thought for a moment before answering, screwing up her eyes and looking as if she didn't know what to say, finally she glanced out at the open-air class in front of the church and tried to explain:

'Paris is an exotic city.'

'Exotic?'

'Yes. To an African, all of Europe is very exotic.'

Then she had talked of her first impressions of Europe, she

thought the trees were exotic in the extreme, sometimes she'd stop at one of them, pick up the leaves which had fallen on the ground and study their shape and colour, she would walk through the woods of Paris and had come to find that exoticism might be very pleasant but it could pall, unless you went beyond and could see within it the people alike the world over, Abionan had been thinking about Paris's exotic nature, and had asked afterwards:

'And the markets over there. Are they the same as here?'

Mariana had smiled:

'Well, that's something that's the same all over the world. At least in all of the world I know of. In Paris, London, Brussels, Marseilles, the markets are all so very different from Ketu and Idigny. Stalls may be larger or smaller, the style may vary and the goods too, but overall they are similar, they have men and women selling and shoppers studying what they are going to buy. Over here we do more haggling than there but things are broadly the same.'

Abionan had been glad to know that there was some point in common between Idigny and Paris and it was with a smile that she said:

'That means that if I went to Paris I wouldn't be too put off. If they have markets, I'll understand it.'

It had been a time for a great deal of talking, Mariana and Abionan had talked nearly the whole day long and had gone on making their observations on things at night as well, from time to time someone would complain and from a stall further down would come a voice:

'Stop talking. It's time to sleep.'

The two would then lower their tone and Mariana would talk of France, of the studies she was doing, of the many doubts she had, she was interested in everything Abionan had to say, she enjoyed discussing the latter's hopes for the kingdom of Ketu and when it was daylight and they were in Idigny, Victor would join in the conversation, he would talk less than the women but passed his opinions with the calm assurance of one who had come to a definite, distinct conclusion on the matter in question, they had been weeks of great happiness, at the time she hadn't thought much about it, she scarcely had a chance to, Mariana was becoming more informed at every moment and when it came to selling, her friend was efficient, she made a point of making a good sale, she had learnt how to argue

with the hagglers, pulling faces, showing surprise and indignation
when the customer offered far too low a price, one night Solange
had asked Mariana why she was doing all this, the latter replied:

'Well, it's really a scholarship.'

'A what?'

Mariana was quite serious:

'I'm not joking. A scholarship is when you receive tuition free of
charge, or support for your tuition, and go to a good school, abroad
usually, and learn something useful that you can use back in your
own country.'

There was a brief silence. Solange had asked:

'And so you did all that sort of thing studying in France?'

'Scholarship? Yes, I did.'

The explanations had been protracted, Mariana's voice seemed
different:

'I live in my house which is my grandmother's house. I am studying in Paris. From time to time I go to Zorei where my father was
president, I know everyone there. Aduni's a small city. But in
Europe I wondered what do I know about Africa? A little more
than the European specialist on Africa who thinks he knows the lot.
Sometimes he does know a great deal, it's just that he understands
nothing. So then I made up my mind to become a market seller and
spend a while following the normal round of markets from Ketu.
Abionan's my old friend so I joined up with her and she thought it
was an excellent idea.'

Mariana made a gesture, throwing open her arms:

'So here I am.'

Solange seemed to have understood:

'So that was it.'

Victor Ajayi had readily understood too, he wasn't one for asking
questions, he now and again enjoyed paying attention and he would
listen, patiently following the words of Abionan and Mariana with
not a blink of his eyelids, he looked as if he realised that the others
wanted to be heard but he would tell stories and talk about Shango
and Obatala and the witches who came down to earth to harass
people, he was also in the habit of explaining the carving he made
and would sketch out in wood a line of a face and say why he had
made that cut, Abionan had only to arrive in Idigny for Victor to
drop everything he was doing so as to keep her company, he would
spend the whole day with her, he would sit himself down near the

stall and be present in all the business, he would make remarks and smile depending on what had happened in the market at a given moment, he would take his friend to eat with him which he would make in a set of pots and frying pans on trivets, for the woman it was perhaps the happiest and most peaceful moment she would lean against the wall, sitting on the ground and following every stage of getting the meal ready, young Mariana had been accepted by Victor as a part of Abionan and the three went around together, they would visit Eshu, go inside the church, eat lunch side by side, the priest from Ketu would sometimes join in the group but only at the end of the afternoon and the four of them would talk together, Solange and Omitola were amused by it and one day Francesca had asked:

'What is it you talk about so much?'

Abionan and Mariana had laughed at the look of astonishment which Victor gave on hearing the question, on the way to Iro Kogny one night Mariana had remarked:

'It's one of the nicest things I've seen.'

'What is?'

'That passion that Victor has for you.'

'Do you consider it is a passion?'

'Maybe not. Maybe that's not the word, passion gives the idea of suffering allied with love.'

They had remained for a moment in silence.

'The best word is devotion. He follows behind you, does everything you want, listens, answers and cooks for you.'

Another pause, Mariana had looked Abionan straight in the eyes:

'Did you ever sleep together?'

'No. It's never crossed my mind. Anyway I only want to have a child by my husband.'

'Yes. I don't think that Victor's thought of it either.'

Mariana wanted to know if Victor had been with his friend elsewhere than Idigny.

'Often. From time to time he accompanies me to Iro Kogny, sometimes he spends quite a time going with me to Ketu and Opo Meta. He knows Obafemi, the two of them drink beer and palm-wine together.'

She explained further that he didn't feel as happy when away from Idigny and she too preferred to meet him in his own town, set among his own things and doing his carvings, Abionan would spend part of the afternoon with him watching him take a knife and chip out bits of wood and start making his masks, the world seemed to have lost its sound, lizards would come in the room, shake their heads as is their way, then a harsher, more rasping scrape of the knife against the wood would startle the creature which would run out, Mariana had been brought into these pauses of silence, for her Victor's style of making carvings had a still greater interest and she would follow the movement of his hands, and learnt to distinguish when he was working happily and when he seemed little engrossed in what he was doing but Abionan had answered:

'He's always the same. He's always happy.'

'Perhaps so. But I can detect changes from one time to the next. Some pieces he does with more joy.'

Abionan would talk with Victor about her dream of having a son to be king of Ketu, the first time they had discussed the subject his voice had been calm:

'I should be most happy if that were to come about. Who can tell, maybe I'll teach the future king of Ketu to work in wood.'

'Of course you will. I'll make sure of that.'

The conversations they had had about her dream were all very realistic for Victor, there appeared to be no more doubts that his friend's son would be king for he would talk only of certainties, how the king would act, how he would be looked upon by the market women, and this was good for Abionan for as long as Adeniran had been alive, her objectivity was stronger but his death had not lessened the conviction of Victor, who had a face both soft and hard at the same time. Mariana had said:

'He seems to have carved his own face.'

Her colleagues at the market respected the presence of the couple at the stall and refrained from talking too loudly or approaching the couple.

'Have you noticed,' remarked Mariana, 'that you're treated differently in Idigny?'

'Differently, how?'

'They leave you two on your own, they don't interfere and don't make jokes.'

Mariana had examined the man, he was small, thin and slight, his eyes shone brightly, his beard was partly grown and he would wear a pale shirt which was sometimes dirty with wood splinters, he had steady movements and could remain quite still, sitting on the stool for hours looking as if he had turned into an object.

There was no doubt that the other market women did leave the pair alone and Abionan began to notice how they all drew away, Victor too seemed to evoke people's respect perhaps because he spoke little, in the period when Mariana was accompanying her from market to market he had spoken more and a fresh subject seemed to crop up at every moment, but silence had prevailed on the majority of occasions, one afternoon the three had remained in silence for more than five hours as he carved a set of guelede masks, one of the masks represented a hippopotamus on its head and the man spent ages improving the animal's figure and the chippings had shot on to the floor, another mask had a braid of wood looking like a hat and there was a mask with a cross and a man on its top part, to start with there would be a noise still coming from outside, then it was as if the world had come to an end, and silence seemed to come out of the very mask that Victor was carving, Abionan was later to see those same carvings of Victor's being used in a guelede dance, it was at the time when the witches ran wild through the world and tried to make mischief, anything could happen but the dancers with masked heads would help distract the witches, charm them for the day, so that they would meantime forget or give up bothering men and women, all of Idigny's inhabitants would be in the market square watching the masks rise and dip to the movements of each step of that strange dance which had always reminded Abionan of the way Victor had made a piece of wood become suddenly more important than anything else round about, she liked to run her hand over the face of the mask and over its nose and its lips, over the markings on each side, but there were also afternoons with a lot of things to be said, usually with the priest there present with whom Mariana delighted in talking to and answering, and talking without getting any reply, on one occasion the priest had wanted to know:

'What was your father like?'

She seemed not to be going to answer, the priest had explained:

'I've always had a great curiosity to know what President Sebastian Silva was like. I was with him only once, at the Water House, and I was so impressed by what he said. It was a meeting of Zorei politicians. Every word that he spoke was simple and clear, I felt that everybody listening was thinking that he was merely repeating the opinion of them all.'

Mariana stayed silent and the priest went further:

'I left with the impression that only a great man is capable of saying the things that we are all thinking.'

Here Mariana had decided to speak:

'It's funny that you have such an opinion because I was about to consult you about some thoughts that my father left behind, which I intend to publish.'

'Thoughts?'

'Yes. Thoughts more or less like Mao Tse-Tung's. You've seen the booklet of quotations of chairman Mao Tse-Tung? Well, I'd like to publish the sayings of my father under the title "Thoughts of President Sebastian Silva".'

The priest had said that if Mariana wanted to lend him the original he would like to read the thoughts of the president.

'Lend. I don't lend, oh no. But I can read them out here amongst ourselves. The exercise books which he wrote them in are in Ketu. I'll bring them with me next time.'

She did. The group consisted of four, Mariana, Abionan, Victor and the priest. They were in the small room in the priest's house, poor and with almost no furniture, Mariana rested one of the exercise books on the table that stood in the middle and started to read:

'Listen to this:

"Politics as conceived and undertaken by Europeans, is an eminently dishonest activity: it promotes injustice, tolerates calumny, incites lying and in many instances condones crimes of violence".'

Mariana had lifted her head from the exercise book, looked at the priest then turned some pages over and read:

' "The difference between the democratic and the totalitarian regime is that the former, even when politically dishonest, enjoys institutions which have the strength to fight for a minimum of respect for basic human rights. Secondly, the thesis of the one correct solution, sometimes the "final solution" for any problem accepted as dogma by the party in power, does not allow for an individual with a different opinion to exist. So if he cannot exist, how can there be any human rights?"'

She had turned some more pages:

'"For the African by and large, politics is perhaps a still primitive means of supplying his daily needs of food, drink, home and shelter from bad weather, plagues, sickness, wild animals and others who are enemies of the community in which he lives. Perhaps that is why African societies generally accept, admire and applaud powerful rich men, the courageous and the fine talkers, who are found to be capable of assuring such immediate needs."'

Mariana had commented:

'Then after that, written in a different ink, comes this question in parentheses:"'

"'But won't it be the same elsewhere in the world too?"'

The priest who was gazing at the half-cracked ceiling, had said in rather a quiet voice:

'It's quite different from what I thought he had written.'

Mariana had just looked at him as she went on:

'I imagined he would have pored over his problems of government, over why he had done this and not that. That sort of thing.'

Mariana replied:

'But I think that is exactly what he did do. Although it might seem that he is putting everything into very general terms, my feeling is that each one of these thoughts arose from a direct and immediate problem of government.'

The priest looked dubious:

'I expected him to talk about problems of the market, for instance, the market selling everyday items, like the four markets which Abionan covers every week. Or matters connected with occupations like Victor's who spends days carving wood sculptures, something which is going shortly to disappear because no one any longer is learning how to make carvings from wood or clay, or anything else.'

'He did deal with Victor Ajayi's craft. One minute.'

Mariana had thumbed through the exercise book, she finally found it:

'Listen to this:

"The African does not dance: he is the dance. The African does not carve a figure out of wood: he is the figure he carves".'

A silence.

'And here's another one, similar:

"The African who carves a figure from wood, makes it out of himself. By making himself, he discovers himself. By discovering himself, he comes into being".'

The priest had asked:

'Read those two again.'

After re-reading it, all had remained silent for some minutes while Mariana went on looking through the exercise book.

'Here's a thought that complements the last one:

"Hasn't every religion always functioned as an instrument for man to come into being – that is, to take on the wholeness of his own self? The difference today between the European and the African is that religion has for the former been transformed into a social convention. For us, religion forms part of every one of life's moments. European religion discarded pleasures and joys as things to be condemned, sins. For us, joys and pleasures, including those of sex, form part of the cult that we make to the gods."

And this one, written straight afterwards:

"The basis of African life is joy. Natural, communicative joy, something that the European has through too much theorising, long ago lost."

'There are other thoughts on comparative politics, a lot about religion, some about how people behave. I'm going to have to sort the book out. Put together things which are on the same subject, make chapter headings, perhaps give a few explanations. Look at this:

"The European adores making revolution in the lands of others – especially in Africa and Latin America. Perhaps he considers that Europe has already reached such an advanced state that it needs no immediate reforms."

'And again:

"Even the European revolutionary can be a colonialist in relation to Africa and the regions of the world where Europe had colonies. Basically, for any European, we in Africa, Latin America and Asia are all children, we don't know what we're doing and Europe's got to show us the way".'

The priest scratched his cheek and his growth of beard: 'Yes, it'll be worth doing. It'll be worth to publishing your father's thoughts in a book. Publish it in France and England and have it distributed throughout Africa. They are African thoughts above all.'

Abionan had imagined her son, the Adeniran shortly to come, becoming king of Ketu and writing down similar thoughts, dealing with the problems of the city, discussing what had to be done and she saw herself, a little older, accompanying him, finding out what he was doing, giving him support, looking after the exercise books in which he had written his thoughts and it was a pity that Aduke was no longer around to see her grandson as king of Ketu and to be with him as well, mother would understand her grandson, she would love her grandson and she would go with him to the seaside, she had remembered one minute of the last day, of mother's reconciliation with the sea, of the death that came on the smell of the salt and the sun, a clear, luminous sky the like of which she could not recall seeing before and far off a vividly coloured procession with red, green and blue robes, it must have been a wedding, snatches of an incantation came over the beach, a drumbeat marked out the step of the procession, mother seemed contented and Abionan imagined there was a smile on her black dry lips, when the second Adeniran existed she would relate to him what his grandmother had been like, she would describe every minute of that pilgrimage, that quest for the sea, that walk in the waves, the gay hues of the folk in the distance, the sound of the drum, the sun and the salt and she had noticed that Victor was answering one of the priest's questions:

'I liked them very much. I don't know that I understood them all though.'

He stopped for a moment:

'Thinking it over, I don't think I understand them all but it was as if I had. The words are resounding again here inside me.'

The priest asked Mariana to read some more.

'This one's like the others I've already read:

"Hypocrisy is the basis of European political philosophy. No one over there seems to have the slightest interest in improving man. The tiny few who think in terms of improving the human being and his institutions, are usually treated as utopians".'

Mariana had rested a little, the priest made coffee, Abionan looked outside, a tree stood out against the thatched roof of a mud house and later on Mariana had read out some other thoughts of her father, in the end she said:

'Listen to this one which I read out to a teacher of mine in Paris:

"Not long ago a European friend was saying to me that he was convinced that we needed to defend ecology and even interrupt progress, perhaps destroy machines. But what that friend wanted was to impose an 'African way of life' upon the world because ecological man is par excellence the African, whose gods require a specific environment for their survival – one of trees, fruits, rivers, leaves, roots, one of sand, cowries, stones, hills, of all the things whose combination produces the harmony capable of promoting and maintaining the existence of themselves, the gods. And what is good for the gods is good for men too".'

But what stuck in Abionan's memory was this thought, which Mariana read out soon afterwards:

'No European has yet looked me in the eye. Could the feeling of guilt be that strong?'

Idigny was also the place that Abionan found most like those she had seen on her journey with mother, not that the similarity was anything physical or visible but because there she felt the way she had felt in the markets of Nigeria, as would happen with the music and the chats that she had heard for the first time in one place and then whenever she heard them again the place would come back into existence in front of and inside her with its smells and its colours and she would again feel happy or unhappy, cheerful or sad, depending whether she had been cheerful or unhappy in that particular place, she was in the habit of going round Idigny with delight, she would visit other stalls in the market, during the afternoons she spent with Victor Ajayi she would talk a lot, he would say nothing while she would speak of parts of her life that her memory would at that point bring back, the man knew every section of the journey which Abionan had made with mother, from time to time he would ask a question, what was Ibadan like?, was the Oshun river very big?, what did it feel like sailing down the Ogun river in a canoe?, Abionan remembered the face of the old woman who had gone with mother and her in that voyage by canoe with Abeokutá appearing in the distance.

Sometimes Victor would explain to Abionan about the figures he was making and their names, he would pick up one of the masks and say that one was the first to be brought out at the festival, it was called ato-baká, the others were munchá, tetidé, okunrin, aribu, ishuaro, the wolf-mask bore the name of alopanjá-elidé and the last one was woogba-woogbarosan, each had its function, Victor would raise one of them up in the air, turn it around for the woman to see the details and, Mariana would say that Victor Ajayi's was a sacred art, once she had explained:

'Just like the images in the gothic churches of France, mainly the wooden images – that's what Victor's making.'

Once his head was down, the small knife in his right hand and the left gripping a piece of wood, it wouldn't be long for Abionan would see a face loom out, a snake coiling itself around the figure's head, two birds with upturned beaks but when the two spent more time in the market and Abionan's stall became packed with customers, the man would help by handing across cassavas and sweet potatoes so that the woman could continue arguing, now on that day after learning that the priest was in Ketu, Abionan goes and sits on her stool, Victor is on the ground in front of her, a customer with plaited hair appears, one whom Abionan doesn't know, she may be a newcomer to Idigny, and she thinks the cassava very dear:

'They're a lot cheaper in Iro Kogny.'

'Go and buy them in Iro Kogny then.'

The argument went on for a good ten minutes or so, the sweat was streaming from Abionan's face, when the other woman moved off with the cassava it seemed she had earned far more than just the sale, Abionan looked up at the sky, big clouds were travelling leftwards, where would her husband be at that hour?, maybe drinking beer opposite Ketu market, but the time to make herself another son, to make the king of Ketu exist, was now approaching, Abionan looked at a group of small boys who were running past, Adeniran would have been in their midst had he not died, he'd be shouting and running about and, when it was time to eat, she went out with Victor who would walk at an easy pace, now the front of the church was flooded in sunlight, children were screaming in the square and the man put a piece of meat on a trivet, tossed some leaves on the meat, then he warmed some cassava meal in a frying pan, the woman ate the gari with her hand, the meat had got a half-burned taste, the leaves had a strong smell and she remembered mother making meals on the journey, Oshogbo market again appeared before her and she thought of Mariana, for she had promised her she would go to Zorei and visit the house which had been the president's, one day she had left the round of the market people for some time and had actually gone there, she had spoken previously with old Mariana who had never again set her feet in the city where her son had died and she could still see her eyes looking at her at the moment she had put the question:

'Are you going to Zorei?'

'I am. I want to see the places where old Sebastian lived.'

'He wasn't as old as all that.'

And there had followed a silence.

'He died very early.'

Abionan had found out that Sebastian's grave was near the house on the dunes that stretched away to the sea in the distance, the wind tossed sand on your feet and she had noticed that old Mariana was from time to time glancing about, as if seeking the spot where the grave lay but the old woman's voice was calm:

'I have never been back to Aduni since my son died. For that reason, many people think I'm living in the past. That is not true. Before he died, my son had a fine life, it was worth him existing. I don't go to Aduni again precisely because I do not live in the past. My house is here, I am old and I don't go out much. Aduni is the past. The girl goes there a lot. I think that's good. For her Aduni's the future.'

She looked at Abionan:

'And you should go too. The girl knows everyone in Aduni.'

The girl was coming into the living room and Abionan realised how greatly young Mariana resembled the other one, the conversation changed its topic because the girl as the old woman would call her, wanted to hear some tales of Shango and flashes of lightning, the old woman recounted a festival of Shango she had seen in Brazil.

'That was many years ago. My grandmother Ainá took me, I have never forgotten the dances nor the drumming.'

But she could not recall any lightning, though she did know of a story that took place in Ibadan on one stormy night, lightning struck a house, while everybody was out, no one had died but the house had remained sacrosanct because Shango had chosen it, there were ceremonies, people turned up from afar to pay homage to Shango and shortly after there were a thousand people lining the streets and hills that surrounded the house, the owners could not get back in, pieces of black stone started to be sold, it was said that the lightning had grazed them and old Mariana had related:

'I went there one day with daughter Ainá to see the house and the people, we slept in the street and I felt a serene joy at being surrounded by so many people in silence, for they spoke little and only the children were running up and down, it rained a lot that night, it was not known how news got around the crowd that Shango was going to reappear and order a flash of lightning to strike the same spot again but no one moved a muscle, rain was falling on the pair of us too, soaking we watched the water streaming down in the darkness, down people's heads, clothes, mats and food, everything was soaked through, the next morning the sun seemed stronger and rapidly dried out everyone's clothes, the house which had been hit by the lightning arose again as new, everyone was beaming and children were playing in the puddles of water,' and old Mariana's voice had a strange note of serenity as she said:

'I don't know why, but I felt happy in the midst of that crowd.'

Today, on the day of Shango that she is spending in Idigny, Abionan eats the meat prepared by Victor and sees a two-edged axe of Shango upon a woman's head, her breasts are large and pointed, and the man said it was not yet ready:

'It's a commission from a babalao in Pobe, but the face isn't very good in the lower part.'

He showed her the feet of the carving, took a knife and used it to chip bits off the wood, he worked away in silence there and when they returned to the market the activity had slackened off and the smell of food was strong, it had been at a festival of the new yams at Idigny that Abionan had seen a man go into a trance, he remained the whole day under the spell of the gods and when the woman returned the following week she found the man still in a trance and had learnt that the trance had gone on for seven days, nearly two whole Yoruba weeks, in Idigny she had also once seen a procession accompanying a dead man, those bearing the body passed through the middle of the market and went down all the back streets, she had an explanation from Victor that the dead man was from Lagos where they too had a custom of bringing out the dead through the streets escorted by musicians and singers, all of them praising the dead person, the yam festivals were merrier, even women became dizzy with drinking so much palm-wine, she had once been amazed at seeing mother drinking palm-wine as well, she had been with her on another journey, to Togo this time when Abionan had been a little older than on the journey round Nigeria and she felt to be almost a grown girl, they had started off one afternoon when it looked like rain, but it hadn't rained, and mother had said:

'Let's go right away. It's not going to rain today.'

It had been the rainy season and the road had small rivulets that ran down from the hills, mother had insisted on going inland, away from the sea and they had crossed the Ibeme river in a large canoe, larger than those on the Ogun river, mother was always different when travelling, as if she was another person and more the owner of herself, at home she would seem smaller, with her head bent and everyone ordering her about, away from home she was different, Abionan would watch her face and mother gazed at the things around her with more self-confidence, there had been no need to take a lot of money as she would sell at the markets along the way, the existence of markets wherever she went also gave Abionan the reassurance that the world was secure, languages might change but the markets remained the same, on the road to the Ileme river, she had no longer understood everything people said but the tone of voice and the way they raised their hands and wagged their fingers, was quite enough for you to understand anything and the girl had been learning to understand without paying any attention to the words, their clothes were different too, there were more colourful headties, but they had not gone through Abomey because, said mother, the inhabitants there had destroyed Ketu, and war between the two cities featured in the tales which Abionan adored listening to, in one township near Ileme they spent ten days, in Zagnanado the girl had made friends with another girl, taller than herself, with a lovely face, mother had said that she was a Fulani, she must have come from still farther north where there were cattle, Abionan had known the girl's name but couldn't quite remember it on the rest of the journey so she had asked mother:

'What was the name of that Fulani girl?'

'Didn't you remember it?'

'No.'

'I never knew it in the first place.'

They would come across baobabs on the road, mother liked to sit beneath one of them as they ate and at one small roadside market they had lingered two weeks, there Abionan learnt how gari, cassava meal, was made, she spent days assisting the women with gari production she would go about with her skin impregnated with gari, her face turned white, the women who made the gari liked dancing, and there were drums beating every night, Abionan slept on the floor with her head resting on mother's legs, as she heard the drums she would see sleep coming and sometimes she would go in amongst the trees which encircled the market, once she encountered a big snake, and an old woman who was coming by the same way motioned for the girl to stand still, she seemed to be saying with her hand held up, 'don't be afraid' the snake passed on its way and went back into the undergrowth at the side, lots of people were passing on the road, women with calabashes on their heads or colourful headties, they passed small lorries that unloaded potatoes, yams, large boxes, tins, and the smell of dried fish from one stall close to where mother worked had followed the girl wherever she went, Aduke got used to selling palm-oil but Abionan would like the potatoes and yams which felt nicer in her hands, the oil got stuck to your skin, she knew a young woman in Ketu who thought otherwise and liked the oil trickling down her arms, loathed having meal against her skin and found a potato skin coarse, once she had witnessed a strange sight; a man eating a huge snail, the creature was twitching as it was being swallowed down by the man, that market by the edge of the road had its own customs, from time to time groups of women with their breasts painted dark would arrive, there were drooping breasts that looked like the pieces of meat which men sold at the butcher's stall, they would talk into the small hours, the girl would wake up in the middle of the night and hear, though not understand, snatches of conversation that seemed slow and restful, perhaps they were telling tales, mother would talk as well, she had learnt lots of words in their language but people turned up who were talking in French, people who would arrive by lorry and tell of what was going on in Cotonou and Porto Novo, there had been a revolution in the big cities and now there was a new government and a new king too, mother had explained that the country didn't have a king, the king was the chief of Ketu, the one who did the real ruling was called a king, but nobody commented any further on what had happened in the big cities, perhaps it was not important, the women of the roadside market spoke too loudly, they would shout and from time to time there were fights with one swearing at another, the lorries reeked of petrol and brought men along who would flirt with the market women, making quips which made them all laugh and it was at the roadside market that Abionan had seen mother have some palm-wine, she had picked up a calabash and with spout in mouth had drunk down a fair amount, she then had become quite squiffy and fell asleep before the girl had done, the latter remained awake in front of a stall lit up by a big lantern where two men were playing aio, their hands dropping seeds along into each hole, one of them gasped with glee and astonishment, the other was studying the row of twelve hollows, six along each side, before starting to play, she had watched the pair for hours, now the one, and now the other, and by the end of the night, the man on the right had won three times running, he was a fat man and his beard bristled from his skin and seemed well grown, but when you looked at him face on the beard could hardly be seen, for the man would turn his face towards her several times, he asked her a question she didn't understand, mother seemed to have forgotten the palm-wine the following morning and had said:

'It's time we got a move on.'

'Where're we going to?'

'To a place called Atakpamé.'

'Is it a long way?'

'Fairly.'

The girl had hung her head and poked the earth with her toe, she wanted to know:

'What are we going to do there?'

'I'm going to work and you are going to help me.'

They had left by the same road where they had seen the lorries loom into and out of sight, they had eaten that day on a dry spot, the soil had hardly any growth even though it was the rainy time and they had slept at a bend of the road from where they could see a single house, then green started appearing, they had walked across a large field of maize and one afternoon had come to a plantation of a different sort, mother had said it was coffee and added:

'We must have got to Togo by now.'

'Is that a city?'

'No, it's a country.'

'Like Nigeria?'

'But it's on the other side.'

The girl had run off to see what coffee was like, there were some small fruits on the plant and she picked one and tried it, it didn't taste like coffee at all, mother said that you needed to dry and roast the beans for the coffee to come out, the land dropped away to a wide river and lots of people were waiting there for a canoe to cross by, a man had informed them it was the Mono river and mother had decided to stay until the next day, at night they had made a bonfire, people came along and gathered all around and on the other side of the river the land was undulating and green, when they reached Atakpamé they found the trees were taller, the city lay in a hollow and from above you could see rooftops and streets, roofing of zinc and thatch, houses with two floors, mother and daughter slept on a hilltop, heavy rain seemed to be on the way and a wind got up just as night fell, the world grew chilly, Abionan tried hard to get to sleep, and she thought about what that foreign city would be like with its different language, mother had said they wouldn't stay there long although it was great fun travelling, the girl would every now and then miss being at home and in the market at Ketu with its trees planted in the right places, she hadn't remembered quite when she got herself off to sleep, but then she had opened her eyes and it was morning, the sun was blazing on the houses of Atakpamé below, mother looked up a Yoruba family which had left Ketu many years earlier, the woman who received the two of them had a scarf on the top of her head and a chubby face, and had listened to what mother was saying and asked:

'Are you coming to live in Atakpamé?'

'No. Just passing through.'

'The best thing's to sell something over on that corner.'

And she had pointed to a spot where there were people selling on packing-cases large and small, two or three stalls ranged round a bend in the street.

'Is it a market?'

'No. Just a get-together to sell. It's a good spot.'

They had chatted a little longer the woman made a suggestion:

'My brother can go over and show you what to do.'

She shouted orders:

'Casimir.'

There had appeared a man with a long face and a little white hair at the sides, he had screwed his eyes up to look at them, and listened to what his sister was saying, then said:

'I'll come along with you.'

He went off ahead, with Abionan and mother following behind, and when he reached the street corner he looked to either side, seeming to be choosing:

'I think that corner's the best.'

He took the woman over there:

'You'll need a good packing-case.'

He seemed to be thinking a moment:

'So, you'll be selling what then?'

'I don't quite know yet. Anything. I've been used to selling peppers but I can sell anything.'

'Then come over here.'

The man had a rapid step and they crossed a main street with people in long wide robes, they spent the whole afternoon looking at one thing and then another, they found a high packing-case and mother decided that she would sell peppers, matches and small bottles of beer, Casimir spoke the language of the place, got a supplier, a short fat man who went around nibbling a twig with small leaves, to agree to mother paying him afterwards, at the end of each day, as night fell the girl was tired and mother was too, so they ate gari and dried fish and slept on the very corner with their mat on the ground.

Mother had already seen to a customer the next morning when Casimir turned up beaming all over and amidst a whole mass of remarks, he had said this:

'I've decided to take you two under my wing.'

He felt happy, talked a lot and the girl decided to explore other streets, she heard Casimir calling out:

'Stary nearby.'

She walked around all morning, and she saw houses painted white and had come back when she felt hungry, in the afternoon Casimir's sister came along to see how they were getting on and asked:

'How's Ketu doing?'

Mother said that the city was growing, the market was doing fine though there were transport problems and the roads were in a bad way, but that didn't bother people, the other woman wanted to know why she had left Ketu with her daughter.

'I don't really know. Every so often I have the urge to go off travelling somewhere, to meet other people and see different markets from the ones at home, you know how it is. I've made a lot of short trips, but this is my second long journey.'

The other gave a look of bland incomprehension and didn't say a thing, Casimir had grinned wryly:

'My sister asks too many questions.'

Mother said no, she hadn't done and she could ask away, it was the simple truth that she simply did not know where that urge to travel round the roads and markets came from.

While mother was selling, Casimir had started asking Abionan questions, after all he too had a mania for asking questions but from the outset the girl had liked him and she laughed at the things he said, one one occasion he had inquired:

'Where does your father live?'

'My father's dead now.'

'Ah.'

And he had gone on asking things, whether she could read, whether she liked travelling with mother, what she thought of Atakpamé, how long they would stay.

'That I don't know, mum never stops anywhere for long.'

The next day he had taken the girl out for a walk and then they went out of the city, the trees seemed greener than those in Ketu and they saw a big bird swooping low, Casimir chuckled merrily and he said there were times when he'd never seen an oró bird.

'What does oró mean?'

'It means forbidden. It means that no one can eat that bird. Atakpamé folk don't eat oró creatures.'

'How funny.'

'It's not really so funny. There are a lot of things forbidden in Ketu too.'

He had paused before asking:

'Did you know that Shango people can't eat white beans?'

She had learnt many things from him, for he would explain everything and at night he would stay up late talking with mother, Atakpamé had a bustling noisy market and the girl would go there as often as she could with Casimir who would introduce her to everyone, she soon came to understand lots of words from their language and from the first days mother proved capable of striking deals and steering through each stage of the business, Casimir had been amused by her, and one night she had heard him talk to mother about the sayings he had learnt among the people and which he loved to repeat, this was one of the first:

'When the poor man's house catches fire you must put out the fire straight away otherwise the fire will end by reaching the rich man's house as well.'

Then there was this one:

'Insects are quite right to eat leaves; there must be a limit placed to the beauty of plants.'

Here is one Casimir had said when he was alone with the girl:

'Mother is gold, father is glass.'

Abionan had asked where he had learnt all those sayings from and he had explained:

'They are Yoruba sayings that I have cherished all my life. I know quite a few of them. There's one for every occasion.'

One day Abionan had laughed at one of Casimir's sayings:

'The hungry man doesn't whistle.'

'What does he do then?'

'Keeps serious,' answered the man, 'Hunger's a serious matter.'

That day the girl had eaten with even more appetite, Atakpamé market had goods she hadn't seen before and she would stop by the stalls and eye every object, she noticed that mother and Casimir talked a lot together and now he hardly ever strayed far from the spot where she sold peppers, matches and beer, he got into the habit of going off to buy what she wanted, meat, meal, pieces of material and, one day mother had told Abionan that the man wanted to marry her, he had proposed that the three of them go off to live in Lomé, a big pleasant city, the girl asked:

'Is it by the sea?'

'It is, but that wasn't why I refused. If I really had wanted to get married, we'd have married and gone and lived in Ketu.'

Abionan observed that the man turned sad, at least for a few days, he laughed less and told less stories, but later he became his normal self again and on that journey mother and daughter had become more united than ever, Abionan thought about having a father as well, it could be a father who was like Casimir, one day she asked whether he had been born in Ketu:

'No. I was born in Whydah, my name is Casimir de Sousa, but I went to Ketu when still a small boy, it was there my sister married, afterwards her husband found a job here in Atakpamé, I had nothing to do in Ketu so along I came too.'

Abionan could see that women worked harder than men, Casimir seemed not to do anything and he had the whole day to himself, when mother decided it was time to go back, the man became once more sad, he never left the pair again, on the morning of parting he saw them off over the hills, and Abionan can remember his figure standing on the road at a bend, the girl could still see him from afar, she walked on a little and looked round, mother scolded her:

'Look where you're going.'

The rains had stopped, there was a makeshift market on the banks of the Mono river and mother and daughter had spent three days looking at what was going on, there had been a dance that lasted all night long when dust rose from the ground beneath the leaps of the dancers, once they had crossed the river the countryside seemed familiar again and Abionan could recall certain stretches of the road, it was as if the day before had returned and at the roadside market the women greeted them with merry laughter, they told them things and asked how the trip had gone, the girl had forgotten Casimir, she thought it was nice being in the middle of women who talked so loudly and played around, one of them called Angélique was in the habit of telling everyone how idiotic her husband was, idiotic and lazy with it, he would spend the entire day drinking beer at her expense, one day Abionan saw a big man come up in clothes covered with alternate red and white stripes, the man had stopped at Angélique's stall, had a few words, while the woman looked at him a moment, then grabbed a piece of wood while the man ran off with her on his tail, the whole market roared with laughter and a very old Yoruba woman made shrill cries:

'Beat him. Beat him.'

Another had said:

'He's so big and such a coward.'

The women had formed a cordon across on the other side, the man was unable to get out of the market and he ran back the way he had come and he went past the girl again with Angélique after him, it proved a diversion for the whole morning, the women had gathered round Angélique's stall and one of them wanted to know what her husband had done:

'He asked for some more money.'

Abionan noticed that no more men would come along that lane in the market where they were, there seemed only to be women doing the shopping and late into the night people were still making their comments, someone had asked Angélique:

'Where do you think he's gone?'

'Let's hope he's gone and got himself a job because no more money's coming from me.'

Abionan had been finding that market very entertaining and she remembered Ibadan for she was greatly entertained there too, the lorries that came enlivened everything and the men who came on the lorries were different from Angélique's husband, they were all working, they worked hard, heaving boxes, sacks and drums off the lorries, the women would joke with them as they would at times poke them, the smell of petrol was for Abionan to become a sign of joy for the lorry brought news from afar, from people who nobody knew and the girl had lost count of the days she had spent at the roadside market and when she arrived back in Ketu she would often recall it, it had been a strange time in which Abionan would for hours amuse herself gazing at the trees and the sky, she began to notice the clouds which passed, both big and small, long and fibrous and on one scorchingly sunny day, she had felt wet, mother had run up and said that Abionan had now ceased to be a girl to become a woman, at that time Ketu market was rife with reports of persecution, there had been threats to close down stalls, cut back the number of stallholders but Abionan couldn't remember how the crisis had ended, at home mother was always complaining, saying that it was an asinine thing to try and boss the market, the uncles had laughed and Oladeji said:

'Whether with the market or anything else, it's the same old story.'

There was in Idigny a calmness that she didn't find in the other markets though a lot of business was done there too, but quietly, or could it be the presence close by of Victor Ajayi which had the power of calming everything? so that when the priest appears, Abionan is quietly in thought, drawing her comparisons between the markets.

'Were you looking for me in church today?'

'Yes.'

After a silence.

'But how did you know, Father? I didn't leave any message.'

He laughed:

'The little girls playing in the square saw you.'

The priest sat down on a stool which Abionan pulled out from underneath the potato shelf, the woman opened a straw bag:

'The fact is that Mariana asked me to have a word with you.'

'How is she?'

'She's very well. She should be arriving from France next month.'

'What does she want from me?'

'Hold on and I'll read it out.'

She took out a piece of paper:

'It's a letter from her that I received some days ago. It says here "Ask Father Tom if he'd like to write a foreword to the book of the thoughts of my father. If he accepts, I'll be honoured."'

There was a silence which the priest finally interrupted:

'But why me?'

No one said a word and Victor's face looked as if he was not following what was being said.

'There must be so many people she knows in Paris.'

'She must want an African to do it, Father.'

'But even among Africans, there are other people here who understand about politics and government.'

'As the one who asked is coming soon, you can talk to her.'

'I should be honoured, of course, but I'm nothing but a poor parish priest. What an idea.'

He looked down at his hands and thought a little:

'It was a shame she didn't leave the scripts with me. How exactly did that thought on the African gods go, who needed food taken from the same place as where they are worshipped?'

And, continuing:

'I shall need to re-read all of it again to do a good foreword.'

They talked on a little and Abionan said:

'It'll be good when she comes back. I miss Mariana a lot.'

'So do we all.'

The priest's voice was clear. He continued as he looked at Victor:

'I'll finish by referring to Victor in my introduction because of that thought which says that the sculptor is the sculpture.'

Abionan remembered other times when Mariana had read passages out of that exercise book, with the priest, Victor and herself all sitting round, Mariana's voice would enounce the words:

'Sometimes the European wishes to impose his political and social institutions upon us in just the same way as in olden times he wanted forcibly to convert us to Christianity. What he wants today is for us to become a society with social structures similar to those of Europe that the European regards as perfect, which is clearly not in accordance to reality.'

There were thoughts on cars and motorbikes:

'Imitation of the European by the admiring African is inevitable. And here we come to the passion of today's African for the machine, cars, motorbikes, any machine in fact. This adaptation has been too rapid with the result that I don't know to what extent the African generation of today has really mastered the machine.'

Mariana observed:

'This one's similar.'

'Whenever I see a man from Zorei driving a car recklessly, I have the feeling that they both – the man and the car – belong to irreconcilable categories – and it is to man's credit that he seeks to reconcile them.'

There was a passage which was a story: 'In Africa, education comes before all else. How can we Africanise our skilled people if we do not prepare our nation for it? Once I dismissed ten Europeans who were typists in a government department because I had been told that there were Africans to replace them. The day that the Africans started work, I saw one of them put his hands on the keys and then stop. I asked what was up. Answer: "I thought you only had to put your hands down here and they would start striking the letters." I wanted to know, "But haven't you learnt to type?" He looked at me in astonishment, "Do you need to learn?" That is one of the missions of anyone who has a place in government in African countries today – to convince everyone that it is necessary to learn and give them the equipment with which to learn.'

The priest stayed a little longer and after he left Victor said: 'He did like being invited to write.'

'Yes he did.'

Solange came up to find out:

'What was it you asked the priest to do which he didn't want to?'

It was hard work explaining.

'It wasn't we who asked him at all. It was Mariana. I read him a request she had made by post.'

'Ah.'

A woman's voice attracted Abionan's attention, it could only be Antoinette, the one who had a mad son, or was he really mad?, he went about gaping and from time to time he would fall down drooling from the corner of his mouth, mother had taught Abionan from childhood that mad people are sacrosanct for the gods had chosen the people to be mad so that they would spend their life doing their mad things to test the others, so she was quite sure that mad people knew more than the others did, but what they knew was so much of the gods that a man could only understand it through madness but Abionan had always been afraid of mad people and when she saw one she would shrink back without saying a word, Antoinette had noticed this before and made a point of teasing her, when she came near she said:

'I think I'll take some large yams today.'

She sat her son down on the ground and Abionan looked at the boy, whose eyes were not looking at anything, then she watched Antoinette choosing her yams and asking the price, once Solange, who was also afraid, suggested that the woman left her son behind at home when she came to market but the latter didn't like the idea:

'He has never been away from me for a moment since he was

born. In the bedroom, the living room, the street, the market and when I'm getting meals ready he is always by my side.'

Omitola asked:

'And when it's time to make love?'

'I've never had a man since he was born.'

From time to time the child would laugh for no reason at all, but would turn quickly serious again and Abionan, even more seriously, just couldn't keep her eyes off him, Victor remained calm, Antoinette sat down and said in a firm voice:

'Well then, are you or aren't you going to sell me the yams?'

Abionan unfastened her gaze from the boy:

'Of course, Antoinette, it's just that I'm miles away.'

She turned down the price offered, it took quite some time to strike the bargain and the presence of the child alongside made Abionan lose all enthusiasm for the deal, as soon as Antoinette moved off she stared at the mother and child as they walked down the lane, what would it be like being mad?, why was it that the gods liked the mad?, and what if her son were born mad?, he might be a favourite of the gods but he would never become king, Victor went out soon after and said he would be back later, Solange and the other stall-mates approached, one thought that having a son like that was the worst punishment there could ever be, another took the view that the child should be put away, Omitola said:

'You said that because you've never had a child.'

Solange:

'In fact Antoinette copes with the situation very well.'

'What does she do?'

'Men's work.'

'What?'

'She embroiders and sews.'

They went on talking about children, Solange cast a sidelong glance at Abionan, who declared:

'There's no need at all to look at me like that, because I am having another son.'

'Who of course is going to be the king of Ketu.' Francesca jibed.

The women laughed and Abionan with them though she did reiterate:

'Of course.'

Solange wanted to know:

'And if you have twins, which one will you choose for king?'

143

'I'm not going to have twins, oh no. But if I did, I'll think about that when the pair of them come along.'

They talked on calmly and they joked about everything, Abionan forgot about Antoinette's son, then a group of masked egunguns, though none of them were wearing pretty masks, only cloths over their faces, went past some way from Abionan's stall while she thought of Mariana, it would be good to see her friend again and go back to Zorei, walk over the beach again and go into the cemetery on the sand, stand on the exact spot where mother met the sea, she felt a gap in her life when she thought of her, she was dreaming of mother, of when she was on another journey sometimes to places which Abionan felt sure she didn't know, but places also appeared in the dream that she could identify, Ibadan, once she thought it was Ifé, and Oshogbo, several times she would dream of Atakpamé, where would Casimir be?, you kept meeting men and women all along the way, then you heard nothing more of them, and didn't even remember the names of many of them, sometimes what you are left with is a scene, the snake in the middle of the bush with the old woman raising her hand, canoes sailing down the Ogun river, stones surrounding the shrine of Oshun and the drunkard who had stolen mother's pouch, people without names, places and things would linger in her memory and come into the dream and she had also dreamt of the little boy after he had died, she would see Adeniran on the ground beside her and knew a danger was threatening her, but at the same time Abionan would remember in the dream that the little boy was dead and she would feel a sharp pang in her breast, how could she get him back?, what could she do for time to turn back and her to be able to prevent him dying?, for if he had been poisoned, it would be easy to avoid Adeniran coming to eat the poison, a small child ran past in front of Abionan, the market again became wrapped in a great silence, one of those that come on in the middle of the afternoon in a pause between two surges of business and from time to time, there were five, six or more customers to serve all at once, one trying to push in front of another, sometimes just women or else women and men, one day in Ketu she had counted fifteen people all wanting to buy at once, then would come a break, and no one appeared, and the woman had time to think about her own affairs, she had now reached one of those breaks, Abionan arranged her skirt between her legs, leant back against one of the struts of the stall, shut her eyes and thought about going to Iro

144

Kogny earlier than normal that day, she wanted to get at least eight hour's sleep and remembered the journeys with mother when she could sleep at will, she opened her eyes to see the priest coming down the lane, he waved a greeting to several stalls and then sat down by Abionan.

'I've written a letter to Mariana. I think I'll need to send it to France?'

'There might not be time now. Send it to old Mariana's house.'

'Listen, here's the letter.'

'I was honoured at your invitation to me to write an introduction to the volume which will bring together the thoughts of your father, President Sebastian Silva. He was one of the greatest and best men of the generation of Africans which brought about the independence of the countries which today form our community. The thoughts, which I came to know of from your readings, impressed me greatly. I would however like to have a copy of the text to hand so as to pore over them, reflect on what they mean and thus be able to do a conscientious job. As I have learnt of your forthcoming visit to Benin, I would very much like to meet you as soon as possible. I would be quite happy to come to your house at Agué should you so desire. Or else I can wait for you in Idigny if you plan to come here. Let me repeat: I felt moved and honoured when Abionan read me the invitation that you had the kindness to make to me in your letter to her. God bless you.'

The priest looked up at Abionan who said once again:

'But do send the letter to Aguá.'

And then, after a pause:

'I do hope Mariana will think it better to come to Idigny, then I can be with her too.'

The priest still persisted to the point of leaving:

'I don't know why she chose me.'

She watched the priest walking off and recalled Fatogum, now she needed him to cast lots again to find out what she ought to do for her son to come quickly, she had above all to go back to her husband and make the birth possible, but when to go back?, there must be a most favourable date, and others might not be so favourable, even the day of performing the act ought to be chosen with the utmost care, there were days, and nights, when everything seemed to go wrong, so why go back to her husband on a day like that?, when would be best?, a day of Eshu?, or of Ogun?, or of Shango, like

145

today?, or who knows, Oshalá could be the best patron for the child's upbringing to get under way?, she would have to wait two more days because she could only make the proper consultation in Ketu, this time she could not leave anything to chance, the child would need to be protected at every moment and she would never leave it alone at home, even less with the uncle around, he would eat only food that she had prepared herself, it would perhaps be a good idea to get away from Ketu for a while but she could only contemplate a trip, not a move, she would travel as she had done when mother was alive, with her son going over everything mother had done with her, she would go to Nigeria, down the Ogun river, she would spend weeks, or months, in Abeokutá, she would sell at the Iba market in Ibadan, she would go to Ifé, Oshogbo and Oyo, the child would know the world before he reached the time to become king, she would take her son to Aguá, old Mariana would have to give him her blessing, she would visit Aduni and she would travel with young Mariana but after each trip she would return to Ketu, there were markets everywhere, she could sell potatoes and yams anywhere or peppers or matches, or even beer, although she didn't really like dealing in drink, she would sell in Atakpamé and at the roadside market or in places where mother had not been able to sell, in Porto Novo and Cotonou, she would even sell on the seashore, the beach, it would be a delight to be able to return to all the places she had known but with her son this time, watching the second Adeniran running from one stall to another, she kept imagining scenes in which mother was now her and she was transformed into her son, she remembered the king of Oshogbo, the Ataojá, her son would eat at the house of the Ataojá just as Abionan herself had done as a child, the rice had had so much pepper that the girl could hardly stand it, her son would go and watch the dances that she had seen at Oshogbo which lasted the whole night long, he would run around in the Shrine of Oshun and along the banks of the river, she could remember quite precisely many of Aduke's remarks on these journeys, mother better than anybody knew how to sell and perhaps Abionan would meet Adimu who was still making clay figures, her son would meet Victor Ajayi and Adimu, he would see how magnificent were the horns of the cattle she had seen in Ibadan and he would gaze down upon Atakpamé from the hill where Aduke and she had slept, he would learn to read, and he would talk with the two Marianas, he would read the book by President Sebastian Silva and he would go to Aduni to see the places where the president had worked, he would wander over the square where the country's independence had its celebration, from early on he would get used to playing near his grave in the dunes of Aguá, with the wind wafting up the sand and the crosses saying who was buried here and who there, the boy would be amazed at the Iba market in Ibadan, and he would see the magicians at Ojag'bo and the market in the bush, he would follow the musicians as they played like all children did, and he would hear the preachers who would gather in the market to speak of their gods, Abionan had learnt to dance when she had returned from her first long trip mother wanted her to dance to the orishas and she had danced and she felt like another person when she followed the drums and the chants, the boy would see the dead animals in Iba market and the monkey skulls, he would learn to be afraid of nothing except treacherous uncles, drinking would be dangerous although it was quite proper for a man to drink, Aduke had also drunk on the trip to Atakpamé and other women drank too but in much smaller quantities, but it's men who drink and when a man drinks he can steal women away, perhaps it wouldn't be too bad for Adeniran to drink just a little, just to show he was a man but he could not be one to be overpowered by anything, whether drink or woman, the boy would see the temple of Shango at Oyo, he would watch the battle of the two armies of Ejigbo, the men holding long poles and the king dressed all in white and he would hear the priests singing oriki in praise of Oshagyan, he would learn about the methods a town would use to bring rain when the drought lasted too long, he would go through the smoke when they set fire to the house during the festival at Ejigbo but everything might have changed now, perhaps they no longer danced in Oshogbo or raised fires in Ejigbo but the markets would be there for markets don't die.

She got up, crossed the market and went into the bush not for from Eshu's organ, she had a favourite spot there, where she often remembered how she'd squatted right down by the tree, she would leave the child quietly on the ground, he as if waiting for mother to finish, in Ketu there was no problem as it was home territory, in Opo Meta, Idigny and Iro Kogny she had selected the nearest patch of bush, and on the journeys from one market to the next the four women – she plus Yatundé, Solange and Omitola – would stop at certain points on the road, for there were places where you could have a bathe, others where they did what they had to, in silence and

147

at those moments Abionan would think her thoughts and make decisions, when she reached the stall, Victor was sitting there, she told him that the priest had come back.

'He wrote a letter to Mariana and wanted to read the letter to me.'

'It'll be good to see Mariana again.'

The woman started to pick up the yams that were left over, the potatoes were sold out, the sun beat down on parts of the stall and that was just the way that Aduke would clear up her stall in mid-afternoon, her hands would move more quickly now, lightly lifting the yams, pulling off the bits of earth that clung to them, she remembered the short trips she had made with Aduke, to Kete, Igana and once they had stayed on in Affamé where the market took up a vast area, and the girl went off to dig sweet potatoes, holding an old knife and when the potato appeared you'd get a great thrill, from Affamé they had gone to Kobejo, the women who covered those routes would also return every four days to the same locality, at Briki and Ifanhin she had seen fresh fish, but mother had quickly set off for Itajebu for she never again wished to venture near the sea except at the last, on the final journey with mother which had been the one that remained most powerfully in her memory, in Pobe there was a thatched house which was always empty which the chief of the town let mother and daughter stay in when they passed through, the bare earthen floor was more comfortable than cement to put your mat down on, Pobé smelt of many things, of pepper and of food, of bush and of people and when it rained the smell of the soil was stronger in Pobé than anywhere else where she'd been, a lizard ran close by Victor's feet as he was making lizards of wood, they seemed to Abionan to be alive and he had once carved a pillar that would be used in a temple in Ilara, Victor had created several lizards running up the wood and the creatures had rounded bodies too, he had received another commission for a big door at Porto Novo, Abionan had seen snakes and lizards and a figure of Shango, with the two-edged axe standing out in the middle, all shaping themselves up, a lorry had been sent up from Porto Novo to fetch the door and Adeniran would one day work in wood too, a king must do everything, how could you tell what was good and what was not if you had no idea about things?, through going about so much with his mother from market to market he would learn how they functioned, what problems they had, Solange had thought of a

148

union for the women who worked in the market, they would have a union when Adeniran became king without the slightest doubt, then she recalled that back in the time she had been with Aduke at the roadside market they had also talked of unions, Angélique had butted in on a stall-mate to say:

'We also need a union for married women for them to put a stop to husbands stealing their money.'

Everyone had laughed, a union of wives against men who made a point of being too domineering was an idea that only Angélique could have had, but what would a union be like in Iba market, huger than any other and with people selling anything that there was to be had in the world, the woman had retained one of the thoughts of President Sebastian Silva on markets:

'The market is the most ancient base of African economy and social life. But its operation must be protected however much it accepts the structural changes which it may well have to undergo.'

Abionan felt that markets didn't need to be protected at all, they protected themselves and that was important beyond doubt, she glanced at the lane which had little traffic, Solange seemed also to be drawing up a balance of what she had sold, Yatundé was in the middle of winding a dark blue tie round her head and Omitola was chatting with a rather stooping old woman while a man was bargaining at the dry fish stall farther on, his bids and those of the stallholder were the loudest sounds in the afternoon, suddenly a child's scream became louder, it must have been the adire woman's son, a lorry's roar added to the overall clamour and Abionan thought of leaving sooner:

'Today I'd like to shut up my stall ready to get to Iro Kogny well before midnight.'

It was the shortest distance in the series of the four markets, even shorter than the journey from Opo Meta to Idigny, Abionan got up, went over and talked to Solange and the others agreed to be on the road earlier, the sun had sunk so far that it no longer struck the roof of the stall, when she came back she said to Victor:

'So you aren't coming to Iro Kogny today?'

'No, but I'll have to be in Ketu the day after tomorrow.'

The woman straightened out her blouse and started packing up her basket and the calabash, she took a sheet of plastic and placed it over the rolled-up mat and set a stone on top of the shelf, put the bench underneath the shelf and when the time to leave approached, the woman went through a mixture of calm and haste, first she went through all the motions as in a ritual, it was a religious act, and it seemed as if all the orishas were standing all around her, observing her every movement and each time she lifted her arms to put away or take out cassavas and potatoes she felt that the cassava was a holy object which the orishas prized, she came to grow afraid of bumping into Shango, Oshun or the hunter god all of whom who were right there examining the way she packed up her things, an order must exist for objects to be placed in, one pre-ordained and chosen by Olodumare ever since the foundation of Ketu, or even earlier when her forefathers had decided to abandon Ifé to found Ketu, an order which must be followed to the letter, one potato could not be placed before another one, the shape must also affect the sequence, a large, fattish cassava had perhaps to be set alongside a long, thin one, it was ever since childhood when she had first felt a passion for the potatoes and roots that Abionan had used to study the details of the stacks on each stall, so that from time to time she would notice an overall imbalance in the pattern, she couldn't say where the flaw lay and after screwing her eyes up to examine every item with her head bent a little bit forward, she would reach a conclusion and re-stack them all, at such moments she had a habit of looking each way as if seeking the approval of Shango, Oshalá or any other orisha who might be nearby, she would smile as if she had heard a chorus of agreement, now as she clutched a long dun-coloured yam she felt it seemed like a man's organ, of those that mark the presence of Eshu along the roads and in the towns, she was afraid that Eshu would disapprove of what she was doing, the ritual of dismantling her goods in one market and stacking them up again at the next was possibly even more important than the act of selling itself, it was the beginning and the end and Eshu, who presided over every beginning, could also rule at the end, she recalled another of the President's sayings which she didn't know whether she had properly understood:

'Independence begins after the independence celebrations.'

A thing starts functioning only after beginning to exist and a most common feeling was that celebrations alone were enough, that the beginning would settle everything without any need for continuity but everything had to be carried forward, there was always another market after the first and in the end it all seemed just like one big market, the women would set out together, arrive together, one stall differed little from the next, but in between there was a movement and the efforts of reaching the following market, might not she perhaps have understood the saying of the President, it was like saying that marriage begins after the wedding, she made an effort of memory to recall each of Mariana's words that afternoon, her friend's dark and serious face looked lovely as she read:

'Independence begins after the independence celebrations. Basically the act of taking the decision seems so important as to appear sufficient in itself. The decision for independence is made, independence fought for then come the celebrations and there follows complete relaxation. And therein arises the danger. And therein lies the whole truth. For it is from precisely that point of the initial act of independence that the effort to construct the new country must be made. Through that relaxation after the celebrations an irretrievable period is lost which is exploited by forces opposing total independence, forces that are not only alien but, sadly, exist and flourish within the country too.'

Mariana and the priest had discussed this passage at some length, Abionan made a mental note of Mariana's arguments and Victor had wanted to know whether there couldn't be a rest between one phase and the next, after all a period of respite was to be expected after a struggle, Mariana had said in a rather low voice:

'There can be no rest.'

And, after a pause:

'Never. What can be accepted, to be sure, is a change of style, and change of rhythm and tempo, but always in motion.'

She concluded:

'At least that's how I understand my father's words.'

Later on Mariana had read for a long while without anyone interrupting:

'I think I'm writing too much. In the new countries of Africa the important thing, is verbal communication. We have to speak to each and everyone, to seize every opportunity to say what we think. In our continent the politician has also to be a teacher. He has to speak constantly, to teach by speaking and by thinking aloud. It is possible that the need for verbal communication is not all that primitive and that it prevails not only in less sophisticated societies. After all, what did Winston Churchill do to uplift the fighting spirit of the English people if not speak? What was Hitler's technique to rouse the German people to the myth of the chosen race if it wasn't to hammer home the same point, speaking, speaking whether with good sense or not? And wasn't Roosevelt's verbal communication decisive in uniting the people of the United States in one single fighting purpose? Political communication is pre-eminently verbal and the African tradition is likewise one of oral history of deeds being transmitted verbally from generation to generation. It is by listening and watching the lip movements of the one transmitting the message that great teachings are grasped.'

There had been more, Abionan looked outside where a goat was being dragged along by a boy in a red shirt, Mariana's voice seemed to belong so intensely to that afternoon that the woman had a moment of illumination, as if she was capable of understanding all things, she comprehended how mother had felt in her relationship with the sea and saw again each moment of that last day, the last hours, the salt-tang again surrounded her and Abionan looked out beyond the houses at Idigny in the certainty that the sea was only a little further beyond, she could only see gentle rises in the ground but she knew that the sea was far away, yet she smelt it close to her and strained her ears to hear the waves coming in, or was it the wind on the leaves?, but soon wind and leaves and Mariana's voice blended into one single sound, her friend was saying:

'I can still remember my father talking. Delegations would come from the interior of the country, people seeking an audience and he would give an audience to anybody, he would talk and talk, today I know that he was teaching them.'

The priest had asked how old she had been when father had died.

Mariana had looked at the floor and replied quite pointedly:

'I was eight years, two months and four days old.'

She looked up and stared straight at the priest:

'I was born on the 10th December 1959. My father died on the 14th February 1968. But I cannot recall when it was that I stopped and worked out exactly the age I was when he was killed. I think perhaps it was on the very day of the burial. There I was on the beach with the wind blowing sand on my feet and my grandmother was clutching me, and I thought "I am eight years, two months and four days old."'

A pause:

'I am shortly going to be twenty and it is as if it had happened yes-'terday. I sitting in the front, the motor car rushing along, my father's body beside my grandmother in the back with the bullet that had penetrated his head which my grandmother had wrapped up in a white cloth. I would look round from time to time and see the cloth stained red, but Jean da Cruz would make me look ahead. Half way there was a baobab and I remember its trunk passing close by the car. When we arrived there were lots of people waiting and my grandmother took out a shawl which had come with her from Bahia and covered up my father with it. There I stood watching my grandmother gripping the hand of my dead father. He was buried on the dune, my grandmother drove off all the people around and there remained only she and I, she was almost hurting me and at the point when she squeezed my arm tight, gave a cry.'

Abionan had heard about that cry before and she gazed at her friend's face as she stopped talking while in the silence that followed, children's cries rose from outside, the woman had thought of her son being chosen to be king of Ketu and running the risk of getting killed, kings and presidents got assassinated, so what could be done to avoid her son becoming the victim of a madman?, and hadn't her son already died once?, wouldn't the first death be enough?, Mariana's voice had resumed the reading, and now lots of children were screaming outside, they seemed to have reached an apex of delight.

'Power defiles and by defiling, corrupts.'

Abionan had lost the thread of the words, she withdrew away into herself, the room was quiet and the people had disappeared, when she came round, Mariana was speaking:

'Some thoughts are no more than notes. They seem to be lists of things needing to be done. From time to time he would ask questions, apparently as if he had yet to reach a decision.'

'How do you evaluate the idea of anticolonialism? Everyone's an anti-colonialist but we need to have one or more slogans that highlight the message. Need for slogans. How to pick them? They must be simple, direct, clear. Making slogans for the people to accept a sacrifice or back a plan of action. Devise a good slogan against corruption.'

Another time, when afternoon was at a close and Mariana had spoken of the importance of the mother, she had quoted the adage that mother is gold and father is glass and had observed:

'How could my father have thought otherwise? He didn't know

his father, he was born some months after his father's death but he had a great mother and to her he owed everything.'

She had paused before explaining:

'My case was different. I never knew my mother and as a girl I was full of admiration for my father.'

Abionan had given her opinion, a father was there to protect, his mere presence gave you spirit, but mother was the important one. She would remember her own and the journeys she made with her, she was already a young girl when mother had taken her to see the river Niger, the river that belonged to the goddess Oya, then Abionan was strong enough to carry heavier loads and it had been a long, wearing journey, there were hardly any markets along the way and they crossed into Nigeria and walked for days on end, they passed through Awereké and they rested at Ogbomoshó, this time mother did not work in the market but spent the day going around the stalls, she spoke little and her daughter chatted with boys, she felt curiosity about any man, she liked to know what they were thinking and how they behaved, at Ilenin they took a train, it was the first one in her life and she watched things passing, a bridge, people, a post, crowded roads and colourful robes that at once disappeared, houses and children running along as if to keep up with the train, mother and daughter had arrived at Jeda on a dark night and they had slept near the station, Abionan woke in the early hours and there were two men arguing loudly, she couldn't understand everything they said but had found out they were talking Hausa, now and again they threw in a Yoruba word and as soon as the sun struck the place where they were, mother had said:

'Let's go and see the river.'

And they did. The waters flowed contentedly by and mother had stayed and watched them for an enormous time, canoes large and small sailed past from time to time and there were people on the bank, a long bridge could be seen beyond and the older woman asked:

'Will the sea be that big?'

'Much bigger, mother. You can't see the other side.'

Abionan recalled the visits she had paid to Mariana, the dune stretching out among the wooden crosses at the cemetery where President Sebastian Silva lay buried, the sea with the endless restlessness in which it lived, the river in which the goddess Oya dwelt was also in ceaseless movement, she had wanted to go out on it, to travel day after day in a canoe as she had done on the Ogun river when she was much smaller, mother and daughter crossed the bridge and went to see the other side, the railway ran on far beyond, a different market appeared on the way to the north, the two women spent three weeks meeting people and talking, Fulanis came by with their long-horned cattle and the herd would gather on some swampy ground, there were goats and kids being taken off to the markets of the south, Hausas appeared with their colourful felas on their heads, Ibo women in long skirts would stop and buy ornaments and, the Yorubas sold wares of every kind and colour, words and phrases leapt from one side to the other, a very old Yoruba woman, she looked like a hundred, told tales about the river and explained that the goddess Oya was violent and it was necessary to be very careful with the waters, she added:

'I know everywhere downstream from here. Previously I lived in Mureji, near where the Kaduna river flows into the Oya, and I spent months in a house which stood right in the middle of one of the islands lying off Eggan. I went back there another time but the house no longer existed. I lived for years in Lokoja and that's a really lovely city. The market there's just like a festival. I know Idah and I also had a stall in Assaba market. Onitsha lies on the other side of the river and it's a lot bigger but I preferred Assaba which is a small nice place.'

'How long does it take from here?'

The old woman counted on her fingers:

'More than twenty days.'

She spread out two hands and gave a toothless laugh:

'Does this river go to the sea?'

The old woman didn't really know, she'd only been down as far as Onitsha.

'I've never heard of any city past Onitsha.'

Mother and daughter had one day got into a canoe, sailed downstream for some hours and then they returned by land, slept along the way, the waters made a nice noise and the old woman from Jeda asked whether they had been to Tada.

'No. Is it far?'

'It's not far and it's a lovely place.'

She had spoken of Tada and the regattas at Patega, Abionan had asked what a regatta was, the old woman gave a look of amazement:

'Don't you have regattas in your part of the world?'

155

And she had told of the canoe races with men dressed in colourful robes, there were dances and bets, important people came from Lagos for the festival and there were canoes full of drums whose beating was in time to the movement of the oars, the old woman spoke with enthusiasm, Abionan had felt she could see the river with its boats of various colours, people shouting and wherever she went, she sensed the river's presence, the waters dominated everything, the hundred-year-old woman would sleep nearly in the river, she would lay out a dark cloth on the edge to lie down and several times in the course of the night she would dip her right hand in the water flowing by, Abionan was surprised she never fell in, mother and daughter had also slept on the bank of the Niger and it was a happy time which was quickly over, one day Aduke had said it was time to make their way back, Abionan bought a necklace of beads from Bida, she tried them on in front of a mirror in a shop, the women took the train back to Ilenin, and stayed there three days before taking to the road and Abionan lost count of the time it took to reach Ketu, all she could remember was that mother wanted to rest a week at Igeyin, the sky took on a blue such as she had never seen and as she recalled the journey she realised that she would never know the name of the old woman who looked like a hundred though her physignomy and her toothless mouth would however remain in her memory quite clearly.

Victor had talked further about the importance of the mother, the priest mentioned the name of Our Lady as being the mother before all others and Mariana had observed:

'The great mother is my grandmother Mariana. Mother to her children, mother to her grandchildren, mother to her friends, mother to anyone who came anywhere near her.'

The last days of Aduke and her reconciliation with the sea, with the journey abroad by lorry, Abionan could not always quite remember in every detail what had taken place but there are times when it all comes back to her so starkly, she knows that her mother will help her to be a mother once more and bring up her son to take a position of king, and at that afternoon's end in Idigny market, she now thinks of her husband and what he will do for her son but she is sure that Victor will be with her always and she feels good to see him sitting there without a word, he was also in effect a husband, one without bed or sex, a husband who gave Abionan a sureness of things, she thought of the struggle lying ahead, first to have her son, then to protect him and make him learn the arts of government, Mariana had made a study of kings and chiefs in the ancient kingdoms and on how they would preserve their chiefdom in spite of the country being different and having a supreme chief, a president or a prime minister, the continuity was important to remind you that the first kings had been chosen by the gods or at least that was how Abionan recalled Mariana's words:

'Every chief shares in a little divinity. In Africa, this little is greater because our kingdoms have sprung from the gods.'

Abionan did her skirt up tighter, everything was in place, benches under shelves, what was left of the potatoes would come with her, she made to get up but Yatundé complained:

'Wait a bit. What's the hurry?'

She sat down again and watched the other one clear up, Solange and Omitola were also coming, and Solange remarked:

'We'll get to Iro Kogny before eight.'

The distance was short, Abionan thought of having a bathe along the way then she looked at Victor who was saying farewell with that same face with which he had asked that morning 'Have you slept well?', now he expressed hopes that the night's walk would be pleasant, that all would turn out well at the next market and the woman thanked him saying 'mo dupé', her voice had a cheerful note because she knew that she would see the man again as he had promised to be in Ketu, Yatundé interrupted the leave-taking:

'We can go now.'

The four women set off walking together, almost beside one another, they went the length of the market lane and the church seemed to be full, two candles burning at the altar could be seen from outside and the priest was shutting the door of the church house, Omitola wanted to know:

'A marriage or a christening?'

Solange thought that it was neither, it must be an ordinary service, the sun was reddening a group of clouds in the direction of the road and Abionan prayed to Shango that her husband would be in Ketu the day after next and would agree to do what she wanted, Yatundé's voice spoke up loudly:

'I think I'll be going to Cotonou after Ketu.'

She walked on some paces and asked Abionan:

'Do you want to come with me?'

'No. Not this time.'

Her friend explained:

'I'm going to visit my brother who's in prison.'

'What did he do?'

'He had a fight in the street and nearly killed the other man.'

'Was he drunk then?'

'Must have been.'

Omitola observed:

'Why is it that men drink so much?'

Nobody replied and the four women walked along in silence for some minutes until Solange said:

'I've heard there's been a lot of fighting in Cotonou lately.'

'Must have been politics,' was Omitola's opinion.

Another group of women was walking along a little way ahead and greetings were exchanged, Abionan became lost to the world, this would happen most often when she was out on the road, it was as if she didn't exist and what was being said around her seemed to come from afar with the words changing their meaning, she could tell that Solange was still relating stories of fighting, people from one party hating people from another and Abionan had the feeling that they were talking about her own family for there was always more than one side to every issue that arose in the family, the uncle who hated his brother would be expecting the latter to adopt the opposing viewpoint but what Solange was commenting on was Cotonou politics, Mariana had once said to Abionan:

'You should take an interest in everything that's going on in Cotonou.'

Abionan had answered that she would do, but she found it hard to think about something not closely affecting her and her friend went on:

'It's there that matters are decided which can sway your life.'

She had gone on and explained further, how could she wish her son to become king of Ketu if she didn't try to find out what was happening in Cotonou?, it was up to Abionan whether it was her dream which was a plan or her plan which was a dream, that Mariana had studied the problem of the traditional obas and had written a work which she called a thesis, one day she had read it out aloud, and she stressed every word drawing Abionan's attention to certain parts:

'Here now: "Independence ended with the ruins of the power of the ancient obas because the obas belonged to an era when there was a kingdom in each city. Ketu was a kingdom. Porto Novo another. On the other side of the frontier, Oyo was a kingdom. The Europeans arrived and abolished the kingdoms, but they did leave the obas a little power. But under independence the obas became weaker still."'

Mariana's voice would be different when she read and Abionan recalled a quiet afternoon in Iro Kogny with almost nobody in the market, Omitolá was sitting asleep at her stall and a lizard with a red head was so still that it looked just like one of Victor's carvings, Mariana had been reading:

'Three forms of society coexist in today's Africa. In many parts of the continent property remains communal. Labour is communal as also are the products of labour. In the larger townships or cities the oba constitutes continuity of the power of the aristocracy. At national level, power is generally democratic but it may be autocratic without belying its popular base. Thus, primitive communism, aristocracy and democracy cohabit in many of our countries with the chief of the commune, the oba of the city and the Head of State each symbolising a rung on the administrative ladder of power. When one above seeks to weaken those beneath him – that is, when the Head of State attempts to impose excessive power over the city oba or the communal chief – the result may be an undesirable social imbalance. For many reasons, which are cited below, the preservation of such a balance is becoming more appropriate with the continuance of the power of each oba and/or king within defined territories corresponding to the ancient traditional kingdoms which preceded the formation of the black African countries of the latter half of the 20th century.'

Abionan was set thinking and asked:

'So can't a king of Ketu be president of the country as well?'

Mariana had given her an odd look:

'Of course he can.'

And here she had laughed and with a chuckle that said:

'You wouldn't be thinking of your son doing that too, would you?'

Now, on the road to Iro Kogny, Abionan hears Omitola say that there were bans on everything.

'It's forbidden to sell without a licence, it's forbidden to cross the frontier without papers, it's forbidden to move round markets.'

159

Solange added:

'I've heard that it's also going to be forbidden for us to dance to Shango and give presents to Eshu.'

'Not going to be. It already is.' interrupted Yatundé.

'In Cotonou and Porto Novo hardly anyone dances any more. Nor do they pay homage to the dead in the old fashion. The people who have studied in Europe say it's a barbaric business.'

Abionan thought that her voice was getting too loud:

'How is it Mariana studies in Europe and yet respects our customs?'

'She's different.'

Solange said that she had seen a festival to Shango in Porto Novo less than a month before and that the festival didn't appear to be in any way, banned. Abionan declared:

'No one's going to tell me what to believe in and what not to.'

A stronger wind came up from the road ahead, would the water be nice for a bathe?, after the first hour on the road, the body would grow used to the movement, there was a sort of soothing in weariness, Abionan found herself walking on without paying any attention to what she was doing, the pauses in the conversation became longer, a phrase here, another there, lots of questions found no replies, perhaps none were necessary and when the next market drew near the conversation became normal again and from time to time one of the women would stumble on a stone and swear, Abionan refrained from bathing and she felt a great wish to lie down, stretch her body out on her mat, open her legs and sleep, she could hear Solange's voice:

'Iro Kogny's getting worse.'

In the pause that followed the lights of the place appeared in the distance.

'That market had little enough business anyway. And of late it's been getting even less.'

'Few people have the money.'

Omitola thought otherwise, it was because many inhabitants of the region had moved to Ketu and Porto Novo and the population had fallen, the four women walked into the market together and Abionan stopped in front of her stall, put her basket down on a shelf, undid her headtie, let down her skirt which was hitched up to her waist and laid out the mat with the lioness printed upon it, Yatundé called out:

'May you not die while you're sleeping.'

She acknowledged the greeting and gave her own, and remembered how mother's greetings had struck her:

'May you not die while you're coming your hair.'

'May you not die while you're talking.'

Once, on the road between two markets, mother had run into a man and a young woman making a child and had given the woman a special greeting:

'May you not die while you're making love.'

Abionan, who was then fifteen, asked why she had not greeted the pair of them, because there were two people and she had addressed only one person. Explanation:

'I know only the girl. I don't know who the man is.'

Abionan lay down lengthwise along the mat, opened her legs and closed her eyes. A dog barked nearby, a sound of running water came out of the shadow and the woman stretched her legs out as far as she could, she liked to lie like that, at least at the start of the night, later she would curl up like a child, then she would wake up a few times and turn over on to her other side, today sleep was slow in coming and she waited and waited for it to arrive, she felt herself being shaken and looked up and saw the child, how could he be at her side if he had not yet been born?, or was it the Adeniran who had died?, the woman thought she was sleeping and dreaming, she looked at the mat and saw herself lying there on it but the place was different, but which child was it, the one that had died or the one that was to come?, she felt that it was all the same, perhaps one was both and both were one, she didn't have much time to think the matter over because she saw the child being taken off in the arms of several men, he went through the air and was passed from hand to hand, there were women there too and Abionan was trying hard to get close but could not quite make it, she fell down on the road and when she got up she realised that the boy was moving far away, she ran and suddenly saw that she was on the bank of a broad river, it could have been the Ogun river but the river seemed to be all the while swelling, it must have been the Oya, canoes were sailing down the middle and on the far side was the crowd with her son aloft in the air, she thought of screaming, then a boat turned up, the paddler had a wide face and motioned as if to invite her:

'You can get in.'

She got into the boat but the crossing had no end, it started to rain, or was it rain?, there was a coolness such as she had never felt before, she turned over in her sleep and in the middle of the dream she sensed she was turning, she thought of waking up and strained to but she didn't, so then it wasn't a dream, her son really was being abducted, the paddler showed her that they had reached the other side and as they were landing she saw mother staring hard at her and saying:

'May you not die while you're getting out of the boat.'

'Oh no, mother, I'm not going to die.'

On she ran again and up a hill, she started to feel tired from so much climbing, there was a force which was stopping her from going any farther, she stopped and saw that there was not a single other person around and the wind struck her face, where would the boy be?, quickly she got up and went to the summit of the hill, a tree was waving about as though it were gusting, she ran down again with no effort and found herself in the midst of Ibadan market with children everywhere, little boys running about and little girls screaming but Adeniran seemed to have vanished, the woman sat down at a stall and wept, Adimu's face appeared before her:

'Don't cry.'

But he didn't seem to be hunchbacked now, but his smile hadn't changed one bit though he had stayed a boy, why didn't he grow like everyone else?, then Abionan realised that she was herself dreaming and that it was mother who was now dead who had told her not to die at the moment she was leaving the boat, Adimu remained a child with cheerful open eyes and if she could wake she would find that Adeniran had died and the second Adeniran had not yet a chance to be born but in the dream his presence, or rather his absence, was quite real, she got up and started to walk round the market, Adimu was walking along at Abionan's side as she saw his hunchback coming back, the noise and women were shouting from stall to stall, where would her son be?, now the market became the one on the road to Togo, lorries were coming and going and in the middle of the road there was a snake which was growing towards the woman, how could she walk by if the snake wouldn't let her?, she waited for the old woman to tell her to proceed and that the snake wouldn't touch her but no woman, whether old or young, turned up, Abionan was alone on the road, just she and the snake, then she saw her son on the other side, in the hands of people who were walking quickly past, she forgot her fear and went on ahead and the

162

snake vanished, the landscape changed and there was a flock of birds, she looked up and saw they were white birds which filled the sky, birds more beautiful than she'd ever seen before, would the birds have carried her son up into the air?, or would Adeniran be one of those very birds?, bright with a strange brightness, moving quickly to begin with then becoming gradually slower, Abionan sat down and discovered that she was really sitting down in her stall at Iro Kogny market, the night was still, what time would it be?, she looked at the clock, it was before ten but the dream had been so vivid and the birds had filled all her field of vision but the noise was real, a rustling of chicken's wings seemed to come from the left and she thought of the times she had talked with mother about Adeniran:

'What will that son of yours be like?'

'I don't really know what he'll be like. But I am going to train him to be the oba of Ketu.'

Mother looked askance at her:

'And will he like that?'

Abionan could find no reply, the trees in the market place of Ketu lengthened in the afternoon and there was a heat which was rising at every moment, another time the conversation struck a different note:

'You can't rely on a man. You never know what they are thinking.'

Mother's voice dropped a little towards the end of the sentence, and Abionan thought of her father whom she had never come to know directly, what had there been between father and mother?, she recalled the men she had liked, one for being tall and handsome, another for being good but in the end she would prefer Obafemi because he belonged to one of the royal families of Ketu and although everyone might tell her all that had ceased to function after independence and the obas were losing more and more of their power, Abionan sensed in the obanate a source of power that would never disappear, how could a king of Ketu fall so low and fail to impose himself upon the city and its market, wouldn't whoever ruled in the market, rule everywhere else too?, the conversation with mother had gone on:

'My son will be different, mother. A son of mine will be like no other man.'

Aduke's gaze saddened:

163

'Oh, but he will be. A son of yours will be exactly like any other man.'

After a pause:

'No one knows how I thanked Ifá for having given me a daughter.'

She spread her hands out a little:

'What would I do with a son?'

As she sat at her stall in Iro Kogny after the dream, Abionan thought of other remarks made on that and different occasions:

'What was my father like, mother?'

'He was a lovely man.'

Silence.

'What else?'

'He drank a lot.'

That was news to Abionan and mother continued:

'He would never stray from the palm-wine stalls. While I was going round from one market to the next he would stay all day chatting and drinking. When he came near me, he had a horrible smell.'

Abionan started imagining father's smell.

'I'd be going around with you strapped on my back and then he'd come and want to sleep beside me. I simply couldn't stand his presence.'

There had also been private thoughts which seemed contradictory:

'Sometimes he was good. He would keep quiet beside me and spend the whole day at the stall, serve the customers, talk softly and not drink.'

Or:

'He had such a jolly face, his eyes would shine a lot.'

Abionan would imagine her son in time to come lying down with a woman, and talking, and maybe drinking, it could be that the woman would find his smell horrible too, how could it be seen for a man to be a man and yet all the same time have those nice manners that women have, that way of listening, smiling and accepting that Abionan would see in the market women?

Another time, it had been in Atakpamé, where mother had spoken of Casimir:

'He's very affable, he'll do anything you ask.'

She seemed to be half dreaming:

164

'He might even make a good husband.'

Quickly following:

'But he hardly does any work. He whiles the whole day away.'

The uncle she hated was also not one to work hard, he would like drinking beer and she ran through various men from Ketu, Idigny, Whydah, Porto Novo, Aduni, Pobe and Sekete, but there were also men like Victor Ajayi and the priest, or like President Sebastian Silva, Mariana lived on her father's memory, reading his thoughts in both a loud and soft voice, she would write about him and Abionan remembered the great names from Ketu's history, king Adira and his ancestors, Leke and Andé, and the struggles between the two secret societies of Ketu, the oba Odjeku, called also Otchum Odjeku, that is, 'sleeping is not dying', of famous men from beyond Ketu, from Europe and America, and there were men who were kings and presidents, perhaps the need for there to be men like that relegated the rest, the ordinary men, to a lower grade, there would be chiefs, those who ruled and decided on behalf of everyone and then the plain mortals who might be drunk and lazy, perhaps the differences among women were as great but mother insisted that not too much importance should be attached to men, whose prime use was really to make children, Abionan could again hear Mariana's accounts of Ketu and her friend had asked:

'Did you know that in Ketu there was a war over a woman?'

Noting the former's surprise:

'They say that Alabá Adira possessed a beauty which was out of the ordinary. She was married to an important man called Kanauan. This Kanauan belonged to a secret society entitled Egbe Ma. A rich merchant belonging to the other secret society, Edgbe Ajudjere-Kunti, he was called Arigbá, fell madly for Alabá. After giving it some thought he made up his mind to abduct her. And abduct her he did going off to live with her not so very far from the husband. A fight thereupon started between Kanauan and Arigbá. And there started a war between the secret societies to which each belonged.'

'Were there battles?'

'Not to begin with. Just threats. King Ad had no desire to take sides, though he did seem to favour Arigbá's group. But then there was war.'

A pause.

'They say that it was on a moonlit night in the dry season. A lovely night. A group of members of the Ajudjere-Kunti society started beating drums at a festival of singing and dancing. It all happened beneath that huge baobab which you know.'

'What, the one on the road?'

'No. The one at Massafé, on the other side of the city. Many people gathered around and there was soon an enormous crowd. In the middle of the festival people started improvising. On the spur of the moment the singers would think up funny, witty verses. As these singers were supporters of the merchant Arigbá they began jeering at Kanauan and the fact that he had lost his wife. The supporters of Kanauan attacked the singers and thus began the war. When night was over, there were forty dead and hundreds wounded. The battle continued on the following days. In every quarter of the city they fought with the weapons to hand. In one house people died, then in another people died, men went forth from one side to kill people on the other, the battles moved out of the city and war began on the farms until one group of Kanauan supporters discovered Arigbá in Issonu. They wanted to bring him back alive to Ketu but Arigbá resisted and was killed, so what came back to Ketu was his head.'

'And the woman?'

'Alabá Adirá was restored to her husband who, I read somewhere, went out round the city to parade the wife who was now his own again.'

'It must have been quite a spectacle.'

'It was indeed. And, naturally, he went through the market with her.'

Abionan had imagined the market women breaking off work, stopping business to see the victor passing by with Alabá Adirá who must too have felt proud to have provoked a war, but would her son come to fall so madly for a woman to the extent of abducting her, would he really have the courage to go and abduct an Alabá from her husband?, but where was the king of Ketu?, Mariana replied:

'The supporters of Kanauan moved against the king, believing that he must have backed the victim, whereupon King Adirá left Ketu and went to live in Meko.'

Abionan knew Meko, for she had sold in the market there, and Mariana had gone on:

'He never returned to Ketu. In fact, a serious problem arose because it was the first time that they had had to choose a new oba when the incumbent was still alive.'

Abionan could see that the clock was showing ten o'clock and thought of going back to sleep again, after all sleeping was not dying, but what a funny name they had chosen for a king, perhaps because he slept a lot, Solange was making a noise at her stall, she must be setting out her wares for the next day, Mariana had also spoken about the eunuchs who were market chiefs, as a eunuch he would have no problems with women and would leave those in the market well alone, the last of the eunuchs had been none other than Oni Ojá, killed during the war between the secret societies of Kanauan and Arigbá. Faced with the problem they had of finding a successor to Adirá, no one had ever bothered thinking about getting a new eunuch but the city's small market, Oja-Kekeré, came to be called Oni-Ojá, would Iro Kogny also have had a eunuch ruling the women?, the need to have a son now made the woman bow her head, there was a sort of pain shooting right through the middle of her, a conviction that life was barren and without meaning, one market after another, stalls and more stalls, potatoes, yams, and cassavas, customers who all seemed much of a muchness, the roads from Idigny to Iro Kogny, the trees half way along the route and Omitola had once said in a very low voice:

'Do you know I have days when I don't know what I'm doing?'

She pursed her lips almost grimacing:

'I don't know which town I'm in nor what I'm selling. I can't remember what day of the week it is, I think it's the day of Eshu, I ask someone and find out that it's the day of Shango.'

Abionan tried to explain:

'You might be unknowingly ill.'

The other pursed her lips even more tightly:

'Could it be an illness? Sometimes I think it must be what men feel when they drink. I look at someone I know very well and I don't know who it is.'

She opened her eyes wide as she asked:

'Would it be old age?'

Mariana, who had been listening closely, had thought it must be nothing but tiredness, she had advised Omitola to go to Lagos, visit Porto Novo, Cotonou and Whydah, take a trip to Lomé in Togo and to Aduni in Zorei, Abionan felt sure that without a son the same thing would happen to her, every market would end up becoming just one more, in every way like the previous one, she glanced around her and thought of tomorrow's work, the customers arriving

167

early, choosing their yams and cassavas, the arguments over the price and here she wouldn't even have Victor's presence to give a sense of calm purpose to every deed, Mariana was shortly to arrive but she might not be coming to Ketu herself for the next few weeks, Abionan was itching to get back to Ketu, have a talk with Fatogum, see her baobab, think of the best way for her son to come quickly as possible, she thought she must be asleep so she lay down on her mat and kept her eyes open for few minutes longer and the lamp on Yatundé's stall lit up the right hand side of Abionan's gaze as she gradually closed her eyes and slept.

Again she dreamt. She picked up the dream again exactly where it had left off. White birds filled the sky, the flapping of their wings seemed whiter and one bird stood out from the others and soared up, as she set her eyes on it, the woman could see her son borne aloft into the air, he was far away, she had to run to reach him and a man with a slow dignified step was approaching the boy, on his body he wore skins and a colourful leather hat, where had she seen him before?, she imagined it would be Odé, the hunter, the chief, the king, the god of the region and it was from Odé that deliverance would come, close to Odé stood Fatogum who was smiling at her, now in front of her there arose a mountain like those she had seen in Nigeria and the little boy was ascending it ringed by people, men and women were trying to touch him and the mother heard a voice:

'He is going to cure all sickness.'

She looked and saw that it was the voice of a young girl in a blue robe, but who was going to cure all sickness?, she thought she had misunderstood but the girl repeated:

'The boy is going to cure all sickness.'

She looked up again and there he was, now encircled by the sick, and the lame, and the blind, there were those who were dragging themselves up wanting to get close and those who were carried by strong youths and all the while the little boy passed from hand to hand in the air, the sick tried to close the circle around him and the little boy seemed to be smiling but a knife appeared in someone's hand and Abionan was afraid, then the landscape totally changed.

It was the peak of the mountain. There was no longer movement, no longer fear. Many people were seated there. In the middle, a very white sheet. The knife was laid on the sheet. The little boy was also lying out with his eyes shut, his hands however were stirring gently as if trying out his finger movements, Abionan was looking at these things quite calmly, Odé was at her side and she wanted to know:

'What was the matter?'

'There was a danger the world would end.'

Odé had to speak several times over for her to understand. The world end?, but from that point on she heard the words more distinctly or else understood them without needing to hear them:

'Ifá has said that only the blood of a little boy could save the world.'

He motioned towards Adeniran:

'He was the chosen one.'

'To die?'

'At first we thought that he must die but Ifá thought it would suffice to shed a little blood and then the world would be safe.'

He pointed:

'Look.'

The blood of the boy ran on to the sheet, Odé went on:

'It was in his arm.'

Abionan made to take the child but the man dressed in skins broke in:

'No. Let everyone see that his blood has been let.'

There was a queue of people, men and women, boys and girls, they filed past Adeniran, stopping in turn, with each looking at the wounded arm and the blood on the sheet and the voice of Odé which Abionan now recognised as something friendly, spoke again:

'It is quite enough to feed the boy well and let him play freely.'

The column of people continued to move along and the woman stayed there quietly, a fresh flapping filled the air but there were no birds, just clouds amidst the silence.

Abionan all of a sudden opened her eyes and felt wide awake, the dream was still close to her with the whiteness of the sheet, the red of the blood and the boy with his arms half open, she could see that the night was full of sounds, maybe it was her imagining noises that didn't exist, she rose from her mat, put her hands on her neck and stared into nothing.

FOURTH PART
IRO KOGNY MARKET

Ojo Obatala, day of Obatala, god of heaven

She spent a sleepless night. She saw when the men arrived with baskets and pots and when the women who lived in the place appeared, they had stalls right at one end of the market, she saw too when the day started to surge, a sunbeam striking the bare flag pole that stood at the entrance, she thought of the dream and the images came back, the little boy lying stretched out as if he had died with the red blood against the pure white of the sheet, but her son really had died and today she was only waiting for a new son to grow inside her body, then she saw again the snake which had stopped her on the road, the mountain full of people and the white bird and she recalled the conversations that she had had about the child:

With Ademola:

'What name is he going to have?'

'Adeniran.'

'Just putting "crown" in a boy's name won't make him into a king.'

'Well, it's the name that I think will fit him.'

She had smiled at her husband and repeated:

'Adeniran. Sounds imposing.'

With mother:

'He has unusual eyes. They seem to see more than we do.'

'Come on now, mother. All children have eyes like that.'

'You didn't.'

With old Mariana, also on the subject of eyes:

'He's got lovely eyes. They remind me of my son Sebastian's when he was a child.'

With young Mariana:

'If he's going to be king of Ketu he'll have to change the market regulations.'

'What's wrong with them?'

170

'Nonsensical taxes, bad judgement in the siting of stalls, and many other things besides.'

Mariana had taken a good look at the child:

'Yes. He has the face of someone who'll be capable of changing everything.'

'How can you tell that from someone's face?'

'Notice the way he sets his lips. That's the sign of a strong and bold person.'

With mother again:

'Why was a man born?'

'I wanted it to be a man.'

On this day of Obatala the morning was beginning softly with Solange asking how she had slept the night:

'I didn't sleep.'

'Why not?'

'I had a horrible dream.'

'How could you have had a dream if you didn't sleep?'

'I slept at first. Then I had the dream and didn't sleep any more after that.'

'What did you dream about?'

'That they were shedding my son's blood to save the world.'

Solange stared at her:

'What son?'

'I couldn't make out whether it was the one I had or the one I'm going to have.'

Solange felt she ought to pray to Obatala to protect both of them.

'What good is protecting the one who's now dead?'

'It could be that he'll return in the next son.'

Yes, he really could. She recalled her fear of that elder god and once she had asked Fatogum:

'What's Obatala like?'

'It was he who made the earth.'

'How?'

'That depends. In Nigeria they call Obatala Orishalá and say that it was he who made the earth into dry land. Before, there was only water and swamp.'

'Is he powerful?'

'Very. The lame are his work too. Cripples, hunchbacks, the blind and the deaf, are all of Obatala, who lets no crime go unpunished.'

171

He had explained further:

'Obatala always wears white. He is the god of purity. He is the father of the other gods.'

That was why Abionan was afraid. Fatogum's voice:

'Obatala created the world in four days.'

Another time:

'In the beginning were the waters. Then Orishalá scattered earth over the world and was assisted in the task by a chicken and a dove.'

'So where did the people come from?'

'Obatala made man out of the mud of the earth.'

'Made them how?'

'Like the sculptor makes his figures.'

Abionan had remembered how Victor Ajayi would linger over marking in the eyes and nose and mouth of his people.

The babalao had continued:

'But Obatala proved unequal to giving life to man. He did not possess that power.'

'How was it that man came to walk about on it?'

'It was Olodumare who breathed life into him.'

And he explained:

'Olodumare is heaven, the greatest, and the chief.'

'Greater than Eshu?'

'Yes, though Eshu rules as well.'

Abionan was surprised to learn that Obatala had been jealous of Olodumare:

'Are the gods jealous?'

'If men are jealous, so gods are.'

She couldn't see that, but had said nothing, who was she to argue with a priest of Ifá?

One night he had repeated:

'Obatala likes the lame, the hunchbacks and the albinos.'

Then Adimu was a very special person. Obatala like the one who had been chosen to be born hunchbacked, and what's more, Adimu made figures, he too picked up the mud and thought up faces out of it, he must be a very beloved son of Obatala, but Abionan did fear albinos, they seemed to be from out of this earth and she had met a number of albinos on the roads, in Oshogbo, in Pobé and at Mariana's.

'It's starting up.'

Abionan looked to one side and saw Francisca.

'Here comes the potato supplier.'

Abionan got ready to make her choice at the same time as she was talking:

'Has business here really slackened? Or is that an exaggeration?'

Omitola answered from a distance:

'You've only to use your eyes. Formerly the market would be full at this time but look around and count how many people are buying.'

The supplier added:

'There are lots of empty houses in Iro Kogny.'

Solange:

'Everyone wants to go to a big city.'

'Like Ketu?'

'No, Ketu's small. Big cities are like Cotonou or Porto Novo.'

Yatundé:

'Everybody wants to be by the sea.'

'Not always. Ibadan is big but it doesn't have any sea.'

Abionan knew now that mother had always been thinking of the sea and wanted nothing other than to see the sea, to sleep beside it and hear the waves, smell its smell, and perhaps she had travelled around inland to disguise her desire for the sea. Once she had said:

'What a beautiful sight the Oyá river is.'

Abionan had observed:

'The other side is a long way off, it's like another country.'

'Nothing's lovelier than moving water.'

The daughter recalled the lagoons and lakes she had seen:

'Still water's nice too.'

Mother had asked a little coyly:

'Does the sea water move about too?'

'The sea has waves, mother.'

'I know that, but do you see water coming from one side and going to the other?'

Abionan thought:

'I've never noticed. The sea is always stirring, but it's different from a river.'

'In what way different?'

She had wanted to say that she should go and see for herself but felt she couldn't as mother would be cross and sad:

'It's a different colour. The water's green and the top part of the waves is white.'

'Green and white.'

'Yes. You'll have to see it.'

She had said the words without meaning to, but mother hadn't seemed to have taken them in and now in Iro Kogny market Yatundé was the one talking as her hands were busy unwinding a brightly coloured tie around her head:

'I'd really love to live by the sea.'

'Why don't you then?'

'I could never make any sense of the markets over there. They sell things from the sea and tins which come from abroad, from Europe and goodness knows where else.'

She paused:

'It's good to sell things that spring from the earth.'

Solange:

'It's good to sell meal. It softens your skin.'

'It doesn't soften it at all, just dries it up. Animals are good, hens which make a noise, something living.'

'It's good to sell painted calabashes and printed rugs that delight the eye.'

A local man came by.

'It's good to sell and buy palm-wine which charms you from head to toe.'

Omitola couldn't restrain herself:

'Ugh, one more drunk.'

The man stopped and looked at her:

'No, not drunk, but a palm-wine just now and again is good, or so I reckon.'

An old woman with a dark blue shawl over her shoulder said:

'It's good to sell herbs. Herbs cure illness, make you live longer.'

Abionan thought of her first weeks in the market and the cassavas and yams that weighed a lot, mother had said:

'You ought to have chosen cooked food: selling buns, acaras like there were in Abeokuta.'

'But it's difficult managing the fire.'

Her husband had thought she ought to sell things in tins and bottles, in Iro Kogny, Solange said:

'I'm afraid of the sorcery stalls, and the monkey skulls and roots.'

The local man:

174

'But they're the best. A market without that sort of stall will soon die.'

'The market die?' asked Abionan.

'Of course it'll die. I've seen many big busy markets full of people and stalls die suddenly without anyone knowing why.'

The man glanced around as if wanting to see the effect of his words:

'It's worth everything to protect the two lucky stalls, the sorcery one and the palm-wine one.'

Yatundé:

'And there was I taking him seriously.'

The other women laughed, the noise of the market seemed to have risen and Solange said:

'What a dream you had, eh?'

'Indeed it was. I think I'll go and make my orders.'

She rose and bought some cakes at a food stall, yes, it was indeed hard to manage a fire, then she went to Eshu's place, talked with him a little and asked Obatala to protect her son who was about to come and on the way back saw that the market was livelier and a very bright sun gave clarity to every object, Omitola was just then saying:

'People have already been to buy at your stall.'

She served two customers:

'Whoever said business was bad?'

'There's no way of telling first thing in the morning. It's from eleven to noon that counts.'

The palm-wine stall was filling up, Yatundé:

'See, the palm-wine man's already on his first calabash.'

The stall was long and roofed in zinc, there were big calabashes everywhere, men in blue trousers and green shirts, others in red-and-white striped shirts or yellow ones, then there were older folk in Yoruba robes, the conversation seemed to be cheerful and at the side stalls a small boy was sitting on an old tyre, a bicycle came by ridden by a man in a green-and-white striped robe, a row of ten or more calabashes cut in half had been set one on top of the other, and the onion and lemon seller was shouting at a customer, drums and casks lay on the ground and Abionan forgot her dream and her weariness, Yatundé asked:

'How about going tonight by lorry to Ketu?'

The distance was farther, Abionan agreed:

'Of course, we'll go by lorry.'

'I'll fix it with Ogunbanjo, the one who's always laughing.'

'Excellent. I want to sleep well tonight.'

An old woman was approaching, who had known mother:

'May you not die while you're selling.'

Abionan acknowledged her:

'How's your friend from France?'

'She's not really from France at all, she's actually from near here, Zorei.'

'What a clever girl.'

'She's very well. She'll be arriving there any time now.'

Abionan remembered Mariana having spent hours talking with the old woman, what was she in fact called?, it was an English name, Sybil, why such a funny name?, the old woman had explained all:

'My father worked for the English, he met the boss's daughter who was called Sybil and liked the name.'

Aduke couldn't resist remarking:

'It's a name that doesn't mean anything.'

The old woman:

'It must mean something over in their country. Where do you ever get a name which doesn't have a meaning?'

Mariana had thought of an explanation:

'I think that Sybil is a name linked with Ifá, foretelling the future and all that sort of thing.'

At that the woman had felt quite proud:

'I knew it had something to do with Ifá. My family's closely tied to Orunmila and Ifá.'

Perhaps that was why she had thought Mariana was so clever and she asked what the meaning of her name was:

'Mariana? It's the name of my grandmother. It's a Christian name, connected with Maria and it can also mean daughter of Maria.'

'Was your mother called Maria then?'

'No. The name was in honour of my grandmother.'

'Ah.'

But the old woman didn't appear to understand why it was that such a clever girl didn't change her name, later she was to say to Abionan:

'It's not because Mariana's an ugly name. It's actually quite a nice one, but surely the girl could have had one name over in France and another back here.'

The old woman asked about Abionan and she spoke of the happenings in Ketu and Idigny, what?, yes, she'd be in Ketu the next day for sure, or even that same night, she had arranged with Yatundé to go by lorry, the other one asked:

'Could you take some medicine for my son?'

'Gladly.'

'He works in a bicycle workshop in Ketu. The workshop's close by the market. Name, address, it's all down here on the paper.'

It was a packet of herbs, so the old woman knew about herbs then?, the other went on:

'Tell him all's well here.'

As she was going off, a group of boisterous youths were coming along dressed all in the same pink robes which Abionan hadn't seen men wearing for a long time, they passed the stall taking loudly and one phrase stood out from the rest:

'She's got the biggest eyes I've seen in my life. Like that.'

And he indicated with his thumb and forefinger the size of the woman's, or maybe the girl's, eyes, Abionan thought of the size of Adeniran's eyes as he was lying in the dream, just of those wide open eyes, the bustle and noise of the market seemed to calm the boy down. Solange spoke:

'Let's see whether they're going to the palm-wine stall.'

'No, they won't be. They're too young.'

The group was lost among the stalls, a chicken ran fluttering out in front of Abionan, the chicken had helped Obatala to scatter earth over the world and ended by being also food for the men that Obatalá had moulded out of mud, mother's last days came back to mind, would her death have been in some way linked with her little boy's?, mother who was never one for saying a lot, had at the end said even less.

'Does it hurt?'

Aduke had put her hand on her stomach:

'A little.'

'We must find some medicine to stop the aching.'

'No need. It'll pass.'

'What could it be?'

'It must be the illness that's going about.'

Abionan was afraid to say the word, the illness that killed everybody and had no cure to stop it, how did her mother know?'

'The babalao's felt it and said something's grown inside.'

Abionan had gone along to talk to him:

'Look at the colour of her face. It's like earth. The colour of earth. That's a sign of the illness.'

Abionan had agreed, the colour of Aduke's face reminded her of the organ of Eshu that stood in Idigny.

'Where do you want to go?'

'Nowhere.'

'A trip to Ibadan perhaps?'

A pause.

'To see the market again, at Oja Iba?'

'I want to stay here.'

This had been shortly before the reconciliation with the sea, the afternoons in Ketu seemed more beautiful than they had ever been, and Abionan suspended the round of the four markets to keep mother company.

'Maybe old Mariana knows of a remedy.'

'No one knows all that.'

One day:

'Do you want to come with me to the market?'

Mother had done. She had sat herself down on a low stool, she carefully followed what was going on and listened to the talking, the earth colour spreading down her neck.

'Shall we go and talk to the babalao?'

'What for?'

'Well, he knows a thing or two.'

'Leave him to care for the others. There are a lot of sick people about.'

Another time:

'Would you like some pepper on your rice?'

'Put some on.'

Later she had exclaimed:

'Eating's fun.'

In the end she ate no more. She wanted to but couldn't. One afternoon:

'Daughter.'

'Yes, mother.'

178

'Stick a pin in my finger.'

'Whatever for, mother?'

'I want to see if it hurts.'

'Of course it'll hurt.'

'Try.'

It hadn't hurt.

'Why not?'

The babalao had said there might have been more than one reason, but, compared with the other illness, it was of no importance. Not a great deal anyway.

Solange:

'Take your mother to a doctor. A babalao is no good by himself.'

'I have done.'

'And what did he think?'

'He confirmed what the babalao said.'

'Did he mention the fingers as well?'

The doctor had produced the explanation that the extremities can become somewhat numb in old age and he had prescribed a medicine for the circulation.

One night:

'The dogs are barking a lot.'

There was a succession of barks marking out the shadows.

'Why will that be then?'

Abionan replied that she didn't know.

There were pauses in the barks, the silence seemed the deeper afterwards and then mother declared:

'It's cold.'

'That's the draught from the window.'

She had gone to shut it. For several days she had hardly spoken. She looked at things, stared at the walls and sometimes at the sky, and Abionan had eventually asked:

'Say something, mother.'

The woman had smiled:

'It's all right.'

She had paused:

'It's nice to keep quiet.'

Was she in pain?, but in those days, her last ones, mother hadn't complained of any pain, she would keep putting her hands on the spot where the thing was growing inside her, she had looked as if she was weighing it up, trying to tell what size and shape it might have, it had been almost like the act of a mother expecting a child.

Solange interrupted her friend:

'Are you thinking about the dream?'

'Not at all. I was thinking about my mother.'

'A great woman. She knew everything to do with markets.'

'She certainly did. And she sold in lots of places in Nigeria and Togo.'

For that was what mother was missing in her life's last days, the market was there stretching out in the sun and the stalls full of activity with the noise of people and things and animals, Aduke had once spent a while thinking back over distant markets:

'Do you remember Oshogbo?'

She screwed up her eyes:

'And it wasn't just the market there but the river too, the river and the Shrine of Oshun. Both the river and the shrine. The waters flowing by. People gay. Dances.'

'I could have easily stayed on longer in Oshogbo.'

Or:

'Ibadan too.'

She talked about Abeokuta, the Ogun river and the stones:

'Do you remember Ifé?'

Abionan had done.

'And the drunk who robbed us at the festival of Ijebu-Odé?'

She had gone straight on to start describing the roadside market with the lorries arriving, it was as if Aduke had been re-living it all, then she had a sad turn:

'I'd have to be very old to see my grandson become king.'

Abionan had looked at her in surprise:

'What did you say, mother?'

'He might go and become king and I'd be old and weak in the head and wouldn't even know he was king.'

'You shall be there when he becomes king.'

'Perhaps.'

The local man who had gone off to drink palm-wine, was coming back with a chicken in his hand, Yatundé shouted:

'He's a lot happier now.'

Solange remarked:

'See if he's got the chicken drunk too.'

The man turned towards her with an angry look, he was about to say something, seemed to change his mind and walked on, Omitolá remarked:

'He might have hit you.'

'A man hit a woman in the market? Never. He'd get the biggest hiding of his life from us all.'

A small boy chased after another, bumped into the post of a stall, the zinc roofing threatened to fall down and a woman's shout could be heard:

'Come over here, you little devil, come here.'

Abionan imagined that she must be a catholic mother, old Mariana had explained to her that in Brazil the orishas had become mixed up with the catholic saints, Obatala was Our Lord of Bonfim and the descendants of Brazilians in Porto Novo would gather together every January for a festival where they would worship Obatala and Our Lord of Bonfim at the same time, with everyone dressed in white, and Mariana had promised to take Abionan along to the festival, Fatogum had declared himself against mixing up orishas with saints:

'They're two different things.'

Another day:

'Our religion is closer. For them, God lives far away. Ours are in that tree there.'

He pointed to an iroko, his voice enunciating each syllable:

'In every big tree there dwells a god.'

Abionan wanted to know whether there were any in the small ones too?'

'Only lesser spirits in the small ones.'

So the baobab beneath which she had been born and had buried her son, was the home of a god and old Mariana had one day said to her:

'To me the baobab is the tree of death. When I went to fetch my son's body, it was the only thing I noticed on the way both there and back: the great baobab on the road.'

Another time, however:

'No, I don't know. I've come round to thinking that after dying, my son went to live in that baobab.'

'Wouldn't he have preferred the beach right in front of us?'

Mariana had gazed at the cross on the dune:

'But the baobab stands on the road leading to Zorei. He would have liked to be not far from the land that he freed.'

181

One afternoon Victor Ajayi had left off carving a wooden Shango to say:

'Trees are wood. And with wood I make figures.'

'Aren't you frightened of destroying the house of a god though?'

Victor smiled:

'The trees I use would be no good to a major god, only to the lesser spirits.'

Then he told the tale of a man who wished to cut a branch from a tree but was afraid of being attacked by the spirit which dwelt inside, so he put a little palm-oil fairly close to the tree and when he reckoned that the spirit had left the tree to go and drink the oil, he quickly snipped off the branch and away he ran.

Abionan thought it quite wrong to deceive a spirit like that, it'd have been wiser to seek its permission to remove the branch.

'And what if he wanted to cut down the whole tree?'

'Then the spirit would have nowhere to live.'

Those had been fine moments, the moments when she had talked at greater length with Victor Ajayi, and the other plants, how could they be used without permission?, and the animals which people slaughtered?, mother thought that you shouldn't take it too far, herbs were on the earth to cure illnesses, animals were there to be eaten, and roots?, as her life in the market was tied up with roots, potatoes, yams, big and small, and cassavas, Abionan had come to regard plants and animals as under the protection of the gods and to ask their permission every time she needed them, once she had even wanted to change her line of business, she had thought about selling mats, a mat-maker had come to see her and had laid dozens before her:

'Look at this one.'

It was a green-and-red mat with a design in the middle.

'And this one, look.'

Yellow all over with red ends.

'And there's another.'

Red with a white square in the middle.

Mariana had put her off changing her trade:

'Mats are made from living things too.'

And they were too. So there was nothing for it, Mariana had nearly screamed at her:

'Look here, think. There's not a single thing around you that's not living.'

182

And indeed there wasn't, stones perhaps, but then Fatondé had told her that stones were from Shango who loved them dearly and would from time to time make them grow so Abionan had continued to sell roots.

'That's the finest yam in any market from Ketu to Ibadan.'

The customer stared at her in disbelief.

'You can take it. There's none better.'

Every time she passed near the mat stall she would recall that period of her life, the man who had come to see her hadn't any animal mats, but Abionan liked her one with a big lioness but stopped thinking about it as a customer with a big nose turned up and while she was bargaining with her, she could hear Yatundé's voice:

'Here he comes again.'

It was the palm-wine man, now without the chicken and he stopped at Abionan's:

'I want three large sweet potatoes.'

Yatundé quipped:

'See if he's got the money first. People who drink lots of palm-wine generally don't have any.'

The man took some money out of his pocket, showed it all around, Omitola commented that he might be rich and the man grinned revealing his white teeth:

'Not that I'm rich, but I've got enough to buy up the whole of your stall.'

Solange:

'He must have quite a few wives.'

'I've three of them.'

He held up three fingers and went on:

'If you want to be the fourth, you've only to say the word.'

Yatundé:

'He's a wit if nothing else. He keeps us entertained.'

Abionan had sorted out three fair-sized sweet potatoes, the man picked them up, examined them one by one and felt their consistency, he didn't argue and left in the direction of the palm-wine stall and Yatundé couldn't refrain from saying:

'He only came to buy potatoes to wend his way back to his favourite stall.'

Solange enlarged:

'He's deceived three wives and bought a sweet potato for each of them and now he'll spend the rest of the day drinking.'

183

The women laughed, the man now looked round, a pig escaped from a stall on the left but was soon caught and Abionan thought she'd better eat, the dream ran again through her head, which of the little boys could save the world, the one who had died or the one who was to come?, and why must someone die to save the world?, the priest at Idigny would always say that Jesus Christ had done precisely that, yet Odé, the hunter, had assured her that death was not necessary, a bloodletting would do, who knew whether he had been wrong and Adeniran's death had been to save the world?, so what had to take place had already taken place and she would in peace have a second son whose blood would not even need to be shed, Abionan bade them:

'Shall we eat?'

Yatundé accepted, the two left the market together, the smell of boiling oil was strong, they asked for some abarás and a little rice but Abionan said she wasn't too hungry:

'I think I'm sleepy more. I was awake all night. I shan't last the whole afternoon at the stall without nodding off.'

There was an iroko not very far from the market and Abionan started wondering which god lived in its trunk, she remembered mother having told her that the name Iro Kogny came from iroko, she broke off her thoughts to ask Yatundé when the lorry would leave for Ketu:

'At eleven.'

'That's late to leave.'

'I hope it's not full.'

'It usually is.'

They spent minutes in silence with people passing nearby, and the heat had risen:

'Shall we go back?'

Abionan agreed, she was to find the stall full of children playing on the ground, the image of Adeniran lying in the dream was still clear in her head, how had she seen it in such detail if it had been but a dream?:

'Do you believe dreams?'

Yatundé opened her eyes wide:

'I do. They exist.'

'Of course, but are they a warning, and do they have anything to do with what is happening in our lives?'

'They must do, don't you think? Otherwise why is it that we keep dreaming?'

Abionan sat down on her bench, during mother's last days, she had sat down like that, sometimes with Aduke nearby and Abionan would pretend not to be looking after her though really she was, Aduke's body had seemed steady, but the earthen colour had become more marked and her hands seldom left her lap.

'After we die do we go back to the places where we lived?'

Mother had continued without waiting for an answer:

'Because if I come back, I shall go round all the markets where I used to be.'

She had smiled to herself:

'It'll be a new way of travelling.'

'You're going to do a lot of travelling yet, mother.'

Aduke had stopped smiling:

'Not a lot, I don't think. But I will make one important journey.'

'Where?'

'You'll know when the time comes.'

And she had done.

The palm-wine man was coming back carrying the sweet potatoes, Yatundé didn't utter a word, business was slackening off and Omitola remarked:

'Didn't I say there were less people.'

Abionan looked down the lane between the rows of stalls:

'It might be just a passing thing.'

But if the markets were one by one to die off, wouldn't there shortly be not a single market remaining in the world?, Abionan imagined the stalls empty with dangling hides, and tumbledown shelves, and stools with no one on them.

'Only if everyone else dies too.'

She realised she was speaking aloud but no one was bothered greatly.

'If that man goes to drink a third time, then I'll complain again.'

The others laughed at Yatundé, Abionan thought that perhaps she was married to a drunk, the palm-wine stall was full up, men were coming and going, youths were sitting on the ground, sometimes a wave of guffaws came over from there, Abionan shut her eyes and at the same time saw the little child lying on the sheet with arms outstretched and blood staining the cloth, she looked about to see whether Odé was still nearby, but all there was was the boy, then she saw Odé saying something to her, he seemed to have already started speaking before she could hear unless it was that she could understand without even hearing him:

'Fear not. He is safe.'

She woke with a start, she could hear Yatundé talking with Solange, could the dream be continuing in broad daylight?, she was frightened, how could she sleep if the dream kept returning?, a big cloud was crossing the sky and she was remembering how she was afraid of it raining on the journeys she had made with mother, she would keep gazing up at the sky in fear of clouds and once in Ketu mother called her to see a rainbow, it was Oshumare himself, the good of the rainbow, the bright coloured snake which arched over Ketu, Fatogum had spoken to her of the importance of Oshumare but why was she thinking about that now?, she shut her eyes and then she knew why, in the middle of Odé's words she had nearly seen a rainbow in the dream, anyway there seemed to be one to the right of where her son lay and she wanted to dream again to check whether it was Oshumare protecting the boy.

She recalled mother's voice hailing Oshumare with almost a jerky rhythm:

'Arrobobo.'

On the same day she had shown her the rainbow, mother had returned to the theme that the orishas had to be remembered every day and looked at her hands as she said:

'The gods also die. If we don't give them food, if we don't think of them and stop making the traditional sacrifices, the gods will move farther and farther from us and go and live far away, somewhere else and we shall no longer know ourselves but shall be left unprotected.'

Her voice dropped a little as she explained:

'As for actually dying, I don't think they do. Maybe it's we who die for them, which comes to the same thing.'

The reports that they were going to ban the religion of the orishas hadn't shaken young Mariana:

'In the first place, I'm a citizen of Zorei. And, anyway, when a religion is banned, it goes into the catacombs.'

Abionan hadn't known what a catacomb was and the other had explained, Abionan more or less understood:

'You mean people'll start worshipping the orishas hidden away where no one can see them?'

She had gazed in the direction of the earthen Eshu and gave her opinion:

'That'll be hard.'

She picked up a sweet potato:

'Eshu has to be above the ground and in the open air.'

She couldn't believe there was a ban:

'Nobody will have the nerve to persecute people who worship Shango or Ogun or the Hunter.'

This time Abionan had scarcely heard Mariana's observation:

'Man is capable of anything.'

Mother had perhaps foreseen that there'd be difficulties in the future, and that the orishas might be forsaken and she felt a commitment to prepare her son as king of Ketu, to fight on behalf of the orishas and his people.

On that day following the dream and with the images of the bloodied child, Odé and the rainbow still vivid in her mind, Abionan thought that perhaps her son yet to be born would be persecuted and passed from hand to hand, seized by the crowd who would draw his blood and that they would shed his blood upon the summit of a hill where his body would lie on a very white sheet but he would be an adult and not a baby, he would not be able to keep his arms and feet up in the air like he did when he was small, they would spread his body out like that of old Mariana's son and young Mariana's father which had been taken away by car and then wrapped in a sheet which had come from Brazil and perhaps it was natural that a chief and king should come to be persecuted and, if one person's blood could make the world a better place, it would be the blood of a king, a minister, or a chief, Yatundé's voice attracted Abionan's attention:

'Didn't I say so? He's back again. And he's changed.'

Everybody roared, the man passed close by the women without looking to either side, he was now wearing a shirt embroidered in bright blue and red, and he went straight over to the palm-wine stall, Abionan detached her gaze from the man and thought again about her mother who had one day given her this advice:

'Don't treat things badly because everything that exists can do you harm in return. Don't fling your comb on the floor in anger,

187

don't break glasses and don't throw your clothes down on the ground.'

Some moments later, she had repeated:

'Treat things properly.'

All her life Abionan had followed mother's advice, she was in the way of being careful how she handled pans, and calabashes, and clothes, and cups, she was even more careful with potatoes, cassavas and yams and her stall would be kept spick and span, when one of Victor's carvings rose into the air he would grip it with a mixture of strength and delicacy and Mariana had been amused when she learnt of this way her friend had but then calmed down and reflected that it was all advice of great wisdom:

'Your mother was right. Her advice can be applied to trees, leaves, rivers, grass, and flowers. After all that's what we need to do today to defend what surrounds us. I think we should have big posters printed in colour saying "Don't abuse things".'

Abionan had been to Zorei with Mariana who had been urging her to do so for months, she had wanted to show her friend round the city of Aduni, the Palace where her father had lived and died, the old houses built by the Germans, the big market on the main square and the church put up by French priests, these had been days at the same time both happy and sad, Mariana had talked about her dead father, Abionan had been thinking about the son who was to come, on the way they had remained quite silent, the city drew near and Mariana got the car to stop in the square and pointed to a tree.

'That was where my grandmother sat for several days when my father was imprisoned by the French.'

The two women had gazed at the seat in silence, Abionan liked Aduni which had spreading trees in nearly every street, the houses were decorated in bright shades of green or red, or yellow or blue, the whole effect formed contrasts such as she had never seen, they stayed in a flat over the shop that old Mariana had founded over sixty years earlier where an old old man was selling drapery, Abionan went round the living room and the bedrooms and her friend had explained:

'On the site where my grandmother opened the shop this office block was built with a flat for ourselves but there remained the shop on the ground floor. I think it must be the oldest in Aduni. And my grandmother has another shop next door.'

Nearby a hospital could be seen, Mariana said:

188

'That's where my father was born.'

Afterwards she showed her the Palace:

'And there he died.'

They received permission to visit the Palace and Mariana halted in the middle of a room and stared down at the floor:

'It was just here.'

She had gone on to explain in an almost neutral voice that father had been killed at that precise spot in the room, there had been a rebellion and to that day it was not known for sure who had fired the shot but the regime had since changed and now the president was an old family friend, the secretary of the political party founded by father, Abionan was that afternoon to spend some minutes facing into a twilight such as she had not seen before, the whole city seemed to be covered in colours, the red, green and blue of the houses changed their shade several times, a very deep silence arose out of things and from a window of the flat the friends watched the night fall, the lamps light up and the shop downstairs close, the market beyond had a deserted look and only when night had drawn in did the magic fade out and they resumed their conversation and Abionan had wanted to know:

'Do you mean to live in Aduni in future?'

'My permanent home's the Water House, but I make long stays here.'

'For politics?'

Mariana thought before speaking:

'Maybe. My grandmother said I must do what I think right. My father captained the independence of Zorei, I was born here. Perhaps the right thing would be for me to come and work here, either in politics or in some activity that helps others.'

Later on, Mariana had gone and looked out a thick exercise book which was in the drawer of the long table which Abionan had seen immediately she had entered the flat:

'More thoughts of the president?'

'No, these are stories.'

'Stories?'

'Yes. No one knew that my father had written things like that.'

She opened the exercise book:

'They're African stories.'

She held it up:

'Look here, his handwriting is clear and calm.'

189

'Are they stories like we hear when we're children?'

'No. These are different. They all have the same character who's called Sousa.'

Abionan remembered various Sousas she had known and Mariana agreed:

'That's so. You find Sousa everywhere. It's a very familiar surname in Brazil, Benin, Togo, Zorei and there was the celebrated Shasha de Sousa from the days of slavery who lived his life in Whydah. There are thousands of Sousas among the descendants of Brazilians along this coast. A children's book came out in Nigeria called *The Adventures of Sousa*. I kept the name of its author, Kola Onadipe, because my aunt Ainá sent the book for my grandmother to read. In my father's stories, which I don't think he ever considered having published, Sousa is a youth who goes out and about learning things and finding out what life's all about. I have a feeling that quite a lot in the stories is autobiographical. He attributes to Sousa many thoughts which he must have had himself here and in Europe.'

Mariana picked up the exercise book:

'Listen to this:

"Sousa went out of the house without saying a thing to anyone. He wanted to see a big city. The place where he was born had only fifty-seven poor houses. Not even that many, in fact, because one of them had been struck down the middle by lightning. So, Sousa's village possessed fifty six and a half houses. The boy walked the whole day long. At nightfall he came to another village like his own. The same sort of houses. Women in similar clothes. The same small children running about everywhere. He sat down in a clearing and counted the houses. There were twenty-nine. Fewer than in his village then. He saw an old woman with a wide face. He went up to her and asked:

'Where can I get something to eat?'

The old woman replied:

'If you have money, I'll give you a meal and you can give me some money.'

Sousa stuffed his hand in his pocket and brought out a wad of notes. The woman examined the notes one by one. Then she looked him in the eye and said:

'This is old money. It's no good now.'

'Why's it no good?'

190

'They've made a law in the capital and this money has been replaced by a different one. As from last week.'

'What shall I do then?'

'You'll have to go to a bank in the capital and change the old money into new money.'

Sousa started thinking the problem over. How could he eat? The woman looked at the boy and said:

'If you want, I'll change two of these old notes for one new. I'll make something on it just in case there's another change in the law. Do you want to change them?'

Sousa agreed to. He felt he was being robbed but agreed. The new note was in different colours. The boy thought it was silly to alter money. He asked:

'Why have they made new money?'

'Because we're an independent country now.'

Sousa mulled on the idea of independence, he couldn't see anything about it that made any sense to him. The old woman had robbed him but she did seem to know a few things. He inquired:

'So weren't we independent before then?'

'How do you get by knowing nothing? You didn't know they'd altered the money. You don't know that we've been independent for three days now.'

'Where can I see the independence?'

'In the capital. There're ten days of celebrations. They're going to last another week yet.'

Sousa decided to eat up quickly so as to get to Aduni in time to see the celebrations. He ate his meal and took the road to the capital. He walked on almost till the morning. When he couldn't keep on any more, he lay down on the ground and slept. He dreamt that the celebration was already over. He awoke with a bit of a start and thought he was wasting time. He went on all day. When he was hungry, he ate what was left over from the food the old woman had sold him. The sun was strong. Sousa was sweating. He ended up with a soaking shirt. He took it off and went on his way with a bare back. The road began to fill with people. When he saw Aduni in the distance, he stopped in amazement. Sousa liked to count things up. He would count how many children were playing a game. He would count the cocoa beans on his uncle's plantation. He would count how many birds were flying over the village at dusk. He would count the houses wherever he was. In Aduni he wouldn't be able to count

191

up all the houses. There were too many. Nevertheless, he did start counting the ones in the street he took. One, two, three, . . When he reached thirty, he saw that the thirtieth was a large house with one floor on top of the other. Would he count it as just one house? Or would it be two? A nice noise seemed to be coming from the end of the street. Sousa looked and saw a group of men in brightly coloured robes playing instruments. He asked what it was. The city boy standing beside him said:

'That's the band.'

Small children were following the band. Sousa did the same. He started counting how many children there were. Over twenty. He stopped at twenty because he thought it would be better to count the men in the band. Twenty-one. The music stirred Sousa. The band arrived in a big square. Sousa saw a still bigger house, filled with flags. He counted the flags. Twelve. One was taller than the others. It was red and white. Others had three colours. Beneath the flags, a mass of men in dark clothes. He counted the men. Fifteen. He asked a fat one with his arms folded who they were:

'The president and the ministers.'

'Which are the presidents and which the ministers?'

The fat man looked scornfully at him:

'What an ignorant young man. There's only one president.'

He took Sousa by the hand and pointed it to the middle of the group of men:

'Do you see the one in the lighter clothes? He's the president. All the rest are ministers.'

Sousa counted again. They were one president and fourteen ministers. Sousa made up his mind to prove that he wasn't so ignorant, he asked:

'That's the independence, isn't it?'

The fat man pulled a face and moved away. Sousa saw the happy face of a girl with three vertical marks on each cheek. He went up to her and said:

'What a fine celebration.'

She nodded that it was.

'How many more days have we celebrations for?'

The girl looked into his eyes. She had a very happy voice too.

'The celebration itself is only for today. What came before were the preparations for the celebration. What comes afterwards will be the continuation of the celebration.'

192

Sousa was very glad to have arrived in Aduni on the day of the celebration. He forced his way through the midst of the crowd and managed to get into the front row of onlookers. He heard two speeches. He didn't understand a lot because he knew little French. He spoke really well only the language of his village. He thought to himself that he really needed to learn French which seemed to be the language of independence. Hadn't the speeches been in French? Everyone understood the village language, which made life simple. When the band set off down the streets again, Sousa walked along behind. There were now fewer children. Only eight. In the middle of the night, Sousa saw that the band was withdrawing to a large house. He was left on his own. Not quite on his own. Sitting near him, in front of the large house, was a pretty little girl. She looked like his little sister. The little girl looked up at Sousa and asked:

'Isn't the band going to come out again?'

'I don't think so. It looks as if the celebration's over.'

The little girl agreed in a voice full of certainty:

'There can't be a celebration without a band.'

The two continued gazing at the door of the large house. Sousa asked:

'Can you count?'

'Of course I can', replied the little girl.

'How many windows has that house got?'

The girl counted them:

'Five.'

'No, it's got six.'

'Five.'

'It's got six. What's that on the end then?'

'That's not a window. That's a hole in the wall.'

'But it's used for a window.'

The little girl laughed:

'A window's a window. And that's a hole.'

Sousa proposed:

'Let's change the subject. How many sticks has that fence got?'

'You can't see. It's too dark.'

'Let's go up closer and count them.'

They went and counted:

'Eighteen.'

The little girl answered:

193

'No. Nineteen.'

'Why nineteen?'

'And that bit there?'

'That's part of the next one. Can't you see they were tied together?'

The little girl asked:

'How many leaves has that tree got?'

'Even in daylight, you couldn't count them.'

Then the little girl said she was tired of counting. She said good-bye. Sousa was left by himself. He began to think about his village. They wouldn't believe him when he told them he had seen the independence celebration. The president. The flags. The ministers. Most of all, the band. He was going to be a happy man when he saw the incredulous physiognomies of the whole of the family.

Sousa thought it was time to go to sleep. He sat down on the ground looked up high above and started to count the stars in the sky.'"

Mariana had stopped reading, she and Abionan had gazed out at the lighted square and the market seemed busier now, there was light in the windows of the palace, the heat was increasing and Mariana had commented:

'An amusing story.'

'I thought it was really funny. Are they all more or less like that?'

'Yes. I've no idea what my father planned to do with them. He placed Sousa in different situations. One is about Sousa in Aduni market. In another Sousa falls in love. In many of them he travels. There's one where he goes back to his village. Perhaps Sousa represents the young African, from here, Benin, Togo, Nigeria or Ghana. The African who's starting to see the world and to find out what people are like outside his family and village circle. In one story Sousa enrols on a French course.'

Later, with her voice resounding clearly in the silence of Aduni, Mariana had remarked:

'The stories of Sousa have nothing at all to do with the thoughts. possibly my father would have one day published these stories but it could also be that he wrote them to retell to me or to retell to groups of children or even to grown-ups. Do you remember that thought of his that the African leader has to talk, to teach by talking and to be a teacher? Well, that's it. Maybe he was wanting to teach something through these stories.'

194

On the day that they had been to the main market of Aduni, Mariana had also read the story of Sousa in the market:

' "Sousa could see, from the start, that the market at Aduni was far busier than the one in his village. In the latter there were exactly twenty-five stalls. Twenty-three not counting the two that had been left vacant since the death of mother and daughter when crossing the river. Mother and daughter had stalls next to each other. Sousa stopped at the first stall in Aduni and grinned at the woman. On the shelf he counted eleven big yams. The woman asked:

'How many would you like?'

'I don't want any. I just want a chat.'

The woman called over to her neighbours:

'Just look at this. This one here just wants a chat.'

Sousa grinned at the women who seemed to like him. At the following stall there were baskets upon baskets of peppers. He saw that they couldn't be counted. There must have been two thousand peppers, large and small, in each basket. It would be great fun for himself and a group of children to count up all that great mass of peppers. Then the onion stall came into view, something Sousa liked a lot. He picked up an onion and sniffed it. The next stall was for maize. That was followed by a bigger stall, for palm-oil. Sousa could tell the dried fish stalls farther on by the smell. He saw the one for salt. He stopped at the one for black soap. At the one for obis and orobos he talked to the stallholder. He bought three obis. He bit one of them. The bitter taste reminded him of his village. He sat down by the smoked meat stall. The meat's good smell spread around everywhere. It made him hungry. So far he had counted thirty stalls. He sat down and counted how many customers bought meat. He got to nine but there were some who passed on without buying. Some while later, he had counted sixty-six passers-by. Back in the village you would need several hours to get to a hundred. To start with, the village had exactly one hundred and ninety inhabitants. Many worked in the market. They were all his relatives. Brothers, sisters, cousins, uncles, aunts. To be sure there were outsiders from neighbouring villages and plantations, who came to shop or sell in the market where Sousa's mother sold. Everyone in the village had the name of Sousa but would be called by some other name. Only he insisted on staying Sousa.

When he was hungry, he bought some smoked meat and ate it slowly. The women from the obi stall sat down beside him. First she looked at him. Then she asked: 'What are you doing?'

'Nothing.'

'Nothing?'

'I mean, nothing at the moment. But out in my village, I work.'

'What do you do there?'

'I pick cocoa beans and lay them out to dry.'

'Is that why you have that smell?'

'What smell?'

'Of cocoa. Everyone who works with cocoa gets the cocoa smell on their body.'

'I never knew that.'

'Well, they do. Do you see that tall woman?' she asked, pointing:

'Now she smells of dried fish. She works with dried fish all day long. People who eat only fish also smell of fish. My first husband came from a place where they ate only fish. He never smelt of anything else.'

Sousa passed his opinion:

'Everybody smells of one thing or another.'

'Yes, but some smell good and others smell bad.'

Sousa counted one more person and said aloud:

'Ninety-six.'

'Ninety-six what?'

'Ninety-six people have passed here since I arrived.'

The woman asked what he was counting people for:

'I've done it ever since I was a child. An aunt taught me how.'

The woman didn't seem to understand. Sousa couldn't explain either, but said:

'I learnt to count like that. I started to count everything. At my mother's stall in the market, I'd count how many people came, how many went and how many bought. On the road, I count the stones, the rivers I cross and the houses on the way. When I've nothing to do at night, I count the stars in the sky.'

'Ninety seven. You're neglecting your job.' the woman interrupted.

'Very true. Ninety seven.'

'You'll soon have a hundred.'

'I have already.' said Sousa pointing at three men approaching.

The woman said goodbye. It was time to go back to her onion stall. Sousa closed his eyes and slept all afternoon. The noise of the market lulled him to sleep. Sometimes he would open his eyes and

196

imagine he was in his village, the market seemed just the same with its mixture of smells and colourful clothes and children running about".'

Mariana had stopped. Abionan had wanted to know:

'Does it end there?'

'It does. I don't know whether he meant to continue it or whether that's all there is.'

She had flicked through the exercise book before adding:

'Each story has a different setting from the next, but Sousa is a common point that fits one to the next. As they've been written down by hand, and in an exercise book, you can follow the sequence.

Aduni market is different from the markets of Ketu and the other places around Ketu. There is more foreign produce here. Lots of things from Europe and America. More expensive goods.'

Mariana lifted her eyes from the exercise book:

'Did you notice that in the story about Sousa going round Aduni market for the first time my father doesn't refer to a single foreign product?' Only local goods appear, things made here on the spot, things to eat.'

Old Mariana's shop had been still busy, Abionan liked to pick up the lengths of cotton material that lay on the counters, she adored watching the process of selling and one afternoon Mariana had nudged her and pointed at a youth coming into the market:

'I don't know why but I have a suspicion, almost a conviction, that that one's Sousa.'

'Sousa?'

'Yes.'

She had looked at her friend with a smile:

'Sousa has come to be so real to me that from time to time I see him in Aduni. I was quite sure that was him.'

Abionan had suggested:

'Shall we check?'

The pair of them had run over to the market and saw the youth whom Mariana had indicated, they followed him about for a while, and he began to eye them with suspicion so they put on an act and pretended to be examining the goods on a palm-oil stall, Abionan thought not:

'I've a different idea of Sousa.'

'What like?'

'To begin with, my Sousa is taller. He's a tall slim young man.'

'To me, he's thin too, but not too tall. Like this one.'

Another time they had tracked a youth answering Abionan's description, tall and slim, he stopped by some atabal players, they did too, and when they heard the boy's voice speaking Fulani, Abionan gave her opinion:

'Impossible. Sousa's got to talk Yoruba, Ewe or Fon. Plus a bit of French as well, of course.'

'But I've already met a Sousa who spoke Hausa and Fulani.'

The pair had talked to people who had worked with President Sebastian Silva, they listened to accounts of the events of the first days following independence when euphoria had gripped the country, an old man who lived on the square facing the palace had said with his eyes wide open:

'In the first months people went about smiling.'

Mariana asked:

'Then what?'

'Then, as your father said, the effort of building a new country burst the energy of everyone.'

Mariana had continued reading tales of Sousa, one night:

'If I were to choose my favourite, it'd be this one:

"Sousa was sitting by the entrance to the market when he saw Ainá. He didn't yet know that she was called Ainá. Whom he saw was a young girl with a black face that didn't shine very much. It was really a rather matt black. That was the first thing about her that made an impression. He followed her. The girl went down a street lined with trees. She disappeared in a door. Sousa scratched his head and made up his mind to wait. He waited a long time. He even waited on to the following day because the girl didn't reappear and he ended up sleeping in the street. When he awoke he recalled the object which had brought him to his exhausted posture. As he had already waited the whole night long he thought there would be no harm staying where he was. There was movement in the girl's house. An old man went out into the sunshine. Three boys and five girls started playing in the street. There were shouts of varying volumes in the air. Women in brightly coloured skirts were rushing past. Sousa reckoned that they must be going to market. Until the girl appeared, he thought about his village. A river ran past the fifty-six and a half houses. Perhaps it wasn't quite a river, just a stream. Sousa used to bathe in the stream and when his body was wet he would shout for joy. In Aduni he didn't bathe much. Everything is harder in a big city. He saw the girl cross the street. She was wearing a different skirt. The material had gay flowers. He quietly got up and followed the girl. So they walked on, he behind her for half an hour. In the square in the centre, she stopped and looked at the boy.

Sousa grinned at her and said happily:

'Your skirt's got forty-two flowers.'

'My skirt's got what?'

She cast her eyes down at her skirt, clutching it with one hand as if she was counting the flowers too. Then she burst into a giggle:

'But what a crazy idea.'

'There are. Count them. There are forty-two.'

'Did you count all round?'

'I did.'

'What for?'

'No reason.'

He pointed across to the palace:

'Do you know how many windows there are in the palace?'

She shook her head.

'Thirty. Twelve at the front. Ten at the back. And four on either side.'

He motioned to the first stall:

'The top shelf always has nine bottles of beer. When the woman sells one, she takes another from underneath and fills up the space on top.'

He turned his finger towards the hospital, not far off:

'It's got six doors. One at the front and five at the back.'

She looked at him smilingly:

'What's your name?'

'Sousa. And yours?'

'Ainá.'

'It's got one less letter than mine.'

'Is that good or bad?'

He thought a bit:

'Well, the number four isn't too good.'

'Why not?'

'I don't know. I was taught from childhood that four isn't good.'

'Which is the good one then?'

'Six. Six's very good.'

'And five?'

199

'That's good too. Not as good as six but it's all right.'

'Why?'

'Because my name can have five letters. I've only to put an "h" on the end: a - i - n - a - h.'

He studied the matter, tilting his head over to one side:

'Yes. You can. Four might not be too bad either. It depends on the person, the day and the year.'

She asked where he had learnt all these things:

'From an old aunt who knew everything about numbers. I think it was because of her that I got this craze for counting.'

'So, do you like it?'

'Counting. Oh yes, I've only to count something for it to become easy to understand.'

'Easy? How?'

'Take the palace, for example. I count the palace windows and it's suddenly as if I knew all the people who live in there. I count the goods on a shelf and then I feel as if the owner of the stall has turned into my friend.'

He looked at her:

'Do you understand?'

'I do.'

Ainá laughed as she asked:

'And as you counted the flowers on my skirt, did you think you've become my friend?'

'Of course.'

As her face turned serious, he added:

'At least, that's what I hope.'

'Who can tell?'

Ainá left the boy and walked over towards a big building. Sousa asked if he could accompany her.

'I'm going to the dentist. If you want to count how many teeth I have in my mouth, you can come.'

She went into the building. He decided to wait for her at the entrance. Half an hour later the girl reappeared in the doorway:

'Didn't you want to come inside?'

'No. It's enough to see you smiling to count your teeth.'

They made a date for the next day.

The morning was bright. She smiled even more. They went down the narrow road. They came to a stream. The boy suggested:

'Shall we bathe?'

200

'Let's do.'

They took off their clothes and went in the stream. Leaves were tumbling from the trees. A lizard stopped on one of the banks. Ainá stood up for a moment. Drops of water dripped from her gleaming breasts. There was a stone at a bend in the stream. The girl said:

'Shall we lie down on the stone?'

'Yes, let's.'

Sousa stretched out beside Ainá. He looked up at the sky. He counted a group of wispy clouds passing among the leaves. He felt that it was the happiest day he had ever had in his life."'

When Mariana had finished reading, Abionan had complained:

'Nothing happens in the story.'

'On the contrary. A great deal happens. And it's a nice one too.'

There had been a moment's silence, until Mariana had observed:

'I think that my father, writing like that was the one with a mania for counting things.'

'Have you asked your grandmother?'

'I did. She said she'd never noticed.'

'It looks as if he would count without saying anything to anyone.'

'He must have counted the windows in the palace, the doors of the hospital and the houses in the square".'

Abionan had wanted to know whether Mariana had read the stories of Sousa to old Mariana:

'I have.'

'Did she like them?'

'She did. After each story she'd motion to me to keep quiet. Once she asked me to read the story over again.'

'Which one was that?'

'The one of Sousa in Paris.'

'I don't know that one.'

Mariana had searched for it in the exercise book and read:

' "Sousa got off the bus that had brought him from the airport. He was happy just to think that he was in Paris. His family in the village would be proud of him. He must be the first person born in that region to have set foot on the banks of the Seine which was where he was. The houses had windows and balconies but they were different from those in Aduni, Cotonou, Porto Novo, Lomé or anywhere else he knew. That one there had seven windows on each storey. Boats of different sizes passed along the river. In a few moments he had counted nine boats.

Sousa left his cases at the terminus to look round the city, he crossed the river by a bridge with tall statues on it. He halted by one of them. The trees didn't look at all like the ones in Africa. The trunk, the leaves, everything was different. He noticed that there were no baobabs to be seen. The foliage was a golden colour that Sousa found very pretty. The girls walked in a strange way. It must be because of the clothes they wore. Very tight. There were young men sitting at cafés in the open air. Among them, some Africans. Sousa took had a good look to see if he could spot anybody from Zorei. But their manner was distinct from what he would see in Aduni. They could already be half Europeans or else came from other parts of Africa. Along the bank of the river, books, maps and figures were on sale.

Sousa saw a church. He went close and came across a whole lot of little images of saints. The doors and the wall were full of saints. He tried to count them but he couldn't manage it. There were saints beyond number. A crowd of saints. They looked impressive all together like that. He thought of the saints which mother had in the house back home in the village, where he had stayed three days before the farewell. Mother had put the money together for him to come and study in France. She had done a deal in the market and sold a plot that she had near the village. All so that he could come and study in Paris.

Sousa went inside the church and saw that the candles lit up the interior very much like in the church at Aduni where he had been with mother when she had gone to the capital to talk to him about the possibility of the journey. Mother had not declared herself either for or against. She had just listened to what he had to say. She had in the end decided that he should leave Zorei and live for a while in France. So there he was.

Sousa thought of mother squeezing his hands. He thought of her making a meal for him to eat. He thought of her fitting a new shirt on her son's body. He saw her sitting in the square of Aduni gazing at the houses, her face calm and with sweat trickling down her skin.

Sousa knelt down, prayed a little and wept." '

There had been a long silence after Mariana had finished reading. The first thing Abionan had said was:

'Sousa was a catholic.'

'Yes. And so was my father.'

The two friends had gone off round the city with no end in view, Mariana would point out:

'This is a house from the time of the Germans.'

Or:

'Here stood the shop of old Haddad, a friend of my grand-mother's.'

Once:

'It is precisely on this spot that my father hoisted the red and white flag of Zorei for the first time.'

'Did you see it?'

'I was ten months' old, or a bit less, at the time.'

'What a shame. It would have been something that you'd never forget.'

'But it is as if I had seen it. From the moment I was first aware of being a person everybody has told me what it was like.'

From time to time groups of women would come to see Mariana to discuss difficult matters, demands and applications, men turned up too and many of them thought that Sebastian's daughter would be the leader of a section of opinion in the country, at those times Abionan would keep out of the way for she preferred not to stand close so as to allow her friend to deal with local problems as she thought fit.

One day:

'The market women want a new law. The taxes are eating up all their profits. Sometimes they make no profit but still have to pay the taxes.'

'In Ketu we haven't quite reached that point yet but we're not far off.'

On another:

'The village of Gapo wants a road.'

At night the pair would talk for hours, Abionan would tell Mariana of the journeys she had made with mother, the latter would talk about her life in Paris, the things she loathed, the friends she had and the walks she took.

'That route of Sousa's in my father's story, I more than once retraced the whole way. I think I know where it was. I would come out of the Invalides terminal, go as far as to the river, cross the bridge, see the people in the cafés, books and maps being sold, go into the church and try to feel the same thing as Sousa felt.

She would explain:

'It was through reading the thoughts of my father that I learnt that in Europe the greatest danger an African runs is of becoming Europeanised in the worst sense. The other day an old colleague who today is in power in Zorei wanted to make a law prohibiting the traditional religions and African forms of worship. He said they were barbaric things. I had to quarrel with him. Changes will come, but from the people. And, anyway, the forms of worship that exist today are not at all barbaric.'

On the majority of occasions, Abionan would not say a word but here she had said:

'Why is it they're always wanting to prohibit something?'

'I don't know. I've thought about it. It could be because the people in government, in any government or regime, regard the people as children incapable of deciding for themselves and need politicians to learn what they want.'

Mariana had looked out at the palace:

'There's no government that wholly good.'

'Not even your father's?'

'Not even my father's. You know why? Because in practice, that is, in important things – laws for the market where you work, taxes, bureaucracies for marriage or to register a baby or bury a dead person – the ruler is not the president or prime minister but a group lower down, where you have the big bosses, the small bosses and the petty officials.'

Abionan recalled how she had buried her son, she hadn't needed any bureaucracy, she thought of mother and the last journey, the smell of the sea overpowering everything, the dune vanishing from view and the drums beating afar in the waning afternoon, now today in Iro Kogny market she senses the urgency of hatching another son inside herself and felt a sort of pain that started in her stomach and kept rising and rising up, suddenly the market disappeared and the woman came to see things quite differently, the green was greener, the red of Solange's dress stood out among the colours, she had always dressed Adeniran in green robes, sometimes she'd put a splash of red on the child, she hears a question from Yatundé and replies almost without realising what she is saying:

'Let's go and talk to the lorry driver.'

'Yes, let's go.'

'He's always standing over the other side.'

'That's right.'

Yatundé noticed that her friend had not moved from her spot and she urged her:

'Come on then.'

'Let's go.'

She gave her a shake to drag her out of the stupour she seemed to have fallen into:

'What's up, woman? Don't you feel well?'

Abionan opened her eyes as if coming round:

'It was nothing.'

Yatundé helped her up, the pair of them set off on foot down the lane and on the air there was a strong pepper smell, Abionan was thinking about what Omitola had said about there being times when she didn't know where she was or what day it was, could something similar be happening to her or would it be the effect of the dream?, with a strain she opened and shut her eyes, she had to last until her son was born, when she arrived by the crooked flag pole she had recovered and felt the impact of the general bustle of the market as if at that moment the world had come back to life, she saw a group of men around a lorry, Ogunbanjo was grinning at the two women, Abionan stopped in silence and it was Yatundé who spoke:

'May you not die while you're grinning.'

Ogunbanjo turned to the other men:

'Another favour coming up.'

Yatundé retorted:

'No favour. Business.'

'If it's business, that doesn't interest me, it'll have to be a favour.'

He kept grinning.

'Well, we want to go to Ketu by lorry.'

That man seemed to be thinking:

'How many are you?'

'Two for the moment, but there may be more.'

The man addressed Abionan:

'So the little girl's not saying anything?'

But the girl did say:

'Just say whether you can do it and how much.'

'That's getting straight to the point.'

He stopped grinning and laughed:

'Let's see now. I might even take you for nothing. That depends.'

'We're not going anywhere for nothing.' Abionan's voice seemed firm.

'Goodness, what a proud girl!'

People gathered to listen in on the conversation. Abionan suggested to her friend:

'Let's decline.'

The man thought they shouldn't decline, perhaps they could come to some agreement, he punctuated his phrases with laughter and from time to time an onlooker would try to chip in on the conversation, at one point Yatundé shouted:

'Outsiders shouldn't pass opinions.'

The heckler replied:

'I'm not an outsider. Ogunbanjo's my cousin.'

There was laughter all round, Yatundé insisted on knowing the fare, they argued non-stop for some minutes and the lorry man wanted to know:

'Who's coming with me in front?'

'None of us. We're going together in the back.'

'So I'll be travelling alone?'

'Take a mate.'

'I've already got a mate to come with me, but I'd rather put my mate in the back.'

He laughed even more as he explained:

'I don't yet know what load I'll have on. It might be something that smells bad.'

'Could well be. We can put up with that. And anyway the bad smell could well be nicer than your smell in the front.'

Laughs were louder than before, they soon came to an arrangement and when would they be leaving?

'I'm going to Nigeria now to pick up some oil-drums. I'll be back tonight. I'll stop by the flag pole at eleven o'clock.'

The women went back, Abionan felt better now, arguments livened up, the sun grew hotter, naked children ran by, a group of atabal players started to move through the market and the drums drew round lots of people, Abionan sat calmly down and remembered the drums that had surrounded mother's moments on the beach as the salt-tang had overwhelmed every one of the elder woman's movements and the slowness of those movements seemed to be caused by that smell of the sea or could it be that the beat of the drums was pinning down the motion of Aduke's arms?, one day she had told Mariana of the moments of indecision which she had had before taking mother in hand and making the journey, her friend had asked – when they were in Aduni, and the palace lay in rest beyond, the square empty and a slight breeze shook the leaves of the large tree which stood in the middle, Mariana's question had come out in a voice that could scarcely be heard:

'Have I read you yet Sousa's meeting with the sea, or not?'

'Not yet.'

She read:

'"Sousa had heard that the sea was very big. He tried to get some idea of how big it was. He would keep asking:

'Does it stretch farther than the square?'

The square was in Aduni. Sousa's friend to whom he had asked the question would scoff at him:

'Beyond the square? It's bigger than a thousand Adunis put together.'

Sousa tried to imagine a thousand Adunis put together but in spite of the craze he had for counting things, he simply couldn't work out the size of a thousand Adunis. Then his friend inquired:

'Where are you from?'

'The village of Zewe.'

'How many days did you have to walk for to reach Aduni?'

'One week.'

'Well, the sea is over a thousand times greater than the distance from Zewe to Aduni.'

'A thousand times?'

'Yes.'

'Do you mean I would take seven thousand days walking along it?'

'You could well do. But as you can't walk on the water you'll never be able to try it.'

His friend was grinning. Sousa was really staggered. He said:

'I'll have to see the sea.'

'Of course you will.'

For a week he thought the matter over. He took the trip so seriously that he even forgot to count things. He saw lots of houses without noticing how many windows they had. He looked at the clouds without attempting to establish how many pieces they were divided into. He worked in the market shifting goods from one stall to another, he helped people move house and thus earned a bit of money. One day he privately made up his mind:

'This money will do for me to get past the sea.'

He set out on foot along a road where there were cocoa plantations on both one side and the other. Cocoa was something he did know about. He stopped by the trees and ran his hand down their golden fruit. Mother would be surprised to learn that he was going to see the sea. She had been on the coast several times before and had previously talked to him about what she had seen but Sousa had never paid much attention to the matter. Not now though. For now he was going to meet the sea.

He crossed the frontier of Zorei with Dahomey. The country might be different but the countryside was the same. People were dressed in a similar fashion. As he understood Fon, he struck up conversation with the Fons he met along the way. Everyone seemed to like him. He didn't tell a single person he'd never seen the sea. But he did pluck up the courage to ask an old woman dressed in a brightly coloured robe:

'Is the sea far?'

'No. It's very near. Half an hour from here.'

Sousa walked slowly along for that half hour. Every moment he was straining his eyes but he couldn't see the sea or even a large amount of water that might look like the idea he had formed of the sea. Just as he doubted whether he was getting close he came across a dune. He said to himself:

'Here it is.'

Beyond the sand there was something which must be the sea. The image struck him only very gently. First he saw coconut trees. Then he noticed creeping plants in the middle of the white sand. He stopped and stared. Then, he saw the sea.

It was the sea, there was no doubt about it. A shade of light green filled the horizon. Sousa went on down to the beach. He stopped with his feet in the water which was coming in and going out. He spotted boats nearer in and a ship in the distance. He stood there gazing for an enormous length of time. An old woman holding up her skirt went into the water and washed her face. Sousa bent down and scooped up a handful of water which he lifted to his mouth. It was really salty. He saw a high rock to the right. He walked across and climbed on to the rock.

The view was better now. He could see farther. He spotted a tall, thin structure standing on a tongue of sand. Fishing boats were drawing in to the land. Sousa could see fishermen taking fishes large and small from one of them. He climbed down from the rock and went over. He thought the fishes were lovely. In the boat there was a net. More people appeared and a group of small boys started to fight over the tiny fishes which the fishermen had tossed aside. More boats came in. Sousa suddenly found himself in the middle of a deal of activity with everyone talking. He couldn't understand what they were saying but he wasn't really making an effort to. There he felt happy. He left the boats and sat down on the sand. He dug his right hand into it. It was nice to fill his hand with sand. He gathered up a bit of sand and started making a mountain. After some minutes like that he gazed again at the waves. He noticed that the colour of the light had changed. The sound of the sea had become now soft upon the boy's ears.

He never knew how long he had remained sitting there. A fisherman stopped by him and started making remarks. Sousa nodded. He didn't mean that he had wholly understood. The fisherman smiled and went back to his boat. The boy wondered what the other side was like. However far his eyes stretched he could not see the end of the sea. His friend in Aduni had spoken of seven thousand days, but even if he could walk it, the journey must be even longer. He noticed that night was drawing in. It was darker on the landward side although there was still light upon the sea.

Sousa got up. He had gone all day without eating. He set off walking, now quite content. He felt fulfilled. He saw coconut trees against the sky. Slowly he counted them. One, two, three, four, five, six."'

Abionan had enjoyed the story, even though nothing had happened in it, Mariana's father wrote things like that, in the stories mother had told her as a child lots of things happened and there were good people and bad people all fighting each other, and the same in the tales of the orishas, Mariana had explained:

'It's what I told you the other day. I think he wanted simply to pinpoint moments in the life of an African youth, a youth from our region. And he must have used scenes from his own life with no intention of telling a story.'

Abionan added:

'What I really liked was when he started counting.'

The two had laughed, the days in Aduni lengthened, one afternoon Abionan had felt she was missing her round of the markets, she announced to Mariana that she would be going back, but she had nevertheless spent three days at the Water House, old Mariana would joke:

'When's the second Adeniran coming?'

'Soon.'

The old woman had remained calmly on the veranda in a rocking chair, gazing at the sea and the dune, and at Sebastian's grave perhaps, after hours without a word, she had shown a wish to speak and commented upon events in Benin, Zorei, Nigeria and Togo, she wanted to know about everything and had listened when Abionan had referred to having visited the Presidential Palace in Aduni and had asked:

'How's the Palace now? A lot older?'

Young Mariana had explained that the Palace had been repainted and a wing had been built on at the rear where the president now held receptions. But father's portrait was still on the wall. The old woman gave no indication as to whether she was pleased at the news or not. She had said:

'What's happened to the room where your mother slept?'

'It's a conference room now.'

'Conference?'

'They spend all the time in conferences now. At least that's what they all say in Aduni.'

President Sebastian had also written down a thought on palaces and once young Mariana had drawn Abionan's attention to it:

'The African requires the outward badges of power. A Head of State living in a poor house can never be respected. He has to live in a palace, and a real palace at that. The richer and more luxurious the better. Through failing to comprehend this trait of the African – that his chief should display pomp and riches – many Europeans likewise find themselves unable to comprehend the political structures of our Continent.'

Abionan had returned to Ketu, and now in Iro Kogny market, the passing urgency of becoming a mother puts her head into a daze, she leaves her stall and goes over to talk to Omitola:

'What did it feel like when you spent weeks when you didn't know what was going on, or even what day it was?'

'I had a headache, but not a very bad one. It was really very slight but it wouldn't go away. It stuck there as if to say "I am here – I am aching".'

'What else?'

'I wanted to think but couldn't manage to think straight. I would shut my eyes and say "I'm going to think". I couldn't manage to make my mind up about a thing. When I was given the money, I didn't know what change I should give back. I slept a lot but it was an uneasy sleep. I kept waking up all the time.'

Omitola looked at her:

'Why do you ask?'

'I think I've got the same complaint.'

'Don't say that.'

'Yatundé just now told me something or other and I answered without knowing what I was answering.'

'It's best to rest a bit.'

'I've rested a lot. But I can't rest as long as I'm not doing what I have to do.'

The drums beat on in the afternoon's heat, Abionan gazed down the side street with its fences reaching to the flag pole at the entrance, some stallholders were sitting and others were standing, some were shouting and others were quiet, the coloured calabashes that came from Oyo brightened up the beginning of the side street and a lorry drove down, she asked Omitola:

'Do you want to come with us to Ketu on the lorry?'

'What time?'

'Eleven tonight.'

'That's no good. I've got to leave early on. I'm making a call along the way.'

Solange was coming up:

'If there's room, I'll come.'

Abionan said there would be, for Ogunbanjo wanted such-and-such and the women would travel in the back, Solange turned up her nose:

'What's he carrying behind?'

'I don't know. Oil-drums from Nigeria.'

The three of them chatting there, exchanging reports and watching the traffic, Omitola pointed to the end of the side street:

'Odette's going to have another baby.'

'How many's she got then?'

'Six, counting the twins.'

'Well, there comes the seventh.'

'She might have twins again.'

Laughter. A tall black woman, with a huge calabash on her head, walked slowly past, when she was far enough away, Abionan asked:

'Who's that?'

'She's married to Adebayo, the man who became rich selling cocoa. Afterwards he went off to Cotonou and spent up all his money. Then he caught a disease there and came back. He can't move from the waist down any more.'

More laughter. When they became serious again, Yatundé:

'The man's ill and we all laugh.'

Solange disagreed:

'I feel sorry for her. Not for him. Wasn't it her who kept on working here all the while he was throwing his money away in Cotonou? And today isn't it her who's looking after him?'

'When they're in difficulty, they come back to us.'

The sun was blazing down on the top of Abionan's stall, the children's screams were dying away, and Omitola started packing up her things:

'I think I'll be off now. I've a lot of walking ahead.'

She rolled up her mat and tied up a bunch of cloths as a voice piped up that Abionan had difficulty recognising, (she saw afterwards that it belonged to that new girl who had taken a stall not far from her) and said:

'May you not die while you're on the road.'

Now the sun could not be seen, the sky had turned red and Abionan leant back against the post and shut her eyes, afraid lest the dream would come back but it didn't, she felt as if the women's conversation was still continuing, was it a dream or reality?, she opened her eyes and saw that nobody was talking, so it could be a dream, she drowsed off once more and, in the middle of the voices, someone started to beat out metal, the noise almost hurt her, she stopped sleeping and with her eyes wide open found herself paying attention to the woman in blue who was saying at the root stall:

'Why get married, son?'

'Well, she's studied in Europe. She'll only sleep with me if I marry her.'

'Keep out of the way of people who've studied in Europe.'

There were various noises, Abionan lost the thread of the two's

212

conversation, now it was Odette's voice down at the entrance to the side street, shouting out:

'Kayodé, Kayodé.'

A boy ran past in front of Abionan, when he got close to Odette she scolded him, studying in Europe was all very well but the village folk were none too keen on it, they would rag those who came back for being pedantic, but for her son to be king he would surely need to spend some time in France?, Mariana had once said that everyone in power in Zorei had been in Paris, darkness was slow in coming and the flag pole at the entrance still caught light at its tip, Abionan recalled another story of Sousa which old Mariana had liked.

It had been a conversation between Sousa and his mother, he telling her that he wanted to go and study in Paris and mother answering that it was a long way away and of what benefit would it be to him, no one from Zewe had done it, he had replied explaining why, mother was little by little convinced, but then they talked about how much he would need to live there, mother mentioned certain sums but Sousa had already thought the matter through, he had talked to boys who had studied in France and had done a sum, she ended by saying that it could be done by selling the cocoa plot near Zewe but he had been against doing it that way, she had replied that there were other plots close to the frontier that she would never sell, it had been a prolonged conversation which Mariana had taken several minutes to read through, Abionan could almost see the two of them there in Zewe, but this time Sousa hadn't counted anything even though they had been talking about sums of money, the word plot came up a lot, and Abionan thought of the plot that mother had left her but there was no cocoa on it, it was dry land where they planted cassava and sweet potato and that was quite as it should be for that was what she sold in the markets, she would go there from time to time, today that land was sacred and she would never have the courage to sell it, the house in Ketu belonged to her too, or at least part of it did, she remembered mother discussing the property with her:

'This piece of the house is mine. Mine and yours. The rest is the family's.'

'Just this piece?'

'From here to that wall. From there on it's your uncle's.'

Then they had spoken about the cassava patch:

'Where we were last month, don't you remember?'

'Yes, I do. There was a baobab nearby.'

'Not nearby at all. The baobab's right in the middle of the plot.'

In the end, mother had quietened down. One day she had asked:

'I want to be buried on my land.'

'Don't talk about dying.'

Abionan had however thought: what if she were to die far away from there?, mother had read her thoughts exactly because she said:

'I'm going to die far from Ketu but I want you to bring my body back and bury me on my land.'

Once, as Abionan had been departing for the Water House, Victor Ajayi had bidden her farewell in these words:

'May you not die while you're far from your land.'

These words of farewell had lodged themselves in Abionan's memory as she had thought: could there be anything worse than dying far from home?, since it now seemed that mother was going to die for she believed everything she said and mother had declared to her daughter that she would die far from Ketu, then she hadn't the slightest doubt that she would indeed die far from Ketu and from then on Abionan had watched every change of mood that mother betrayed, and they were many, now she would smile to herself as if she was recalling nice things, and now she could get sad or else she would close her eyes though she wasn't asleep, she would release sighs and talk of matters that Abionan knew nothing about:

'Do you remember the first year of my marriage?'

How could she have done because she wasn't even born then but she felt sure that she could remember her birth, mother lying under the baobab with her legs apart and she, Abionan, coming out from inside her, Adeniran now lay buried there, she had not buried him on land that belonged to her or to him but the site of her birth was her own, and where else could be so much hers, Aduke had not spoken any further about the first year of her marriage, she seemed to have forgotten the subject but the business of selling would still make her happy or at least she now and again would liven when confronted by a customer who argued a lot and thought the price too high and offered a lower one, she would follow the answers and the answers back and smile at the funnier remarks, Abionan now recalled that the dead of olden times were buried inside their houses, generally in the room where they had lived, the house of Shasha de Sousa I in Whydah was where the Shasha and his relatives lay buried and she had often been there, either with young Mariana or by herself and she had stood in silence before the tomb, Mariana's father had also written a story about Sousa going to Whydah to see the tombs of the Sousas of old, the night on which Mariana had read out the description had been one of the hottest she had spent in Aduni, hot and humid, the air seemed to be soaking:

' "Sousa arrived in Whydah pent with curiosity. Lots of people had told of the fact that the tomb of the first important Sousa of that region, Shasha de Sousa the First, was located there. They were now on the eighth or ninth Shasha de Sousa. He had asked them to open up the house for him. The women who were the custodians of the keys asked him what he was called. When they learnt that his name was Sousa, they had said:

'He must be a relative.'

'That's quite likely. I've found Sousas everywhere I've been.'

The eldest of them came out to the front and opened the door of a room. Sousa was to learn that there there had lived, died and lay buried the first Sousa, Francisco Felix de Sousa, a man of standing, friend to King Ghego of Abomey. The tomb was simple. On the wall, the portrait of Shasha de Sousa I. Over the tomb, a saint. It was the image of St Francis of Assisi. They had told Sousa that the Shasha had had a life full of adventures. He had been born in Bahia, Brazil. He had come to Whydah where he had served as a go-between for the Portuguese and King Ghezo. He had built his own house. He had had lots of children. He had died at 95. He had become rich. He had been respected by everyone. people came from afar to seek his advice. The eldest woman asked the boy:

'Do you want to see the other rooms?'

'Are there some more then?'

What he saw were several tombs all in one room. There were eight. Buried in each of them was a person with the name of Sousa.

'Does anyone still sleep here?'

The woman showed astonishment at the question:

'Of course not. It's their place.' and pointed to the tombs.

Sousa thought it was nice for someone to be buried in their own room. In his part of the world you were buried in front of the house but not indoors. He would have a word with mother about that.".'

That night Abionan had asked Mariana whether there wasn't a story with Sousa married or getting married, the latter said there wasn't.

'Maybe father had wanted to carry on with the stories and show us Sousa with children as well. Or maybe he didn't. If I've got it right, he just wanted to show us a young man before getting married and growing old.'

But there was a description of a birth among the stories of Sousa.

'A birth?'

'Indeed so. Sousa attended the birth of a baby to his sister. As I think that everything he wrote was from his own experience, I asked my grandmother if father had been present at a birth.'

'What did she say?'

'She thought it quite possible. She said that there were lots of births around here and in Aduni. Including my own.'

They went quiet for some minutes because her mother had died in her own birth, until Abionan asked:

'Read me the story of the birth.'

Mariana looked through the exercise book, it was hard finding the page, she skimmed over the beginnings of a few stories and in the end she found it:

' "Sousa's sister, Isabel Sousa, was going to have a baby. The household was therefore anxious. Sousa noticed that mother would not stop still in one place. She'd be coming and going at every end and turn. He couldn't see any reason for such excitement. Where was his sister's husband? No one knew. He had gone to work in Ibadan, Nigeria, six months prior. Nothing more had been heard of him. He could have died. Isabel was huge. Sousa asked her if she thought there were going to be twins. She replied that one would do. Why more? Having one would be work enough. Just imagine two or three.

On the day she had the pains, mother rushed off to fetch the woman who helped babies arrive in the world. The two of them filled pitchers of water. Sousa sat in the doorway gazing at the trees in front. Then mother appeared from inside and invited him in:

'Come and see.'

Sousa felt rather ill at ease, but could in no way disobey mother. He went into the room. Isabel had her legs open, half leaning back, half lying down. She was uttering groans. The woman asked her to try harder and with her hands squeezed her belly, which rose up high. They didn't ask Sousa to do anything. So there he remained doing nothing. His sister's sex opened and closed in spasms or so he had the impression. The hairs of her sex became matted in the sweat

216

of her skin. All of a sudden her sex seemed to burst open, the woman screamed:

'Harder, harder now.'

It opened yet wider and Sousa could see something appearing at the back. There was a commotion in the room. Sousa noticed that a head was coming into view, the women were talking loudly and the head grew and the women gripped Isabel's legs. Then no longer the legs. Now what they were gripping was the head being born and now everything was appearing. They kept pulling and pulling. They boy saw blood come out. He started to feel afraid but he knew that there had to be blood. He didn't pay complete attention to what came next. The women cut the baby's umbilical cord as it cried loudly. He heard mother telling him:

'Go outside now.'

He went back to the door and started to think. So that was how you were born. That too was how he was born by his mother. When she came through the door with a pot in her hand, Sousa stared at her for a long time".'

Abionan had forgotten the details of Adeniran's birth, she was thinking more about the next birth, the one that was to come, whether she could give birth to her son in a public place for all the world to see the future king of Ketu come into the world, she had spoken to it to Mariana who thought the idea was quite correct:

'Though nobody would understand.'

The market at Iro Kogny was beginning to be lit by lamps and Abionan lit hers, a smell of food was coming from all sides, the woman could see fires and heard the sound of things frying up, it was always colder at night and she got a shawl and put it round her shoulders, then turned to the shelves and counted up the cassavas, and at the same time she remembered Sousa, there were five fair-sized cassavas, three yams and seven sweet potatoes left over, so if she didn't sell any more she would take them all to Ketu, but there were still customers around the market and a man in European dress bought some peppers at the stall alongside, there was a row in the palm-wine department and Abionan imagined that the man whom Yatundé had jeered at must still be there, she hadn't seen him come back anyway unless it was during the time they had been arguing with Ogunbanjo over the fare for the lorry ride, then a baby's crying made her look towards the side street, it must be Odette's last child, the sixth one, as the seventh was still on its way, she felt envious of a woman with so many children when she had had only one and lost it, but she wasn't going to lose the Adeniran who was to follow, then she heard Yatundé's voice:

'There's still some time to go. It's seven o'clock.'

'Four hours quickly passes.'

'Not when you're waiting.'

She suggested:

'Shall we go and have something to eat? The smell's making me hungry.'

Off they went. They ate acaras, then they washed their hands in a basin which the stallholder kept at the side and Abionan asked:

'When do you think we'll get to Ketu?'

'Just past midnight.'

Yatundé added:

'That's if the driver doesn't stop on the way too often. If he does, we won't be in Ketu much before one.'

They went back to the stalls, Abionan felt that weariness was falling, getting on top of her, after all she hadn't slept for two nights, but going to sleep now would be risky if Yatundé and Solange went to sleep too they'd miss the lorry, and she consulted Yatundé who proposed:

'You know what we can do? Take our things over by the flag pole and if we get drowsy we can go to sleep on the spot where the lorry's coming to pick us up.

Abionan started rolling up her mat, the figure of the lioness disappeared into the roll and she put the yams, potatoes and cassavas into a basket, she stowed away the stool, gathered up the cloths which she took from market to market and walked over to where the pole stood, leant against it and thought of calling to her friends to hurry up but at that point she fell asleep, she slept and she dreamt, and picked up the same dream where she had left it with the child lying on the sheet, and the blood, and the rainbow, and the Hunter who was speaking:

'He shall be all right.'

The woman wanted to know whether she needed to give her son some medicine:

'No, just water.'

'Water?'

'Water cures everything.'

Odé picked up the child, lifted him up in his arms and the queue of people climbing up to see Adeniran melted away, now the Hunter was walking with long strides and the woman could barely keep up with him, he was carrying the child in his arms and everyone was following behind, then the woman saw that they were by the sea and she came across mother who was waiting for everyone as she sat on the sand, Odé came up close to Aduke and handed her the child, Abionan wanted to shout out:

'No, he's my son.'

But she couldn't manage to make herself heard to Aduke, for there were lots of people in between, then the queue formed up again and each person who approached the child kissed him, Aduke effortlessly raised him aloft, Abionan strained to get nearer but she felt pinned to the ground, then suddenly she noticed the palm-wine drinker grinning at her but the grin was already changing, and now it was Ogunbanjo's, she looked up to see whether the lorry was near, it wasn't and she wanted to ask Yatundé where they had hidden the lorry so she asked and heard the reply:

'No, it's not hidden. It'll be here at eleven.'

Abionan found herself with eyes open wide, leaning against the flag pole with Yatundé looking at her:

'You were asleep but when you asked about the lorry, I thought you were awake already.'

'Yes, I did sleep. I slept and I dreamt.'

'The same dream?'

'The very same one. Or rather a continuation of it.'

'Was it good?'

She thought a little:

'It was and it wasn't.'

How could she explain that what she felt in the middle of the dream was torment?, first because she knew deep down that her son did not exist and that the thought would come over her from time to time within the dream and then again because even though her son was being honoured like a king, she was afraid they would kill him, Odé's protection notwithstanding many things could happen, there were bad people about and there might be someone like her uncle in the crowd filing past her son, a man might appear with knife in hand not just to let the child's blood but to kill him, then Solange came up:

'Three and a half hours for the lorry to arrive.'

Yatundé retorted:

'Don't let's count the hours, otherwise we'll get over-anxious.'

If she had been in Idigny, she'd have Victor Ajayi close by to talk to, and to be quiet with, in Ketu there would be no problems, for there the family stood right beside her, even her husband could provide company but here she would just have to keep waiting, sitting against the pole with the sounds of the night growing ever smaller, the babies' crying disappearing and it was only the dogs that kept barking, here a bark, farther off a bark and a muffled sound of talking coming only from the palm-wine stall and from the spot where the acará-seller was kneading her dough and baking her cakes, now she remembered that her husband had wanted her to sell meals, people who sold meals were always busy, they would always be beset by people, they would the centre of the conversations, and everybody would be merry when the time came for a bite, merry and communicative, and when the time came for a drink, just as she thought that and saw the man from the palm-wine stall stopping in front of the flag pole, Yatundé exclaimed:

'Just look who's here.'

'Yes, it's me, ladies. Have you had a good day?'

'Very good, thanks to Obatala.' Abionan was quick to reply.

'So here we have someone who still believes in Obatala.'

Here Yatundé said:

'I wonder if he's one of those who'll go and denounce what we're doing?'

'Not at all, madam.'

He was a bit drunk, making exaggerated gestures and went on:

'I just like to be kind to the ladies of the market.'

Yatundé:

'So we've become ladies of the market now.'

'You always were. I do hope you've done a lot of good business today. And that you've sold everything there was on your stalls.'

None of the women replied and he walked away, staggering along one stretch and walking straight along the next, Abionan spoke:

'Will he be married?'

Yatundé:

'By that age they're all married. The wife'll be working or minding the children while he's out there drinking.'

Mother would say that father drank but she hadn't been able to know him, Abionan could remember only a voice of a man, would it have been father's?, Yatundé continued:

'My brother drinks heavily. And my first husband too. Not my father though. He was hard-working and religious. He was always around the church.'

'What, a Catholic?'

'He was. He had even wanted to be a priest but didn't have the money to study.'

Solange:

'In my family they don't drink too much.'

Yatundé:

'People who keep drinking are a breed apart. They promise things and never do them. They've no time for anything. Just to hang around the palm-wine stall.'

A lame man passed and Abionan thought that Obatala liked the lame, she closed her eyes a moment and seemed to have slept, then opened her eyes again for she had slept and not dreamt, then she tried it once more and she heard a noise not far to her left, she looked up and saw three bicycles coming along, one youth was saying to another, his Yoruba voice clear in the night:

'We'll be late.'

Abionan thought of the days when she was studying, she would break off her course from time to time to go travelling with mother, she had learnt to read quickly, she liked to pick up books and run her hand over the letters and numbers, she hadn't found French too hard but she had kept on speaking Yoruba at home, she would switch form one language to the other with the greatest of ease since mother seldom spoke French and knew few French words, just enough to make herself understood, Abionan had learnt English in Abeokuta, the French of Atakpamé was different from the French of Benin and also the English of Ibadan was different from Jedá, she had once heard old Mariana talking Portuguese to a group of Brazilian visitors, it seemed to be a hard language and once she had asked young Mariana:

'Can you speak Portuguese?'

'Yes, I can. My grandmother insisted on teaching me from when I was tiny. My father would also speak to me in Portuguese. Not always. Only when we were alone, he and I.'

Abionan had liked geography too, she would learn place-names off by heart, running over on the map the places she had visited with mother, with her finger she would trace the course of the River Niger with the halt at Jedá, and there she would pick up the Ogun

River, run her finger over Abeokuta and she thought Africa was vast, she could never know it all and would put her finger down on Ketu and from there would set off on imaginary trips, she and Casimir had played with maps and once she had found one in a teacher's house she looked but couldn't see Ketu on it and complained:

'This map's all wrong.'

'Why is it all wrong?' the teacher had wanted to know.

'It doesn't show the city of Ketu.'

The teacher had come up and checked and indeed it didn't, she had looked at Abionan and explained:

'It's a small map, it's only got capitals and big cities on it.'

The little girl went on staring at the map and, the other had continued:

'Ketu's not as big as people think.'

Iro Kogny was even smaller, perhaps she could do as Sousa did and count the number of houses and inhabitants there were in Iro Kogny, for there wouldn't be that many, possibly fewer than Zewe, Sousa's village, which she remembered as having one hundred and ninety people, and Idigny, how many people would that have?, she hadn't a clue, but places with priests tended to have more folk but the map was wrong because Ketu was reasonably sized and the city had been the capital of a kingdom, it was a place with an oba, a king or a chief, and what's more it had one of the best markets she had ever known, a lively market, bustling and full of women and small children, with wares of every kind, drums beating, egunguns passing by and young girls going from stall to stall, married women bringing along their new-born babies for the market to see, and the orishas presiding over it all and though they might say the orishas were banned within the market, there seemed to be no bans whatsoever, perhaps the market was the sanctuary of the orishas and the vow she had made to mother always to remember the orishas, to worship them, to make sacrifices to them and to bring presents for Eshu, and not to forget that the Hunter deserved even more tributes because he was the god of the city, Odé, Oshosi, the god of hunting, she had heard it said in Ifá that it was the centre of the world but, be that as it may, Ketu was the centre of the world too, from Ketu the hunter cared for the bush and the wild animals and the men who went out among the wild animals and the bush, Abionan had also liked history but at school they didn't study the history of Ketu

222

which she had only learnt in bits, mother had taught her a little, Fatogum a bit more and older uncles and aunts also know how this or that had come about, like the wars of Ketu and the kings and how the inhabitants of Ketu had ended up going to Brazil as slaves, about Ketu's links with the other Yoruba kingdoms, Ifé and Oyo and the important people of the kingdom, Abionan heard Yatundé and Solange chatting, they were saying what they were going to do in Ketu the next day, Solange was talking about her mother who should have returned from Cotonou, Yatundé was recounting things about her son, the tone of voice of the two of them accompanied Abionan's thoughts for a few minutes, it was like a background against which the woman was setting her memories, the recollection of mother fastening her skirt up over her breasts, left in her memory only the rapid movement of her hand pulling across a bit of skirt for she had seen mother of this in Ketu, Pobe, Atakpamé, Abeokuta, Ibadan, Ife, Oshogbo, Oyo, Jedá, and in so many other places too that she couldn't say where, sometimes the picture had a river behind, it could be the Ogun or the Oya, the Ileme or the Mono, she also remembered her in the act of handing over goods she had sold, an obi or pepper, a bottle or potato, Aduke had a way of clutching what she was selling in both hands and Abionan could see again that gesture before her, in the market at Ketu, at Abeokuta, at Oja-Iba in Ibadan, at Oshogbo which she loved so much, in the little roadside markets, the one on the way to Atakpamé, with lorries arriving and the snake in the middle of the road, today she was going to take Ogunbanjo's lorry, she thought of the lorries coming and going and the delight she felt at that market which was just a market with no village nearby, without any houses and everyone all together sleeping on mats, Yatundé's and Solange's conversation continued, they were talking now about the land one of them had inherited, her son would have to be born to inherit hers and Mariana had shown such confidence about that future son that she had already invited him to come for stays at the Water House and to Aduni too, Abionan had laughed:

'He's not born yet. Let him get born first before you invite him.'

'I know he will be born. A person like yourself is capable of achieving anything they wish.'

'Will I manage him to be king too?'

'Of course you will. One way or another you'll manage it.'

Mother had been of the same view, she had many times said that her daughter had a down-to-earth way of wanting whatever she wanted and this was so strong that it made things happen, one afternoon she had remarked:

'I was never like that.'

'Like what, mother?'

'I never had the strength to want things.'

Another time, cheerfully:

'You have the gift of wanting.'

Let's hope it was so, Abionan was saying to herself during the long wait for the lorry, she thought she could ask now:

'What's the time?'

'Ten fifteen.' said Yatundé.

Solange:

'Not long now.'

The three bicycles came back past, the dogs had gone quiet, the night was imposing its silence, in Atakpamé the stillness had at night been broken by Casimir's voice who would never stray far from Aduke, Abionan would sleep hearing his voice and she would wake up and for a while it would still be Casimir's voice, mother's answer rarely, when there was a respite or a silence it seemed enormous, the lanterns would be put out except for two that shone on the middle of the market now, while a cold wind was coming into Iro Kogny from outside, the pole supported the woman's body who, as she looked upwards, could not see its tip, then the three heard the roar of a lorry approaching, it was Ogunbanjo who alighted from the cab smiling all over:

'See? I've got here earlier.'

'What a miracle.' said Yatundé.

'It is.'

The man motioned with his hands:

'Come on. Get on. It's time to go.'

Abionan picked up her things, the mat, the basket, the cloths, and put them on behind, a smell of petrol seemed to impregnate everything.

Yatundé asked:

'What are those big drums full of?'

'Petrol.'

'How nasty.'

But Abionan liked the smell, it reminded her of the market that was just a market with the lorry men smelling of petrol, she found

224

plenty of room for all three of them, though the drums of petrol took up half the space and there were large pieces of sacking on top of them, the women cleaned up the patch where they were going to sit, the back was open and Yatundé laid her hands on a petrol drum and asked in a very clear voice:

'Are they well lashed down?'

Ogunbanjo's face appeared behind:

'Don't worry. We lash everything down properly.'

The engine started up, at first the lorry bumped over pot-holes in the road but then the motion steadied and the women got used to the movement, Solange said with relief:

'I thought it was going to shake all the way.'

'You'll never get to sleep.'

In the darkness, Abionan tried to see Yatundé's face, but couldn't quite, she replied:

'No, I certainly shan't. I'll sleep in Ketu.'

Her tiredness grew and she felt her knees aching, she decided to stretch out her legs but knocked into Solange's without meaning to, she apologised and the latter said:

'There's enough room for all three of us to stretch our legs out. We've just got to get things organised.'

Abionan gazed up at the sky, there were some stars that seemed to shine brighter than others, she thought that were she Sousa she'd start counting the stars but there were too many for that, and she'd never arrive at a total, when she'd finished counting one patch, she wouldn't remember where she'd begun, then Yatundé asked whether she'd be going straight on to the market or sleep at home:

'I'll stay there in the market.'

It would be better, for she'd sleep on her mat, perhaps without dreaming, and she'd go and find her husband in the morning for a talk, she would see Fatogum, and consult Ifá, she would pay homage to Eshu and the Hunter, her weariness all of a sudden surged, she shut her eyes and tried to wrap herself up in the sway of the lorry, she saw images from the dream, the Hunter bearing the child in his arms and Aduke accepting him with a smile, then she stopped and gave it more thought, would mother really have smiled at the moment of receiving her grandson?, if she slept and dreamt again she would be able to check whether mother was smiling or not, but sleep was hard in coming and she thought that she could even pretend to herself she was asleep, her tiredness seemed to be choosing

225

patches of her body in which to make itself felt, first shoulders, then neck and straight after that her eyes which were burning inside and then her whole head which was full of the images from the dream of the last days, of Victor Ajayi, the organ of Eshu rising from the ground, and the priest at Idigny, the face of Ogunbanjo, and the rainbow, the sheet with blood on it, and the child with its open arms and the long line of people on the mountain, the memories of mother in the act of straightening her skirt and winding it across her breast, of offering her goods with both her hands outstretched and the river flowing past behind.

KETU MARKET ONCE AGAIN

Ojo Awo, day of the secret, day of Ifá and Eshu

I sing of the weary woman arriving back in Ketu with the lorry rumbling down the quiet streets and the market with the remains of the day before's activity, or was it already the start of a new day?, I sing of her at the moment when she reaches the stall and puts her things down on the ground, I sing of her as she feels now at home with the tree in the market place, the houses around and the roof-tops and sky of Ketu as the woman lays out her mat on the ground and thinks of her weariness which being so deep may not let her sleep, I sing of her as she puts away the cassavas, the yams and potatoes left over, her now serene body still feeling the sway of the lorry, I sing of her at the instant she shuts her eyes, though not yet lying down and as she thinks of what she will do when morning will come but first she needs rest, to sleep, perhaps to dream, to prepare for a day that will be decisive, I sing of her as she lays herself down, her hands clasped as if to protect each other with the mat's familiar yet harsh touch against her arms, I sing of her in the fear she has that the same dream will return to her head, for wasn't it there that dreams dwelt?, she asked herself, I sing of her as she screws up her eyes forcing sleep to draw in, her muscles easing bit by bit and a quiver unexpectedly rising up through her eyelids, I sing of her amid that final stillness which takes charge of the whole of her body, I sing of her in the void which invaded her, in that dreamless sleep and in that white utter sleep into which she dropped.

She woke late, or so she thought, Solange enlightened her:

'Eight o'clock.'

'How on earth have I slept so much?'

Yatundé wanted to know whether she had slept well.

'Very well'.

She looked about, the day was bright and the sky was blue, the sun was beating down on the wet ground, small children were running about, she remembered that she had to see her family and above all to pay homage to Eshu, she glanced at the empty shelves but she left market matters for later, she carefully combed her hair, looked at herself in her glass, washed her face in a basinful of water at Solange's stall and went out observing things, the lively bustle of buying and selling, the cars and the bicycles in the street and the holy tree, she went up close to the organ of Eshu, it was as if she hadn't seen it for ages, perhaps there was now a ban on worshipping the orishas, so she looked to either side but no one seemed to be paying her any attention at all, so up again she got and returned to the market place, she bought twelve cakes and now once again before Eshu she made her offering, she set six cakes down before him, as the day was the start of a new stage, the path leading to the birth of her son, she shut her eyes a moment, the noise of Ketu seemed to remain afar, then she rose, and when she reached her family's complex she set the other six cakes down on the ground in front of the house and as she entered she ran straight into Obafemi, the good uncle, which was an omen that the pathways were opening.

'May you not die as you're arriving back home.'

The voice was cheerful and he was smiling:

'May you not die while you're smiling.'

She saw small children everywhere, nephews and cousins who hugged her and Abionan asked her uncle:

'How's Ademola?'

'Quite well. He's only just gone out.'

Then Olaitan was coming up, so the woman decided to keep quiet and the former said:

'Just look who's back.'

She looked at his face, its wrinkled skin was earth-coloured, she couldn't help thinking that possibly he was ill and replied:

'Yes, just look.'

'To what do we owe this visit?'

She would like to have said that the house was hers as well, or at least one end of it was and she took a key from her bag and went over and opened the door, at once she saw the place where Adeniran used to lie, an old chair – it had only three legs – was propped against the wall, and at the back was the mat that she had stopped using when the child had died, a broken jug and bits of things of no value, she and mother had for many years slept in that room there they would comment on what had happened during the day, one night mother had opened the window which opened into the yard and told her daughter that she had dreamt the sea was flowing past and Abionan had explained:

'Mother, the sea doesn't flow past. It just stays where it is, its rivers that flow past.'

'So doesn't the sea flow past?'

'No, it's like a lake but it runs up to you and then goes back again.'

Mother didn't seem bothered.

'Yes it did. In my dream the sea was behind the house.'

And she told of how she had dipped her hand in the water, had felt the cold water between her fingers and had woken up half startled and half happy she was more alive than ever after all, this had been before Adeniran was born, long before the final journey and the unseen roads scarcely seen but merely glimpsed in their details, the daughter feeling that Pobe had passed, Sekete was coming up and that Porto Novo seemed noisy, now Abionan sat down on the floor of her room, shut her eyes and concentrated on the idea that an important day had arrived, when anything she did could prompt the approach of the moment when the second Adeniran would be born but that moment would elude her if she went wrong, she thought about inviting Ademola to come and see her in the market but, at the same time she wondered whether it'd be worth the trouble or have any effect for husbands weren't in the habit of paying their wives visits in the market, though mother had told her that this wasn't actually forbidden, it was merely a custom, but first she needed to have a talk with Fatogum, if Mariana had arrived by now, she would have had some firm support, for even without mentioning the matter the two understood each other, a small lizard, one of the green ones, crossed the room and she wondered how it had got in, she watched as it stopped under the three-legged chair, Abionan stirred from her immobility and cleaned the mat which only now she noticed was covered in bits of dirt, had some plaster fallen off the wall? She sat down again and heard Uncle Obafemi's voice outside:

'Don't worry. She knows what she's doing!'

Whom could they be talking about?, perhaps herself and with whom?, she was going to get up to have a look when Olaitan's voice retorted:

'I've got my doubts.'

229

Yes, it was her they were talking about, again she thought it odd – she had thought so before – that one good man and one bad got on so well, chatting and exchanging ideas and managing to understand one other, she noticed that the sounds of the morning were rising, growing ever louder even though she was situated far away from them, she felt that the precise day had arrived and she needed the peace and quiet to carry her idea forward, she needed mother at her side, the dead did come back though perhaps they didn't though, they did manage to be present at the necessary moment, she was certain that Aduke had been waiting for her there in the room, sitting on the floor as so often before, attentive to what her daughter had to say and Abionan now saw that this was why she had come out of the market at a sure and steady pace, knowing that mother was waiting for her in the room and it was as if she could be seen and heard, she closed her eyes again and rested, her thoughts on the son who that morning had already begun to exist, she felt him returning from the place where he had been and coming back again to open out his arms on the ground in the market, on the ground in the room, on the ground on the sands of the beach, on the hilltop she had seen in the dream and the two of them – her mother and her son – were on all these patches of ground, they were together in the market with the woman selling, the little boy picking strands from the mat with his tiny hands, a louder noise outside made Abionan get up and open the door, a baby was crying, its wet face gleamed in the sun and, the woman asked:

'Uncle Obafemi, please tell Ademola to come and see me in the market!'

'At any time?'

'I'll be there nearly all day long.'

But not now, she thought, now she had to see Fatogum, to find out whether the day was good or bad, would Ketu be fuller than usual today?, or who knew whether there might be something in the air which was preparing her for the moment of conception and that that something would make the day different and give a greater beauty to houses, clothes and people?, now she began to notice everyone's general colour, that man must be from Ghana with his gold and green kanté, the other one was a Yoruba from Nigeria with his cap hanging a bit to one side, the place where Fatogum lived stood near a corner on which there was a group of women selling obis, orobos and meals, there was a buzz of conversation the whole time, certain words stood clearly out in the air and the smell of the food entered the house with Abionan as she saw Fatogum sitting on the floor staring into a corner of the room where there was nothing at all, just the join of the wall and the floor.

The woman stopped a moment, the babalao continued to stare into nothing until he realised that she had arrived, Abionan smiled:

'May you not die as while you're sitting on the floor.'

Fatogum gave his greeting and bade her sit down, he wanted to know what the days at Opo Meta, Idigny and Iro Kogny had been like.

'Very good. I have thought a great deal.'

'Have you really?'

'Yes, I have. I've talked, and sold cassavas too. And I dreamt. Then I stayed awake and thought even more.'

Fatogum looked her in the eyes:

'Were you thinking the same as what you always think?'

She nodded and after a lengthy silence in which they grew used to each other, she started to tell the man how the three days had gone, how she had sensed the presence of mother at every moment, the things that she had recalled, the journeys she had made with Aduke, round Nigeria, in Togo, on the banks of the Niger the lack of the sea, the taboo which was conquered, though perhaps the taboo had prevailed to the end, she spoke of the conversations with old Mariana which she had recalled, her friendship with young Mariana, the thoughts of President Sebastian Silva, the time when Mariana had gone round the four markets with her, the stories of Sousa and the streets of Aduni, the President's Palace and the mania Sousa had for counting windows, doors, flowers and stars, the dream of the child bleeding but, now she knew that she was ready for the return of Adeniran, after speaking she looked at the babalao and waited.

He pressed his hands one against the other like someone tensing their muscles, then asked:

'What was the dream like?'

'The dream?'

'Yes, tell me every bit of the dream that you can remember. Was the blood very conspicuous?'

She thought.

'It was and it wasn't. The Hunter kept telling me so often not to worry that I didn't believe the blood very much.'

'Tell me the rest.'

Abionan did, first the hunt, they had taken her son away and she needed to find him, drag him out of the hands of those who were carrying him, she spoke of how she saw him being borne aloft into the air, of the canoe that took him, of mother telling her not to die, of how her greeting had frightened her, of the hilltop, the sheet stained red, of the Hunter close by and what he had said, the appearance of Oshumare and she couldn't remember having in reality seen such a lovely rainbow, and of the people who filed past before the child, she paused briefly before asking:

'Do you think the dream has some meaning?'

'Every dream means something.'

Then he smiled:

'Your dream is really quite straightforward. It doesn't need any interpretation. It seems to mean that your son shall suffer, and shall bleed, before occupying an important position.'

'Before becoming king?'

'What ought I do to avoid him bleeding?'

'Nothing.'

'What, nothing?'

'There's nothing you can do. When what has to happen doesn't, it can prejudice what's to happen afterwards.'

She frowned as he explained:

'If he doesn't suffer – here he made a gesture that what he wished to say wasn't quite right but continued:

'If he doesn't bleed he might not become king'

She nodded. She had understood. She remembered the blood of President Sebastian Silva, Mariana's description, of Old Mariana with the dead son in her lap but then the blood had flowed after he had become king or president, her son was to bleed first and only after being bled would he be able to become king, she dropped her head and set her eyes on a piece of wood lying on the floor.

Fatogum picked up his cowries.

'Is there anything you want to ask?'

'There is. It has to be today. I want to know whether the day is good.'

'Must it really be today?'

'Yes, it must. Today my son shall start to exist.'

232

'Have you spoken to Ademola yet?'

'No, but I've sent a message for him to come for me.'

Fatogum cast the cowries, looked at the position of each of them, then gathered up a set of four of them which he cast again, he did the same thing over again, all the cowries together and then just part of them and at a certain point he raised his head towards the woman.

'The day's a good one. It's the day of Ifá and Eshu. The day for things that are beginning.'

He further stated that it was a good day for starting a journey, selling in a new market, meeting people, making new friends and a very good day for a child to begin to exist, she explained:

'I'm going to interrupt my trip round the other markets and stay in Ketu. I'll start back in four day's time.

He kept holding the cowries, as if having forgotten that he had cast them only shortly before, he had the look of someone who was about to say something but changed his mind, the woman remarked:

'What was the matter?'

'Nothing. I was just thinking that anyone who has the ambition you have must be prepared for big disappointments.

'If the goal is what I know it's going to be, that's not a bad thing.'

Fatogum opened out a big handkerchief on the floor and put the cowries back.

'When I say that a thing is going to be good I often doubt it to myself and I feel like casting again, to confirm whether it's true, but then I become afraid of annoying Ifá.'

She laughed:

'Anyway I believe what the casting says. I haven't the slightest doubt about it.'

'When the reports came out that they were going to ban the cult of the orishas and imprison the babalaos, I thought about giving it all up and doing something else.'

She turned serious:

'Mariana thinks that in that event people will go down to the catacombs with the orishas.'

He seemed to know what catacombs were and said:

'One needs great courage to do what is banned.'

'No one's going to ban anything.'

He put the handkerchief away in his pouch and Abionan said happily:

'I'm going to bring you some yams round to your house today.'
Fatogum smiled:
'That's a good idea.'
She went on:
'And then I'll cook some tasty meals for ourselves.'
'There's no need. I'm eating very little.'
Abionan noticed that he was thin, too thin perhaps, she wanted to say that he must eat well but felt that the man belonged to another caste of existence, Ifá might well require his own people not to eat too much, though as regards children Fatogum had several so there was no ban on that and there the woman remained in thought, she felt well, the room seemed to be the best bit of Ketu then she thought she'd better go back to the market for her husband might come at any moment, she got up and ran as far as the door and from there she gave a wave to Fatogum, she went out into the street where now there seemed to be more people selling, one of the women who had obis and orobos on a packing-case, looked up at her as if she knew her but the woman didn't stop and one street farther on she saw the holy tree, she thought of the place for worshipping the Hunter and she had to touch the holy tree, the day was still at its beginning and many things could happen, she put her right hand on the trunk of the tree and a small boy in a red shirt stared at her with gaping eyes, when she reached the market, Omitola started saying:
'Your supplier's been. He couldn't wait. He's left everything on the shelves, potatoes, cassavas and yams. He said he'd have a word with you later.'
Abionan sat down on the small stool but didn't look to see where the cassavas were, she took a coloured headtie and began to fasten it round her head, Omitola observed:
'You're not in the mood for work today.'
Abionan smiled:
'I'll do a bit, but not too much.'
But she did see to five customers almost all at once, then a group of atabal players stopped in front of the woman's stall as she rocked her head to the beat, at one point Solange shouted:
'Here comes the little one who steals your cassavas.'
This time, the man passed by without looking aside, Omitola said:
'He doesn't want to work today either.'

Francisca took off her blouse and rubbed a wet towel over her arms and shoulders and breasts, while a customer who was buying peppers stood with his eyes glued to her, she complained:

'Never seen womens' breasts before, eh?'

Everyone around laughed and the man disappeared down a side-turning, Abionan asked:

'Who's that?'

Solange reported:

'Old Louise's son.'

She remembered her, she had had a stall not far away, she had been ill, and today she hardly ever left the house, her son always did the shopping, he must have been brought up right there in the market, first crawling about in the dirt close to mother, then running about together with other children and in a few years' time the second Ademiran would be running about too, she thought of mother sitting on her bench, talking loudly, calling to the neighbours, shouting at her daughter when she ran off, at first she put the matter of sea out of her mind, she remembered when she had wanted to tell her what the sea was like, it had been just after Abionan had seen it for the first time and mother hadn't wanted to hear, but as time went on she herself would start conversations in which the sea came up and later on she had got in the way of recounting the dreams she had dreamt about the sea, in the end she had made the request, it had been on that very spot and the pair of them had been sitting there late one afternoon, and her illness had by then become a part of everyday life and, she had said:

'One day I'm going to ask you to take me to Old Mariana's house.'

'What, the Water House?'

'Yes.'

Her daughter had begun a sentence but restrained herself, mother had smiled:

'I know the sea's just in front.'

'Yes.'

'So I want to go there.'

There had been a pause.

'I want to go, but not now.'

'When?'

'When I say so.'

Abionan had spent weeks thinking about that request, by then mother would no longer accompany her on the round of the four markets, she would remain in Ketu while her daughter sold in Opo Meta, Idigny and Iro Kogny. Abionan had told Victor Ajayi:

'My mother wants to see the sea.'

'But can she?'

'She can't. But she wants to.'

'If she wants to, she can.'

She had a shock because just as she was thinking about Victor he appeared, he was coming up the side-street with that calm step of his, carrying a sack on his back.

'May you not die while you're sitting.'

'And you're not going to die at all: I was thinking of you.'

'About me?'

'Yes, I was remembering when I told you my mother wanted to see the sea.'

'Aha.'

The man sat down:

'I've just come here to deliver two masks. I'm going back at midday.'

Abionan let him relax a bit and then said:

'I'm going to miss a market and not go to Idigny.'

He frowned as if to ask why.

'I have to have a talk with Ademola today and I want to spend some days in Ketu.'

He made no comment and stayed seated, gazing at the traffic in the market, an argument arose three stalls farther on, lots of people went over to see what it was all about, for the stallholder was shouting that her price had not gone up and the shopper was saying that it had risen so much that it was an affront to a market with a name for fair prices, a group of men started jeering at the two women who turned on them in the midst of the rumpus. Abionan heard Victor's question:

'Does Ademola know yet that you want him to come here?'

'I've sent word.'

'As I'm going to deliver these masks near the place where he usually drinks before lunch, I'll have a word with him.'

He rose, Abionan wanted to say not to, it was too soon and he ought to stay longer but he didn't have time and she confined herself to following him with her eyes, she could at least have said 'may you not die while you're walking', but he had got lost among the inquisitive people following the argument, she stayed quietly sitting there, the words of the stallholder and the shopper seemed to be coming from afar and what she felt was a haste for the process of her son's birth to be started, amidst her tranquility she sensed that she was happy, a sort of euphoria took hold of her body, a burning in her eyes made her keep shutting and opening them all the time, she seemed to see more, she could distinguish shapes and colours passing and at one point she looked down to the end of the side-street and even managed see the houses away in the distance, a bicycle went past with the man's Yoruba robe flapping in the breeze like a flag, she remembered one of the stories of Sousa in which he made up his mind to learn to ride a bike, but instead of bothering about balancing, he wanted to count how many metal wires there were in the wheels, the owner of the bicycle was cross:

'Do you want to learn or are you going to count the spokes?'

Sousa had replied that he wanted to do both, Abionan thought that nothing much happened in the story of Sousa and the bicycle, just the boy wanting to learn and to count the spokes, she thought about the meeting with Ademolá, now she was sure he would come because Victor would go after him wherever he was, what words would she say to her husband when it came to talking?, perhaps it'd be best not to think about that but let herself say whatever might enter her head at the time, Yatundé had a jolly voice when she called Abionan's attention:

'Here comes the boy.'

It was the son she had left behind in Ketu and now he was approaching, well dressed in a long vivid robe of green, red and white, he was grinning at seeing mother and Abionan watched the two of them, and felt like a little girl again going up to mother with a smile, she had gone up to her like that in so many places, in Ibadan, Oshogbo, Jeda with the river flowing past beyond, then the river would pass by and go on its way, it left one place and came to another and the water she had dipped her hand in yesterday morning ought today to be arriving at the sea, she had smiled at mother in the market half way along the road, with the lorries coming and going, she remembered once having walked up to mother with a smile, her arms outstretched, mother had lifted her up in the air and then hugged her, she thought that one day the new Adeniran would come over to her with that very same smile, and she would lift him so high and he would be seen by all the market and also by whoever might be in the square or the streets at the doors and at the windows, in the trees and on the terraces, that image of Yatundé's son approaching mother with a smile seemed to linger before Abionan as she took in each stage of the movements, the little boy coming up, starting to open his arms, getting half way there, opening them right out, Yatundé bending to pick up the child, placing her hands underneath his arms, lifting him up against the colourful backdrop of a drapery stall, then mother and son sat down inside the stall and Yatundé starting getting a meal for him, she lit a brazier which she brought out from under the shelf at the back, then Abionan felt she should go back again to Fatogum's house, she remembered the packet of herbs that the woman called Sybil had asked her to deliver, and she went to deliver it, on the way she kept thinking to herself whether Ademolá would have the idea of visiting her at the very moment she was out, but no, because in the afternoon he was in the habit of detaching himself from the place where he drank and ate with friends, the women found Fatogum in the same place and invited him:

'Lets go and sit outside. I've come to cook your meal.'

He smiled and she added:

'At the usual spot.'

The man got up and went and sat down by a mound of earth which stood at the back of the house, Abionan arrived with a piece of meat, three yams and a small bag of gari, she raked up a fire beneath a quite rusty trivet while Fatogum just watched, as noises of various sorts came in from the street, the sun was beating down hard on the wall of the house, everything was hotter, the smell of the meat seemed to form of a general heat and after they had eaten, Abionan began to talk about the son which would come along in more or less nine months, he laughed at her preciseness, she insisted that she was quite sure about that, and at a certain point she stopped a moment as if thinking an unexpected thought, then she asked:

'Do kings always go to war?'

Fatogum hesitated before replying, he seemed to be analysing the question.

'They did in days gone by. Today war is very rare.'

He told her:

'Have you heard that there was a time when we were always at war?'

He picked up a grapnel from the floor.

238

'Indeed there was. The Yoruba people made a lot of war. The chief was called Balogun or Ibalogun which means war-lord. The Balogun was above the law, he ruled everything. The Balogun was the law and he had two aides, one at his right hand, the Otan Balogun and another at his left hand, the Osi Balogun. There were wars in Oyo, Abeokuta Ibadan and Ketu and the chief led the soldiers and negotiated alliances with his neighbours. Before the war started it became necessary to give thanks to Osanyan with a human sacrifice. The one chosen to die would have his hands bound behind his back and be taken to the market where he would parade past all the stalls. As he went around the market, the people would seek blessings for the city and its chiefs.'

'Would his blood placate the gods?'

Fatogum didn't answer straight away and she was thinking of the child with open arms on the sheet stained red, children were born in blood too, but after some minutes Fatogum did decide to say:

'After the victim had been sacrificed, the blood which had been shed was regarded as sacred.'

Abionan thought of her son as Balogun, the War Lord, above the law and capable of solving all problems and conquering obstacles, but perhaps the everyday problems, those of a market and a city, were more difficult, Mariana had said that her son, as king of Ketu, would have to solve the problems of Ketu market and of all the markets around, while she was thinking, she was eating pieces of meat with gari, once it had occurred to Abionan that kings lived a very long time and Yatundé had told her that King Abiodun of Oyo had lived over two hundred years, then Fatogum had explained:

'In those days years were shorter.'

But it would be fine for kings to live two hundred years, her son would do so too, although she would by that time be no longer alive, though she could be at some spot keeping a vigil for her son, on a cloud or a hilltop or attached to a tree like the gods of the trees, the genies that clung to the branches, those that lived in the baobabs and looked after everything happening around them, then she thought it was time to return to the market, she washed her hands in a bowl of water and took leave of Fatogum who remained leaning against the mound of earth, now the sun was even hotter and she went and found Yatundé talking to Omitola, her child was sleeping beside her on the mat, and she wanted to know whether anyone had been looking for her, Yatundé said they hadn't, Abionan sat down calmly, took a comb off the shelf and started combing her hair, a little sweat ran down her brow and she thought of the victims sacrificed before a war, she imagined a man with his hands bound behind his back being taken through Ketu market, stopping in front of her stall, looking her in the eyes before being killed and shedding his already sacred blood, among the stories of Sousa which Mariana had read to her in Aduni was one where the youth got into a war but it had been a make-believe war, Mariana's voice had seemed gentle and brighter that night:

' "Sousa began a war against the street on the side where there lived a boy called Ajagbo. The boy arranged with him that the two of them should go to war. Each would have his own army. The street on the right had twelve boys to draw from. The one on the left had eleven but one of them was tall and strong. He was under ten but seemed to be fifteen so the two armies were matched. Before the battle Sousa counted his troops. There were just twelve. He addressed them on the patch of ground between the streets. All was quiet on the far side. The war would be one of shouting and barging. Each boy had to shout a lot and barge the enemy troops. When the time came for the two armies to join battle, Ajagbo's committed an impermissable foul. One of the boys under Ajagbo's command picked up a stone and flung it at Sousa. The two chiefs stopped it all and decided to try the offender. They sat down between the streets and began the hearing. Who saw the boy fling the stone? I saw him, said one. When they had reached the conclusion that he was the one who had flung the stone, they asked the culprit why he had done it. He replied:

'I was scared.'

Sousa and Ajagbo talked in private and considered that fear was a very powerful motive. They decided to pardon the boy on one condition: he would not play with the others for three days'."

Abionan remembered the war she had witnessed in Ejigbo, a war of poles and shouting, but the two armies called each other names, they insulted one another as the king dressed all in white attended serenely, Abionan thought that only kings should go about in white, she could again see the king with a crown on his head and a smile on his face and she saw again the bonfire they built, she and mother had gone into the smoke, even the food had been white, rice, cakes, and white maize and the rains had started, she remembered mother's words in Oyo, that she was tired but that travelling was worth the trouble, getting to know other markets, seeing the place where they made adirés, visiting the temple of Oshun and Oshogbo, living in the midst of the commotion of Ibadan market but then a shopper turned up who took a delight in arguing the prices so Abionan set aside her thoughts and put on a look of astonishment.

'At that price, never.'

'Have you seen such manners', the man shouted to the other stalls.

'My manners have nothing to do with the matter. Nothing at all. What we're arguing over is the price of the cassava.'

'For that price I can buy twice as many in Cotonou.'

'Go and buy them in Cotonou then – off you go. But the transport will cost you three times more. Off you go.'

'But cassava is produced here and not there.'

Then it was her turn to say:

'See, have you ever met anyone who knows so much about where cassava is grown.'

She was in the middle of the argument when she saw Ademola approaching, the Yoruba robe he was wearing was in bold shades of yellow, he was grinning as he came, he came close to the stall and stopped and started to wait, Abionan looked at him without breaking off the argument and she kept a straight face as the man was saying:

'For that price I'll take those three large cassavas and this small one.'

'For that price you can take two of the big cassavas.'

'Three of the big ones then. I'll leave the small one for you.'

'Not that either.'

They argued the price a little more, Abionan consented to sell two of the big ones and a small one for that price and the man went off with his purchase, Ademola greeted the woman:

'May you not die while you're selling.'

She thanked him, re-stacked the cassavas on the bottom shelf, pulled out a stool, and motioned to it, her voice was bright:

'Be so good as to sit down.'

He continued to grin:

'What formality.'

'Make yourself at home. I've another stool for myself.'

The couple sat down, Yatundé vanished from the stall alongside but Omitola and Solange were talking, Ademola asked:

'You wanted to see me?'

'Yes, I did. Who gave you the message?'

'Victor.'

After a pause:

'He said it was important.'

'And so it is.'

He stopped smiling:

'Important business is generally serious.'

Then it was her turn to smile:

'Not always, today's business could be quite jolly.'

A baby cried in the stall behind and Abionan went on:

'It is important, but simple. It is that I've decided to spend a while without selling in markets. I need to rest for a while in Ketu.'

'Have you already forgotten the death of the little boy and your mother?'

'It's impossible to forget them. I think I can never forget them but life must go on and has to be lived.'

'Where will you want to stay? In your old room? Or in the room where we lived to start with?'

'What do you think?'

'It all makes no odds.'

'My mother's old room is very nice.'

'It's got one advantage – it's larger.'

She rested her elbows on her legs:

'This doesn't mean I'm going to stop selling in the market.'

'Of course not. That'd be impossible.'

'Maybe the best thing would be for me not to go with my companions to the three other markets, but stick to Keto.'

'You could go to Idigny or any of the other cities just now and then?'

'Yes, I could do.'

Yatundé had come back to her stall with her little boy with her, Abionan asked as she gazed up at the man:

'Do you like the idea?'

'I do. I've been hoping you'd make that decision sooner or later.'

He frowned as he added:

'But of late I gave up hoping.'

'Why?'

'I heard you were going to live in Cotonou.'

'Really?'

242

'To keep a shop.'

'Oh that was my uncle's idea. How did you get to know about it?'

'He told me so himself.'

'But didn't he say I rejected the idea?'

'I didn't know you had.'

'He must have spoken to me before you turned it down.'

'He must have done.'

They kept quiet for some minutes. The market also seemed more silent, the traffic had eased off and at a certain point the man asked:

'How's business been here and elsewhere?'

'Steady. not enormous but steady. And how are your operations going?'

'I made a good deal last week.'

'What was that over?'

'I bought twenty bicycles in Cotonou at a reasonable price, I brought the bicycles to Ketu on a lorry and sold them all here.'

'Made a good profit?'

'Adequate.'

'Yes. You also have your market.'

He chuckled.

'It's different.'

'It seems different but if you think about it, it's much the same. It's just the stalls that change. And also your trade lacks stability.'

'What's the good of stability? I do a deal that allows me to live for six months so I can spend six months without working.'

She looked at her own hands:

'I just can't conceive a life without working.'

But she said it with a smile as if she wanted to say what she thought without upsetting the man. Seeing her smile, Ademola agreed:

'You were always a glutton for work.'

She turned serious.

'In actual fact, every one of us does what we are prepared for. In my case, I was brought up in markets. I've always been mixed up in markets.'

They paused afresh, Ademola looked round the stalls and commented:

'It's a good place to work. Cheerful. You can have fun all day long.'

She too looked aside, Francisca Pereira was talking with a young

243

lad, she was gesticulating with her arms and seemed happy, Abionan turned to Ademola:

'It's good when you like your work. But it's hard too. It's no child's play. . .'

Here she smiled at him.

'. . , or man's play – carting our things about all night from one market to market, studying the prices, arguing, having to put up with drunks. . .'

He nodded in agreement, he seemed about to say something but kept quiet, the pair spent some minutes in silence, across the market with its sounds and smells walked man and woman, Abionan felt a great peace descend upon her and she had the sensation of mother close by, looking at her in her usual manner, silent as at the moments when she just would just contemplate things, she sensed her so strongly that she shuddered a little, she knew that the dead came back but not as abruptly as that, she proceeded to shut her eyes so as to concentrate on that presence, who knew whether mother was wanting to return in the form of the second Adeniran?, she had thought that before and Fatogum had told her that sex wasn't important for woman could return in the body of a man, she had been buried on her own land, she was resting in peace and contended and could return in the normal way, the proper rites had been performed and as she opened her eyes she saw that Ademola seemed calm too, at one with all that surrounded them, when he spoke his voice regained much of the affection of the first days:

'What time shall I come and fetch you at?'

'At nightfall.'

'Just after six?'

She smiled.

'That's a good time.'

Ademolá walked off through the stalls, the yellow of his robe moving amidst the people and animals, Abionan turned to one side as if looking for her mother and she recalled Olaitan having said she was wrong to stay tied to mother in her mother's house:

'Married woman go off and join the husband's family.'

But in her case, being closely attached to Aduke from childhood made it essential to keep on the room in which they had lived together, the influence of old Mariana had also brought Abionan to cling to mother, she did however agree with the uncle that once the new son was born, she would need Ademola's family, which also belonged to a line of kings and would be able to help make her son become the king of Ketu, Yatundé's voice interrupted Abionan's thoughts:

'Are you really going to stay in Ketu?'

'Yes.'

'Just for this once or for longer?'

'I don't know yet. That depends.'

Solange approached and the three women drew up their stools, Yatundé said:

'I've often thought about picking just one market and working there. It could be Ketu. . .'

She looked about:

'. . . it could be Idigny. Ketu's better for the boy's schooling'.

Francisca:

'I prefer Opo Meta. It's smaller and easier. Abionan's bound to prefer Ketu.'

'Of course, but I like doing the four markets as well.'

Yatundé:

'I'm afraid I might miss moving about. I'm so used to it.'

Abionan:

'Me too. Maybe I'll stay here just for the next four days. Let's see what happens.'

Yatundé's son was playing nearby, the peace of the afternoon seemed to have arrived, Abionan remembered the afternoons she had spent lying in a maize field in Porto Novo where she could see the cobs with their dangling whiskers, there were cassava plantations at the side and the girl pulled the cassavas out of the ground with a rusty knife, she was without mother because the spot was too near the sea, and she would spend short stays with an aunt who would keep saying:

'That sister of mine's daft. Whoever's afraid of the sea?'

The question 'whoever's afraid of the sea?' came to Abionan's mind from time to time, as, at the end, she had rushed off with mother to the sea, she had fled off with death in her thoughts, death and a strange sense of haste, as if demons were in pursuit, mother had said that demons had come to Ketu from Europe for hitherto there had been no demons in the area, it was necessary for people to appease them because they too had power, but it was only when she saw the sea in the distance that she calmed down, before the very word 'Okun' which meant sea, had scared mother who didn't want to hear it, but she did like all water, she had felt attached to Oshogbo because of the river Oshun, every river had its god or goddess, mother had told her about Yemoja, the Goddess of the waters who lived by the sea, she had seen a shrine to her in Ibadan, there was also Olokun, the god of the sea, a powerful god, but mother would refer only to rivers, she remembered that dipping her hands in the river was nice, Mariana, the old one, had talked one night of a journey she had made by sea, it was not by one of those steamships which arrived at Cotonou but in a sailing ship which needed wind to move and when there was no wind people died:

'First there died a black from Alagoas, nobody knew his name. Then there was a half-caste from Pernambuco, I saw the captain as he ordered the first of the dead to be rolled up in a sheet. The body was thrown into the sea. Next little Joana died. And as more people died, the sea would swallow up all the bodies.

She paused:

'I have seen many people die since I was a child.'

Abionan had also seen bodies being watched over and buried, she knew death as something close at hand and clinging to one's skin, once she had argued with Solange who had said that you shouldn't show dead bodies to children.

'Why ever not?'

'I learnt from my French teacher in Cotonou that you must protect children and not talk to them about death.'

'Nonsense. It's quite proper to show the child that death exists. It will see how things are from early on. Will hiding death from children stop them dying?'

'My teacher said it was to avoid them keeping it inside themselves throughout their lives.'

'But the opposite's the case: everybody does keep the idea of death in their heads throughout their lives. And that is natural.'

The dead on the ship had remained with old Mariana who cherished another death which young Mariana always remembered, it was the dead president in the palace taken to the Water House in mother's arms, the daughter in the front looking round to see the sheet stained with blood just as the sheet in the dream and the child with arms outstretched had been, then she heard Yatundé saying:

'I wanted my son to be a doctor and care for the sick people of Ketu.'

246

'A doctor?' asked Solange 'A difficult profession.'

Yatundé looked at the boy:

'It's the thing I most admire. I like seeing them give medicine and make people stop having the pain they feel.'

Abionan thought of her wish for Adeniran to come and be the king of Ketu, Yatundé wanted hers to make others well but what had Aduke wished for her?, that she'd be a good market woman and not forget the orishas, in the end she had accepted that her daughter's dream was hers too, that Abionan's son would be king, one night mother and daughter had talked till late, there was moonlight over the city and the older woman had asked:

'When you're in Ketu, don't you feel a force rising from the ground which makes you feel stronger?'

'I always feel well in Ketu.'

'There's a mystery here. . .'

She put her hand on the ground and looked doubtful. . .

'Here on the ground or is it in the air?'

Then she had started talking of her early childhood, of how she first became aware that she was a person and explained:

'It was in Ketu Market. I could see my mother's nape. I was strapped to her back. I saw a coloured tie, then I saw the ground, my mother had put me down on the ground, then a dog came up and sniffed me, I put my hand on its nose and it licked my fingers. My mother screamed. I think she was afraid that I'd be bitten.'

Abionan had felt she could ask:

'When did you learn that you couldn't see the sea?'

'From very early. The babalao alerted the family. And I couldn't because even before I learnt that it was forbidden, when I was less than four years old, an aunt took me to Pobe, she had wanted to go to Porto Novo, but on the way I began to look poorly, I was sick and fainted, or so I was told. My aunt was afraid I'd die so she rushed me back to Ketu.'

The market had been quieter than ever that night.

'Every time they tried to take me near the sea, I got ill.'

Young Mariana had told Abionan about a voyage she had made by sea to France, with high waves:

'Between Madeira and Lisbon there were waves twenty metres high.'

'How high?'

'Twenty metres.'

'They said it was a seaquake, the land lying beneath the sea was in motion. No one left their cabins or ate. I was afraid I'd die.'

'Did anyone die?'

'No. Before Lisbon loomed up the sea became calm, but it didn't seem the same. Then we sailed into the river Tagus which was calmer still.'

Abionan thought of twenty metre waves, whatever would mother have said had she known that could happen?, she asked:

'Didn't you say any holy words to beat the waves?'

'How could I know?'

'Ifa's people have quite a few words which drive away dangers.'

'The vessel was French. Would French words have had any effect?'

Abionan thought a little.

'I don't think so. Holy words can only be in Yoruba.'

'The two of them said over words that might be holy. Mariana thought that the greetings of the orishas ought to have quite a special spell.'

'Shango's one, Kauo-Kabieci, has a hard sound.'

And that phrase was also used to treasure what had happened in the past, there was the Baba Elegun who knew the list of all the kings of Ketu by heart and whenever there was a coronation, the Baba Elegun would say over the names of the kings and their histories, his son was learning the list so as to carry on from his father, Abionan remembered that her family also had a list of fathers and mothers who had had this or that son or daughter, from time to time the members of the family would gather, come together for a celebration and declaim the names of their ancestors, Mariana liked the idea:

'I'm going to find out whether my grandmother remembers any names other than Epifânia, my great grandmother's, her own grandmother Ainá and the grandparents who were my father's parents and of their parents so that we can recite them at home when we have a celebration.

The words that Abionan now overheard on the market were:

'Perhaps I shall decide to stay on longer in Ketu?'

Yatundé's voice dropped, maybe she was talking to herself, Solange followed her thoughts:

'It's what we'll all be doing sooner or later.'

A fat shopper appeared wearing an African skirt and a European coat. Yatundé laughed:

'Where will he be from?'

Solange:

'Not here.'

The man had quick movements, he would pick a sweet potato then a chunk of cassava and an old, old woman who was passing found his movements funny, then Francisca asked from a distance:

'What would you like?'

The man replied:

'I want to buy some good cassavas.'

He was smiling now and Abionan retorted:

'They're all good.'

'That's not so, worthy stallholder.'

Yatundé:

'In Iro Kogny we were called market ladies, now this one here's saying that Abionan's a worthy stallholder, something's afoot in the world.'

The fat man looked at her:

'Do you sell cassavas as well?'

'No. Peppers.'

'I don't want peppers. I want cassavas.'

Abionan:

'Then take your pick.'

'That's what I am doing.'

He picked up the potatoes again then the larger cassavas and made his choice:

'These two.'

Abionan named the price, he paid there and then and started walking off towards the way out, his skirt was swinging from one side to the other, and Yatundé thought that he looked like a woman from the rear, Abionan got up and went down a narrow street, she wanted to take a stroll but ran into two egunguns who were coming along, she took another turning and she could see in the street on the other side a group of women and girls, she did a Sousa and counted them up, there were eleven, two women and nine girls, the women in skirts of three colours, red, white and black, yellow and white necklaces around their necks, cowrie bracelets on both arms and one forearm, strings of cowrie alternating with a sort of black bead on their legs, they were sitting down and talking, the girls ranged from five to twelve years old, dressed in different clothes, one in a red skirt and bare breast, her neck covered with green, yellow and white necklaces, another in a dark-blue skirt and necklaces of cowries and yellow and green beads, and yet another, a smaller one, wore yellow with blue and white necklaces and all of them with white turbans on their heads, Abionan stopped for a minute gazing at that spectacle of women and girls together, a group of atabal players started drumming within the market and the women and girls kept up with the beat in a succession of gentle movements. Abionan still watched them as she set off in the direction of the holy trees, the palm-wine stall had few people at it, she put her hands on the tree for a moment and, then walked once all round the market and stopped at the stalls with the articles for witchcraft, she saw a group of old nagos selling the wherewithall for cures, herbs and roots, she went down the smoked meat alley, naked children were rolling on wet earth and went through the mat and cut calabash stalls and when she got back it was to find two shoppers waiting for her, one of them had been a friend of Aduke's.

'At long last. Where have you been?'

'I took a walk once round the market.'

Once mother had chatted with that friend for over twelve hours on end, Abionan who was then a child had played about in the market, run off down the street, visited boys and girls at various stalls but when she came back she found mother and the friend still talking, speaking sometimes in low voices, with heads almost together, how on earth could there be such a lot to say?, the girl had gone off again and played, mother and the friend hadn't stopped talking together, then afterwards she had asked who the other was and mother had said:

'We spent our childhood together, she lived near our house but now she's in Porto Novo.

Yet she seemed much younger than mother, she used lipstick and wore ear-rings, mother would say:

'She was always like that. She's worn ornaments ever since she was a child.'

Mother would do too, but only African ornaments, coloured necklaces from back home, but no face ornaments from elsewhere, like those appearing in the magazines which Uncle Obafemi would bring from Cotonou, today mother's friend bought sweet potatoes without saying anything and at the end hugged Abionan, another shopper argued about the quality of the yams and ended by taking one of the larger ones, the heat had dropped and Abionan sat down and rested her head against the stall's wooden pillar, she could see big clouds travelling slowly past and remembered Mariana who would be arriving from France that week, she needed to go to the Water House to see her and talk with her, this would keep her away from the round of the markets for another week or so and then she would send a message to Victor Ajayi who would perhaps come to the Water House too, lost to the world she shut her eyes and thought of the view to be had from the upper storey of the Water House, the dune to the right and the coconut palms further off, the beach where she had spent the moments of that great meeting with the sea and she recalled Mariana saying:

'When I am here and look out, it is as if everything has gathered around myself, father who died, grandmother who is always here, great grandmother Epifania and Ainá, my grandmother's grand-mother, I feel that they are all here within me, do you understand?'

Abionan did understand, she couldn't explain it but she did, and looked out of the window feeling that the place had quite a different force, Mariana had gone on:

'When I imagine my father writing down his thoughts and the stories of Sousa, I can never see him in the palace at Aduni, I always see him here in this house, writing in the room which used to be his and is now mine. He must have written looking out of the window and seeing the dune out there where he is today buried.'

A pause.

'That's how I see him imagining what he imagined. Even when he was president, he'd often come here, to spend weekends thinking, no one knew where he was and a minister who found this out thought it was all wrong because this is a foreign country and not Zorei, at that time this was Dahomey and he was president of Zorei, but my father attached no importance to that, he continued to come here whenever he could and I can imagine him writing, making up the stories of Sousa, making up or adapting to Sousa things that had happened to himself and when I was little I must have been playing just out there, running up and down the steps and over the dune where one day my grandmother was to give the cry that she did.'

Mariana could have a different face when she was saying what she said, she seemed like another person and there were moments too

251

when Abionan felt different, as if elevated above herself and saying words which didn't seem like her own, on that day she had seen Mariana in just such a light, a similar thing had happened on other days with her friend acquiring a look resembling Fatogum's at certain important times as when he was foretelling decisive events or when he betrayed fear, – and fear it was – or recounting what the cowries or metal plates said, but as the sea was what Mariana knew it to be for to her and Aduke, it was quite natural for her friend to say to her:

'Do you remember the story of Sousa seeing the sea for the first time? It must have been written at this table by the window.'

She had pointed to the exact spot, with the window open and at that moment a bird flitted rapidly across the gap of sky which the window exposed, Mariana had gone on:

'There's also a story of his which was certainly written here. If I had to give it a title it would be "Sousa Alone in his Room" It was nearly midnight. He was in lodgings near the sea. He had been visiting the tombs of Shasha de Sousa and his family. He was thinking about tombs. There was complete silence in the room and all around. Very occasionally a slight sound of the waves reached him. He felt strange being in a room. It seemed like a prison. From the moment he shut the door it was as if someone else had locked him in. He felt jailed, in Zewe he never felt jailed. Everything was open. The house didn't need doors. The doorway at the front was wide and had just a low board that stopped the chickens getting in. And they still sometimes hopped over the board. Banana branches would tap at the window. Not far away stood cocoa trees with their yellow fruits sometimes touching to the ground. Over the cocoa trees stood other trees, bigger ones, protecting the smaller ones. It could be dangerous. A snake might come in the house but that was a rare thing to happen. There was plenty of room for snakes to get around. Here he felt jailed. Jailed and alone. In Zewe he could be in the village on his own without it mattering or he even realising it. Everything enshrouded him, leaves, sky, and clouds, the stream, the houses and the mud of the road. He formed one part of the whole. Now he felt in a tomb. Shasha de Sousa's room had his own tomb in it. This one was merely a larger tomb. He was buried in the room with space around him to place the offerings made to the dead. He lay down and shut his eyes and he avoided any movement. It was vital for him to appear quite dead in his great big coffin.'

Mariana had finished reading and Abionan had said:

'It makes me frightened in an eerie way.'

'It does me, so much so that there can be no doubt that at least once in this room, my father felt exactly the same as Sousa.'

'I prefer Sousa in the happy bits.'

'So do I but the world's not made of happiness alone.'

Abionan opened her eyes and again saw the clouds passing in the sky, Yatundé was speaking, loudly now:

'If my son becomes a doctor, I shall do everything for him to stay in Ketu.'

Solange:

'You won't manage that. Qualified people prefer Cotonou, that's when they don't stay on in France.'

Yatundé gazed at the child who was pricking four bits of wood into a cob of maize and playing with it as if it were an insect, he was pushing the insect along the ground until the cob fell over, then he stood the insect back on its feet and made it hop over a stream of water that ran on the ground and formed the river, Abionan was following the child's play too and she thought about what she'd do if Adeniran didn't want to be king, but why think of that now?, she had before all else to make him be born and become a person, Mariana had once said to her:

'If you son doesn't become king of Ketu, he can be king of lawyers, or king of businessmen or king of maize or king of cocoa. It's always worth being king of something or other.'

But that was not the way Abionan viewed the matter, king of Ketu was what her son must be, Yatundé's little boy had abandoned the maize cob and was now playing with an old tyre, now Abionan felt a bit sleepy and lay out on her mat as she listened to her friends talking, Solange was saying:

'There goes old Olujimi.'

'He hasn't had a drink today.'

'They say he's been ill and he's drinking less.'

'Adewele's coming along behind him.'

'What's he doing these days?'

'He runs a taxi in Cotonou.'

'Any money in that?'

'They say so.'

Where she had been buried, she remembered the burial in every detail, but she didn't want to think of that just now, an ache rose through her chest and reached up into her throat when she rose from her mat and swallowed down some saliva, perhaps she should eat something, have a bit of dinner or maybe a drink of water would be better, she put her right hand on her womb, pressed it and started to breathe deeply as mother had once told her to do, from out of her womb the king would come, the second Adeniran would come and that was the right day, Yatundé broke off her conversation with the others and asked:

'Feeling queer?'

'There was a spot of pain in my chest but it's gone now.'

She rose and went across the market, the sun was still strong and she went into the bar of a relative of mother's called Olufuyi and had a glass of iced water then she stared at the posters hanging on the walls and came slowly back, on the far side of the market place a man in a yellow robe was talking to an old woman, would it be Ademolá? Now she missed Mariana and when she sat down again at the stall the centre of the market seemed deserted and she recalled Mariana reading out the thoughts of her father, for there were after-noons when Abionan could hear without hearing and the sound of Mariana's voice and the figures of the priest and Victor were quite enough for her to feel that everything was at peace in the world, Idigny would be resting in its summer heat, Ketu market would be awaiting her in two days' time and the thoughts of Sebastian Silva were important precisely because they made possible that tranquil-ity whose centre was Mariana's voice reading out the words which a man had written down in an school exercise book just like those Abionan had used when she had learnt to read and count, even dur-ing the journeys she had made with mother she had taken exercise books to study now and again and in Atakpamé Casimir had teased the little girl who wouldn't leave her exercise book behind yet never read nor wrote one single thing in it, one day he had offered:

'I am going to teach you everything.'

'Everything about what?'

'Everything I know.'

'Is that a lot?'

He scratched his head:

'I think so. Anyway it took a long time to learn what I've learnt.'

'Go on then.'

Casimir had gone off to fetch a map and had started to show her the world.

'Here's Togo where we are now.'

'It's very small.'

'And here's our country, Dahomey.'

'That's small too.'

The man wanted to know:

'What do you like? Hills? Islands?'

'Rivers are what I like.'

He showed her the map.

'Here's the river Nile.'

He moved his hand to another area of the map:

'And that's the Amazon.'

'I like the rivers near us.'

'Well look at the river Ogun then.'

'I know that one.'

'Do you?'

'I've been up it in a canoe, mother and I travelled on one for a whole day.'

Casimir would turn into a child when close to her, or perhaps he really was a child, mother had one day said this:

'How can you marry a man who behaves like a child?'

The girl had wanted to say that being a child seemed to her the best thing in the world, but mother wouldn't want her opinion, today Abionan feels that he might well have made a good husband for Aduke, he didn't drink, he looked after her and protected both mother and daughter, he had been the closest thing to a father she had ever known, although Uncle Obafemi had acted as father for a while, later on the girl had asked Casimir:

'Don't you know anything off the map?'

'I know maths. Do you?'

'So do I. What else?'

'I know the history of several countries.'

'Ketu?'

'Ketu's not a country.'

'But it's got a history.'

'What I know is the history of France.'

The girl had showed scant interest, then the man talked about a girl soldier who beat the English, Abionan liked her:

'A woman winning a battle, that's great.'

But Casimir didn't know that much history, just a few odd events, about the soldier girl and the king and the queen who had been guillotined, Abionan had said:

'Killing the king and queen, that's bad.'

'You keep on saying "that's great" and "that's bad" as if you were mistress of the world.'

'I'm only passing my opinion.'

As she sat and waited in the silence of Ketu market, Abionan relived the final journey, the last one, from the moment – it was in the morning – that mother had called her over to say:

'Keep near me.'

Abionan took Aduke's hand, a little cold, and she had wanted to know whether she needed anything.'

'No.'

It had been a bold and arid denial.

Mother and daughter had remained together in the room with the window open and the sun blazing down on the crown of the holy tree, Aduke had said:

'I'm going to make a request, my daughter.'

'Go on, mother.'

She hadn't made the request there and then and seemed to have forgotten about it, she shut her eyes and Abionan grew alarmed:

'Are you in any pain?'

'Pain? No. Just a bit dizzy.'

The daughter fell silent, she had thought of calling the doctor, there was raucous laughter outside and with it a sound of children, she had finally asked:

'Shall I call the doctor?'

'No.'

'Fatogum?'

'Not him either.'

Mother had closed her eyes again and Abionan wanted to know:

'What is this request, mother?'

It had been as if the woman had risen up from within herself:

'Request?'

She looked towards the window and said:

'I want to see the sea.'

'What, the sea, mother?'

'Yes, the sea.'

Abionan didn't know quite what to say, the woman had repeated:

'I want you to take me to see the sea.'

256

Abionan squeezed mother's body tighter still tighter against her as she went on in rather an anxious voice:

'Will there be time.'

'Time, of course there'll be.'

She had propped mother against the wall and gone out of the room into the sun, there were uncles and aunts, cousins and brothers and sisters, lots of people in front of the house, but she didn't talk to them, Obafemi had tried to talk to her but she broke into a run down the street, all the while she was thinking of what to do, it would take two days to get to the coast on foot and mother wouldn't be able to make it, she had gone into the market to look for the men who drove lorries to Porto Novo and Cotonou and had asked at the palm-wine stall:

'Where's Jerome, the lorry driver?'

'In that store.'

She had found him arguing about the weight of a load, and told him they needed to go at once to Porto Novo or Whydah, the man stared at her calmly:

'Today?'

'Right now.'

'Why the hurry?'

'I must go there.'

'I'm not going today. I'm waiting for more loads from the north. Jose da Cruz may need to go to Porto Novo today.'

Abionan had rushed across to Jose da Cruz's house.

'No, I'm not going today. Not till next week.'

'Do you know anyone who's leaving today?'

'Today?'

'Yes, today.'

'No. Unless Adebayo's going.'

It took quite some time to find Adebayo and he too said he couldn't make the trip, the lorry had something wrong with its engine.

After a lot of searching, she came across a man called Ogundeji, tall with a wide face, balding hair and a red robe, who had said:

'Yes, I'm going. I'm going to Togo today.'

'Togo will do. We can get off on the way.'

'But I'm not leaving till this afternoon.'

'Can't it be now?'

As he seemed surprised, the woman had added:

'My mother's ill, I have to go to the Water House with her.'

'Ill? If it's something bad, I can't take her. I can't run the risk of someone dying in my lorry.'

'No. It's nothing bad. Just faintness. If you're leaving now, I'll pay more.'

'How much more?'

'The usual price's three hundred francs, isn't it? I'll pay you six hundred.'

'If you give me one thousand five hundred, I'll leave right away.'

'All right then. I'll give you one thousand five hundred.'

'All right, lets go and pick up your mother. A friend's keeping me company in the cab so you two can ride on top with the maize.'

She had waited for the driver to fetch his friend and had climbed on to the lorry's body, the maize covered up in canvas filled all one part. Ogundeji had explained:

'I was going to wait for some more loads and leave in the afternoon. As you're paying one thousand five hundred, I needn't wait any longer.'

They had arrived at the front of the house, Olaitan had asked what had happened.

'Nothing. I'm just going out with my mother.'

She had gone into the room.

'Mother, I've told them we're going out for a ride. Don't let them see you're not well.'

She was smiling and the daughter had helped her up but Aduke was quite firm on her feet, Olaitan had looked at the pair of them with doubt written across his face while Ogundeji cleared a space between the maize cobs, mother and daughter got themselves comfortable and the lorry set off before the rest of the family realised what was up, Abionan could see the holy tree, the market and the church, then the lorry reached the main road and began to throw up dust behind, the daughter was afraid that the lurching would make Aduke's state worse, but mother shut her eyes and squeezed her daughter's hand, every so often she would increase the pressure to show that she was all right, now branches of trees swept over the lorry and disappeared, mother's clothes had got out of shape with the movement and Abionan was anxious to get her skirt straight, she saw people standing and walking on the road, groups sitting and small clusters of women selling and then a large market appeared

258

and Abionan tried to recall whether she had ever been there, but couldn't place it, at a certain point the lorry drove into a square, Ogumdeji had stopped and came round to tell the women:

'I'm having something to eat here. You can come as well if you want.'

Abionan had left her mother propped up there and asked:

'Can't we go on and eat later?'

'Where? In Porto Novo? Cotonou? We're hungry now.'

He had gone off and Abionan had returned to the back of the lorry, mother's eyes were wide open and she had said:

'Don't worry. I shan't die before we get there.'

The men had gone into a house with just a door, voices could be heard from inside, voices and laughter too, Abionan got off the lorry but she was in doubt whether to go in or not for she was afraid that mother would feel very much alone, so she came back and once beside her, estimated how much more time it would take to reach the Water House, they could get off earlier for there was sea at Porto Novo but they would have to go a long way on foot, in Cotonou they would come closer to the beach, but Abionan wanted to have mother within reach of friends and though the Water House was farther to get to, it did have that advantage, the men were a long time and the daughter asked:

'How are you feeling?'

'Better now. This morning I felt really bad. I got better on the lorry.'

'We're not far now.'

Aduke had turned her eyes towards the square in Pobe:

'We slept here when you were a little girl, don't you remember?'

'I do.'

Then she had remembered that journey with mother, when on the way out she was wanting to get close to the sea but then came the fear which both had felt when the salt-tang reached them and then the journey back when the pair of them had run along in their hurry to be back in Ketu again, the men had now come out from the house and Ogundeji had lit up a cigarette:

'Just one minute more.'

He smoked calmly, taking his time, Abionan had watched the cigarette growing smaller and when the man finished she felt relieved, the motion of the lorry had made mother close her eyes again the dust got worse, the sun grew stronger and the canvas cov-

259

ering the cobs of maize had a nasty smell, a group of young cyclists tried to keep up with the lorry and one of the youths managed to catch hold of the bodywork, letting out happy bursts of laughter, Abionan was thinking about the sea which mother had to see, the ban on her seeing the sea and the need for the journey to be fast, and for the need to get to the Water House as quickly as possible, a young woman with a pot on her head stood out against the road for one moment, Abionan had seen Sakete go by as children had been shouting goodbyes to the lorry, the daughter had been quite surprised to see mother answer with a wave of the hand, Aduke was smiling now, then she had fallen into a sleep that scared the girl but everything seemed to be all right, her breathing was normal and a little sweat ran down her face, Abionan was sweating too and she noticed when the lorry had crossed into the district of Porto Novo, the road was full of people with little markets everywhere, women in brightly-coloured clothes and men gesticulting, Ogundeji was cutting corners tightly and mother and daughter were hurled from one side to the other.

Abionan had been about to catch the driver's attention but he had stopped by a large market, where mother stared at the stalls and wore a look of great curiosity upon her face, Abionan had wanted to know why they had stopped:

'I've to pick up a load here.'

She looked crestfallen:

'What sort of load?'

'A refrigerator.'

'What?'

'Yes. It's a refrigerator I've got to take to Togo. Why?'

He looked at Aduke.

'She's all right isn't she? Nothing serious I hope?'

'Nothing serious at all.'

'It'll only be a minute. The refrigerator's coming right now.'

He had been walking off but had turned to say:

'I think you'll have to get out while the men load the refrigerator.'

The daughter had got mother down and the pair had sat down by a fruit stall, Aduke was looking all around with the greatest attention and had asked:

'So this is Porto Novo market then?'

'One of them. It's the largest one.'

The stall next to them was selling little wooden earrings, there were ibejes, the figures of twins which the girl had played with as a child and shouts came from all sides, women in coloured headties passed proudly by and mother had pronounced:

'It's a lively market.'

'Really lovely.'

'Like the one at Oshogbo.'

Abionan had tried to recall what the market at Oshogbo had been like, but she couldn't, but mother must be enjoying Porto Novo because Oshogbo was always the place she would recall most vividly from previous journeys, five men came pushing a cart up with a refrigerator on it, and Ogundeji's voice had been strong:

'Now you two go up with the rope and haul the refrigerator over to the lorry. We'll heave it up from underneath.'

Mother and daughter had kept watching the men working with their bare backs and sweat running, one would say:

'Steady there.'

Another:

'Pull now.'

Ogundeji:

'Over to the right.'

People had gathered to watch the men at work and at one point Ogundeji had shouted down to the men from the top of the lorry:

'Haven't you any strength?'

Everybody had laughed and a small boy let out whoops of joy, in the end the refrigerator had been lashed on to the lorry and Ogundeji tested the ropes.

'You can come on now with no fear at all. It's properly lashed down.'

He had helped the women on and the lorry had left, it drove on to a long bridge and mother had peered over at the waters below while Abionan had explained:

'It's a lake.'

The road was now bordered with office blocks, factories and restaurants, but Aduke had shut her eyes and seemed weaker, her face was an earthy colour and her lips almost red, Abionan had squeezed her tightly, Cotonou had passed with its busy streets, big shops, tall buildings, and squares with statues in the middle, now the daughter thought that the end of the journey was near, they'd soon be running into Whydah, and, just afterwards, they'd come to the Water House, she had shaken mother who had opened her eyes:

'Are we getting there?'

'Nearly.'

'See? I'm not dead.'

She had smiled wanly, the lorry was near by the Portuguese fort, and a little beyond stood the house of the Shashas, mother had seemed to have more energy and Abionan had banged on the cab of the lorry:

'You can stop just after the bend, by the tip of the dune.'

The vehicle stopped and Ogundeji had helped them down, the girl took the money out from a pouch fastened under her skirt and the man had grinned:

'Have a nice stay at the Water House.'

The lorry drove off and the pair were left standing on the sand and Abionan had explained:

'We have to go in that direction.'

'Come on then.'

They had gone slowly, the sand had ups and downs and they had passed close to the cemetery where President Sebastian Silva was buried with the wooden cross, then a strong breeze had struck them in the face and mother had dropped her head, her feet were sinking into the sand and a matted growth of plants every so often entangled her feet, Aduke had lifted her eyes to look ahead as she was reaching the point of parting between the end or the start of the sand and the waters which rose and fell, she had steadied her eyes as she came closer to her daughter, she was walking and looking, and now the breeze freshened, but this time mother had not dropped her head until the pair of them had stopped at the spot where the waves would lap on their feet, Aduke had broadened her gaze and inhaled the smell of the sea, as she had now little by little lowered her body in an effort to sit down, Abionan had helped her and sat down at her side, afar a boat had sailed by, the colour of the waters was green and the waves were carrying a piece of wood in and out, mother had said:

'I never thought.'

Abionan had wanted to speak but her voice would not come, mother had repeated:

'I never thought.'

And however could she have known beforehand? Abionan too had gazed at it with fresh eyes, it had been as if she had never seen it before, the green met the sky and the waves seemed to possess a will of their own and at that very moment, a celebration seemed to have started behind her, atabals were beating, chants rose in the air and Abionan had turned her head to see a procession of great beauty, with men and women in fine clothes, it gave all the appearance of a royal procession, a king and queen had always to walk ahead of everyone else and the atabals were playing so loud that it could hardly have been a parade of egunguns, or could it? It might have been a wedding, with the man and the women surrounded by atabals players, they would be the bridegroom and bride, now the chanting had come nearer and the procession moved in the direction of the mother and daughter, which was the direction of the sea, Aduke had also tried to twist her head round to get a look but the men and women dancing had by now come closer and stationed themselves alongside mother and daughter, who watched a group of them go into the sea, their feet and the hems of their clothing got wet and a tall youth was dancing more vigorously than the rest, into the water he waded waist-deep, and a stronger wave raised him up in the air, the atabals would not stop playing and there were clothes of every colour, greens and blues predominately, a young girl, almost a child, had fastened a green tie around her head and wore a long skirt coloured red and white and a pink and blue blouse, the dancers blended into the waves and the sound which that afternoon rose from them brought a strange joy to Abionan and yet she had felt that she could not be joyful with mother being there so sick, but she had noticed that mother too seemed joyful, after her first exclamation aroused by the sea, her face had taken on a tone of serene contentment, the dances and the chants had seemed to increase in intensity and it was amid this crescendo of sounds, that Abionan had felt the dance rising through her body, as if out of the ground and the sand, she had a sensation that a power greater than herself was compelling her to dance, she had not danced since childhood, even though mother had insisted on her acquiring the habit of dancing to the orishas, as life had been making her more concerned about other matters, markets and the status of Ketu, and the friendships she had made on her travels, the trips to the Water House and her son who was to be king, then she had got up as if dragged by someone, mother must have sensed that her daughter needed to move away because she had remained all the more firmly seated on the sand at the very moment Abionan had gone dancing off, with arms in air, her feet furrowing the beach in a rather slow dance, her hands lingered a moment in mid-air, then dropped, the daughter would come dancing up till she was almost touching her mother with her hands and then retreat again at once, she had felt herself to be a little girl all over again. Ibadan market was there playing to her dance and every now and then it had taken some moments to pull her feet out of the sand, then she saw that the people around her were not from Ibadan market but the beach, wearing their colourful robes, the drums were also playing to the sea, Abionan was making the movements of the waves, her arms waved slowly, then they waved quickly, the sea ran through her from hand to hand and she was transformed into a continuation of the sea before mother who was gazing at her with eyes wide open, the members of the group had little by little ceased to dance and only Abionan was in motion on that expanse of beach, mother, the atabal players and the entire procession remained immobile, until, with sweat streaming all down her face, the daughter had fallen down beside mother and sat there tired on the sand, still hearing for some time the drums and chants, becoming ever less audible as they left the beach, until Abionan and Aduke had been once again left on the sand and a seagull in a low curling flight almost brushed them both.

Abionan had felt that her mother was relieving her muscles and was looking at her daughter with the look of someone expecting an answer, then she had repeated:

'I never thought.'

The body which by now had no weight, slumped down, the daughter was sheltering it and the tang of the sea grew stronger, the wind had blown up in a fiercer gust and Aduke's hairs had been tossed in the air, her face grew still and her eyes were beginning to shut while she had squeezed her daughter's arm, and said yet again, for one last time:

'I never thought.'

Her eyes had not altogether closed, they had remained open to the sea and Abionan had stayed there with her like that for a long while, mother's body resting on hers, the noise of the waves wrapping up the pieces of thoughts that, though not always complete, were passing through her head and disappearing without leaving behind any taste, Abionan had got up and, gripping mother by the shoulders, set off dragging the body over the sand, Mariana's house lay on the other side of the road, Aduke's feet scraped grooves in the ground, every so often the daughter would stop, rest a little and then continue, in front of the cemetery a man with three vertical marks on either cheek had appeared and he asked:

'What's up?'

'It's my mother. Would you help me get her to that house?'

The man had grasped Aduke tightly and looked at Abionan:

'She's cold.'

'Yes.'

'Why?'

'She's dead.'

The sound of her own voice announcing the death of her mother had seemed to come from someone else, Old Mariana had appeared at the window then disappeared, two men had come down from the Water House and together with the man with the three marks had carried the body up the steps, Abionan came up behind and Mariana had ordered the body to be laid out on the living room table, she found sheets, lit candles and finally asked:

'What do you want to be done?'

'I want to take her by lorry to Ketu. I'm going to bury her where she asked to be buried.'

The old woman had nodded her agreement, Abionan had sat down in the living room with her eyes fixed on mother's face, Old Mariana had closed Aduke's eyes and set the body about with flowers but the girl needed nothing else to be done, she had heard the rumble of a vehicle outside and Mariana had come to tell her:

'The lorry's arrived.'

She had pointed to a short dour-looking man.

'This is Manuel who's going to accompany you to Ketu.'

They had laid out several mats in the lorry, sad-coloured mats, Aduke's body had been carried by the men who laid it on the mats, Mariana had followed the men's work and then said to Abionan:

'The girl's in Paris.'

'I know.'

'Do you want me to come with you too?'

'Please, that's not necessary. I'm so sorry for all this trouble, but she did so want to see the sea. I had to bring her here.'

Old Mariana seemed to have thought before saying:

'You did quite rightly. She had to see the sea.'

Abionan had climbed into the lorry and the man called Manuel had done too, this time the journey hadn't so many jolts, the lorry had driven slowly, but the girl didn't manage to see the driver's face, in Porto Novo, Manuel asked whether she had had anything to eat, Abionan said no but asked whether they could get down as she thought to herself that now she had ceased to hurry, she was left alone with mother in an empty, dimly lit street but the men hadn't delayed, Manuel climbed up in silence to seat himself next to the body and Abionan, as night had encircled them all, the daughter was looking at the stars in the sky and had hardly noticed when they had passed through Sekete, frail lights had come from the houses, and it must have been late, and so she would find everybody asleep in Ketu, she would have to rouse the relatives but Pobe had still seemed to have some life left, in the market there were lanterns illuminating women selling their wares, she had taken a quick glance at an old woman with a baby on her back, would that be the mother or the grandmother?, when she had reached Ketu she directed the driver to the front of the house and then had got down saying to Manuel:

'Wait here while I wake my uncles.'

She had knocked at various doors, Olaitan appeared with a sleepy look and Abionan had explained that mother had died, the former was shocked:

'But how? where?'

'She was ill already.'

'I know, but I never realised it was that bad.'

'But it was. And everyone knew it.'

Obafemi had come up and spoken of practical matters:

'Where are we going to bury her?'

'On the plot which lies by the road to Opo Meta.'

'Why there?'

'That was what she asked me.'

She had paused:

'It's her land.'

The uncle had nodded, his face was serious:

'I know.'

The house had all woken up, boys and girls had been posted around the mat, the woman carried out the body, bathed it and dressed it in a gay dress, Abionan was without a word following everything that was being done, Obafemi had asked:

'When do you want the funeral to be?'

'Tomorrow.'

'So soon? She had a good life, she deserves a celebration:'

'No. I want the burial to be tomorrow.'

Oladeji had gone out to talk to Manuel and had said to his niece:

'I went to arrange with him for the same lorry to take the body out tomorrow.'

'Thank you. You've done the right thing.'

She had spent the night looking at Aduke's face and had scarcely thought of anything else at all, a blank formed in Abionan's head as from time to time she would recall a phrase or a scene but could not link one with another, flies had come into the room and it was almost morning when she had seen Ademola.

'I've only just now heard.'

Abionan had nodded, meaning to say that she understood his absence, but hadn't wanted a lot of talking, her voice hadn't come and she realised that a celebration had been started, Obafemi was offering drinks to those arriving, they had made cakes and sweets, a group of atabal players were beating their drums near the house, the children of the family would come in and out of the room and at times they would run about gaily making piercing cries in the street, the odd person would come up and talk to her, but where would her market friends now be?, today as the day of Ogun, so they must be at Opo Meta, but she soon had recognised five, and then suddenly there would be ten market women all together in a corner, there were some of those who never moved out from Ketu and they had come over to talk to her, one by one, wearing their working dresses, there had been three with children strapped to their backs, in her memory she could hear Mariana's voice telling her that she had done right to have taken mother to the sea and that last journey had still remained with Abionan who could smell the smell of the canvas, the stop at Pobe had been a moment of anguish but that at Porto Novo had not made her suffer because there was a market close by with the fruit of the stall and the refrigerator, where would Ogundeji's lorry now be?, mother had made her last journey in it, and she could see Mariana with that quiet efficiency of hers, she had gazed at mother lying out in the room, she was even thinner now, her face more earthen, but serene, the tone of voice in which she had said the final 'I never thought' had haunted Abionan's ears who had suddenly realised that mother had now become a little girl, it was a little girl's body that lay there in the room, and when one of the little girls of the family passed by, it was Obafemi's daughter, she had noticed that the two of them resembled each other, the running child and the dead child, Aduke's body had shrunken in size, not that it had ever been very large and Abionan had remembered being surprised when she had found that she was taller than her mother, she had been used to looking at her from below but one day she had discovered that she was looking down at her from above, she had grown bigger than her, but now she had noticed that mother had returned to her infancy and the body that they were going to bury had come back to be the body of a little girl, she had seen the coffin arrive, three strong men had gone into the house with her, but it was a coffin which was too big for her, mother was going to disappear inside it, the body had been placed in the coffin and Abionan got up, went into the room where she had lived with mother, and had chosen the headtie that she liked most, necklaces of cowries and green, red and white beads, she had taken a green-and-yellow striped skirt and as she came out of the bedroom she had seen Fatogum arrive, he had remained in one corner and Abionan placed mother's clothes inside the coffin, she felt someone tap her on the shoulder, she turned round and saw Obafemi who took her over by the door and asked:

'And the market? Shall we go with her to the market?'

'Of course.'

'But it can't be today.'

'Why not?'

'No. Only on the third or the seventh day following the death.'

Abionan had seemed vacant, Obafemi had added:

'Don't worry. When we bathed it, we dealt the preservation of the body too. We also made a tiny mark on her right shoulder for her to be recognised should she be born again into the family.'

The man had lifted the clothes that covered the dead woman and showed the daughter the mark. Fatogum had come up:

'Your uncle's right, only on the third day.'

Abionan had wanted to accept the custom, to feel happy at the death of someone who had had a good life, but she knew that mother had missed something and her life had not been as good as the others had thought or as what she deserved, only Abionan could know how mother had lived, and how she had taken things for the daughter had understood her silences and her journeys, day in and day out, she had followed her sickness, so how could she pretend that everything had been fine and that a celebration was in progress?, but then it had crossed her mind that mother might also have been happy, who could ever tell whether having had a daughter almost constantly at her side and seeing the same places with her, eating the same meals and sleeping on the same mat, who could ever tell whether all that had not made her blissfully happy?, then she had shut her eyes and agreed:

'All right then, let's wait three days.'

She had remembered:

'We'd better send the lorry back to the Water House.'

Obafemi:

'I spoke to the man about returning. He said that Mother Mariana's orders had been for him to stay here till after the burial.

So everything had been settled then, without her they had decided without her that she should remain inactive and would have to wait three days, then she had looked outside where Obafemi, Olaitan, the aunts and nephews were setting out chairs for the guests and visitors, calabashes of palm-wine had appeared upon the tables, cakes and sweets and bottles of beer, the atmosphere got merry, a neighbour came over to bring her across to those at the table, the girl had gone over and heard another neighbour, Akindele, say in a loud voice that mother had been a great woman, and praised her in the style of a chant or poem, Fatogum had sat down by her and didn't say a word, Ademola had also welcomed the guests, perhaps mother was present there at the party, the daughter had wondered to herself whether Aduké would have liked what she saw at the celebration of her death or whether she would have pursed her lips one against the other in her customary manner of registering displeasure at what was going on?, she had heard people talking louder, Oladeji had reported to her that a stallholder in the market had fallen into a trance, would she have been under the spell of an orisha?, she had looked at Fatogum as if to ask him, the babalao had made a gesture that he did not know, Olaitan had also turned up to say:

'That's not right. The authorities don't want any more trances in public places. Even less in the markets.'

People had run over towards the stalls and there were shouts, shortly afterwards they had come past carrying a young girl who seemed to have fainted, her skirt was trailing over the ground, and the party had filled up again, more beer had appeared and in the afternoon Abionan had shut her eyes right there on the spot and slept, she had dreamt that she was in a big house, full of rooms and she was looking for mother through a whole number of rooms, but she wasn't in any of them, she could only see groups of women in the passages, some were going into the room on the right, others into one on the left, she knew that mother was amongst them but she went into the rooms and saw different people, then she went into a room and came across mother lying dead and had found that it wasn't a dream, she was standing before mother's body in the living room, how had she got there was standing before mother's body in the living room, how had she got there?, had she walked in her sleep or had someone taken her?, she had sat down but couldn't sleep or she could have slept without realising because all of a sudden she had looked out of the window and seen that it was night and the party outside had seemed livelier still, drum beats were mingled with voices singing, Abionan had remembered that she had an instruction to give and she had asked for Ademola to come and see her.

'On my mother's land on the road to Opo Meta, there's a small house with a tree in front, do you remember?'

'Yes, I do.'

'I want the grave to be dug in front of the front door, roughly between the house and the tree.'

'Leave that to me.'

Ademola had gone off, Abionan saw him talking with Obafemi, the two had gone out together into the night, the woman had returned and withdrawn into the living room, there she had seen old Uncle George, all of ninety years of age, he had come out of the front of his room to see the party, he had seemed only to have just learnt that Aduke had died, he had sat down by Abionan without saying a word, shortly afterwards he had pointed to the body and spoke:

'How can you die so young?'

Abionan had thought of her child's death for it was as if her child had died a second time, she had lost him in the market and she had lost mother by the sea, the little boy had been buried at the foot of a baobab which wasn't on her land, though it was the spot where she had been born but mother would be buried on her own land and would not be far from the child, both would be sleeping close to the road which ran from Ketu to Opo Meta and thus deep down in the depths of herself, the deaths of Aduke and Adeniran conjoined, it

270

had been one single death, the little boy had died and now the little girl into which mother had been transformed had died too, Uncle George had fallen into a deep sleep and snored every now and then, with the noise of the party outside only Abionan was awake for the old man was sleeping to keep the dead woman company, the new day had been gradually dawning and from the street had come the noise of a lot of people going to the market, Abionan had spent the next hours quite still and the whole house had returned to stillness, Yadori, the eldest aunt, had stayed part of the time with her and Ademola and Obafemi had come into the living room but they had gone out and Uncle George had sat down on the pavement in the sun, he had talked a bit to himself, things with no sense at all and at a certain point Abionan had heard him say 'my mother' and straight after reeled off a string of Yoruba words which she hadn't been able to catch, the day had come to an end without her being aware of it and it had been already night and the drinks had returned to the party, it would be the last one and they would be able to get on with the burial the next day, Abionan had rested with her eyes closed but without sleeping, the presence of Adeniran had become stronger, she sensed her son lying on the floor of the living room and now that mother had gone she was in an even greater hurry to give birth to a son, it must have been then that it had occurred to her that mother could well be born from her, she could even be her son, Aduke would be transformed into Adeniran, the second Adeniran, and perhaps the first one had died to allow her mother and his grandmother to come back into the world through the daughter's womb, she had been the mother and now would be the son, the two ideas had blended quite clearly in her head and she could see vividly how the birth would unfold as she looked at mother's body and thought of the mark on her right shoulder, then she had got up and tidied up the clothes and necklaces and in the morning she had seen Victor Ajayi, Yatundé, Omitola, Solange, Francisca and Tomori, who had stayed close to her, Yatundé said:

'Today was the day for Iro Kogny, but we didn't go. We left Idigny for Ketu direct.'

She paused.

'Will it be tomorrow?'

'Yes.'

They had stayed with her for the rest of the early morning, Victor Ajayi had quite motionlessly glanced at her now and again and

271

when the sun struck the wing of the door, movement had increased in the house, women and men arrived, the lorry had been standing outside and Abionan had got in the front, the men lifted up the coffin which had not yet been closed, Abionan's companions kept behind, and the procession had come out of the house, crossed the street and gone into the market, the business of buying and selling came to a halt, the women stood waiting for the coffin to pass by, Abionan saw the bread stall, the palm-oil stall and the meal stall from where a smell of peppers was drifting, mother's body was paraded past the food stalls, then they came to the stalls for shoes and ceramics and for hand painted materials, for soap from the coast, for lambs and for pigs, for salt and for onions, for maize and for dried fish, for herbs, for obis and orobos, then in front of the central stall where mother had worked and where Abionan now stood, the body made a stop, one of the women picked up some pieces of yam, two potatoes and one of the bigger cassavas and put it all inside the coffin, ahead stood the white flour stall and then came the one for white maize, then for smoked meat and the tailor's stall, the one for lace and blouses and the coffin turned off down the narrow side-street on the other side and took to the road once more, now the following had swollen, with women and men and children and a stronger wind had started to blow up, – Abionan had felt she was burying her son as well, but a child didn't enjoy the rites of death that older people did and so she had then opened a hole in the ground on which she had been born and buried Adeniran in the silence of the small hours, no one had seen the moment when she had rolled the child's body up in a cloth and thrown earth in on top, – filing, parading through the market, had been the body of mother and son at one and the same time, together the two of them had received the tribute of the stalls and the stallholders and of the holy tree, the lorry would wait in the street and Abionan again saw the man named Manuel, the body was placed in the back, Abionan also climbed on, and sat down beside it, behind came another lorry with Victor, Yatundé and a very large number of women, farther behind five or six cars and a third lorry to end up with. The procession had moved on to the Opo Meta road, where would the uncles and aunts ,be?, they must be coming on in the cars, she had seen the road which she was in the habit of travelling between the first and second markets, she was ready and waiting for the baobab to appear, she had detected clues to its approach, it stood a little way past a house

272

painted red, the house had now passed, when the lorry turned a bend and she saw where the child lay buried, she felt the beginning of tears, the deaths were two and not merely one but the tears did not however come for she seemed to be dry inside, then she had realised that the lorry had stopped and Obafemi had asked her to get down which she did.

'Let's give a hand.' said Obafemi.

Ademolá and other men came up, they dragged the coffin down and set it down on the verge by the road, not far off Abionan could see the little house that mother had had built and in front, the open grave.

'This way.'

At uncle's word of command, the man had gone on to the plot, with Abionan behind, there were small bushes everywhere and just one larger tree beyond which lay the grave, the coffin had been deposited on the ground, the daughter had stopped and looked into the bottom of the grave, higher up the yellow earth showed bits of root, Manuel had jumped in and helped the coffin down, they had started to toss in the earth, the sun was beating down on Abionan's face as she remained there until the ground was flattened down and then she had thought that she would come back to place a stone or a piece of wood there, perhaps with one of Victor Ajayi's carvings, bearing the name of mother and her dates of birth and death.

Ademola and the uncles had surrounded her, Abionan announced:

'The house is empty. I'm sleeping here tonight.'

She looked around her:

'I don't want anyone else.'

And she had added as her face softened.

'Please.'

She had gone to talk to Manuel and thank him for what he had done, she had made to give him something in recognition, which he refused, she insisted and the man again refused:

'Mother Mariana would be angry with me.'

Abionan had spent the rest of the day without eating, afterwards everyone had gone and she went up to the grave and tidied up the earth, looked for some stones round about, put them down on the spot, when she thought that their pattern looked neat, she had sat down in front of the house and remained still, motionless almost, watching the day go by and the night draw in, and the people who

273

were passing on the road farther off, two days later she had been in Idigny talking with Victor Ajayi:

'I want a figure to put on my mother's grave.'

'What figure?'

'An Oya. Isn't it she who watches presides over the dead?'

Victor had started on the figure the very same day, he had taken a good bit of wood and worked till nightfall, Abionan had watched the head emerging, the hair parted on the crown, the eyes of the figure had appeared once Victor had tossed out several chippings of wood, the pointed breasts were taking shape, now you could see that it was a woman, the rest of the body, the navel, the legs and the clearage of the sex Victor had cut out with a finer knife, on top of the head a piece of wood had been left which Abionan had still not grasped or quite understood what it was, it turned out to be a kind of receptacle, the man had explained:

'It's for you to place your offerings in.'

The figure had been ready the next day: Abionan had returned to the grave, set the figure of Oya upon a bed of stones and stood back from the grave, she saw that it looked all right and when she had reappeared in Ketu market weeks later – for she had spent days without talking to a single person, keeping quite still for hours on end, gazing at trees stirred by the breeze, and the clouds moving over the sky and she had scarcely eaten – the market had greeted her with its same vivacity, and now here today, as she waits for Ademola to appear in the side-street, she is thinking that the time is ripe for her to have a bath, she runs out to her mother's room, takes some herbs which she knows will be in a drawer on the left, has her bath and on her way back to the market she smears ori on her arms and her neck, mother had always insisted that her daughter rubbed the greasy substance on her body, now as she begins calmly to comb her hair, Yatundé, who was looking at her from the side, asked:

'What's all this? A second honeymoon?'

'Maybe.'

Then Tomori was coming and she at once started explaining that she had not been round at all the markets the previous week because she had had urgent business to do in Porto Novo, how was Idigny?, and Victor Ajayi, quieter than ever? was it true that Abionan was also going to leave out the other markets and stay in Ketu most of the time?, as they were talking Ademola appeared walking down the now almost deserted street, he came up close to

274

the women and greeted them with a nod, Abionan said goodbye, a first trace of night darkened the inside of the market, here and there the lights were lit and children were playing in the family complex, Uncle George was sitting out on the pavement, Abionan talked to him as he strained his eyes to see who it was, he recognised her by her voice and Ademolá said:

'He sits here till nightfall. Round about eight he goes to bed. He wakes early with the children and the chickens.'

Chickens had helped in the creation of the world, Fatogum had taught.

Obafemi was coming out and saw the two of them, he asked Abionan how things were.

'Very well.'

'Yes. You seem happy. You two must be feeling really fine.'

The market was a happy place, the woman thought.

Ademolá went in the front, she showed him the room where they had lived together in the beginning, she saw that everything was neat and tidy with a pretty bedspread on the bed and said:

'Mother's is a lot bigger.'

Mother is gold, Casimir had explained to her, but mother's room had no bed, just a mat, Abionan was used to mats, she felt all wrong on that floppy padded thing called a mattress and had found Ademola making love to her on top of that thing quite unpleasant, but she had to some extent grown used to this, though today she was quite able to sleep on a mattress, something which had formerly always been beyond her means, Abionan saw that Ademola had done everything possible to make her happy and she admitted as much:

'It looks all very nice.'

However:

'But let's talk outside first.'

They each took a chair, set them side by side, one of the cousins who was seven years old, went up to Abionan, said something that the girl didn't understand and ran off after the other girls.

Ademola asked:

'Do you miss both him and her very much?'

What on earth was the use of explaining, he wouldn't understand, for him missing someone was perhaps like being unable each afternoon to have the beer to which his body had grown used, she nevertheless smiled:

All of night had fallen and his voice was pleasant:

'It was a shame.'

'What was?'

'That you didn't take up the shop in Cotonou.'

'Why?'

'It would have been a good place for us to live.'

'What do you mean?'

'Of course. It's a big city, a go-ahead place.'

What was the point in arguing, if Ketu was right there sharp and clear in front of him and he simply couldn't see it, arguing would change nothing but she did all the same observe:

'Big cities do have their drawbacks.'

He didn't ask what the drawbacks were but started as if trying to persuade her:

'It's better for the children to study.'

'That's true, but only at the right time.'

She thought a little:

'But you can live in Cotonou.'

He wanted to know how:

'By going to keep uncle's shop for him.'

Ademolá laughed and the tone of his laugh was pleasant:

'For one thing, he hasn't asked me. Secondly, I don't think he'd trust me enough:'

'Isn't there a third reason?'

'What?'

'You wouldn't like to stay in a shop the whole day long.'

He laughed even more.

'That's right.'

She thought of Yatundé, Solange and Omitola who must by now be on the road to Opo Meta:

'It's best that we go on like this.'

'Really?'

'You doing business from time to time, going to Porto Novo and Cotonou as and when necessary, and myself in the market.'

'All four of them?'

'Or perhaps just in Ketu.'

Olaitan came up from the street and saw Abionan and Ademola.

'Well how about that? The couple of you all nice and cosy together.'

'That's it.' retored the woman.

The uncle gave a suspicious look.

'So you've decided to live at home again?'

She seriously:

'No. I'm just visiting.'

'So I see.'

Ademola didn't seem to pay any importance to the other but waited for him to go away:

'You never hide the fact you don't like him.'

How could she say that Olaitan could have been responsible for the death of her child, Ademolá wouldn't really understand and there was such a lot he didn't understand:

The man made an invitation:

'Shall we have something to eat?'

They did. They crossed the street as they made towards the market, there was a house that sold soft drinks, alcohol and meals, and that was where Ademola went in, Abionan ate without knowing what she was eating and on the way out it was her turn to make an invitation:

'Let's go and see how the market's going?'

'Empty.'

'Not altogether.'

She went in at the front, women and children were sleeping on mats, lanterns lit up slices of the insides of the stalls, two men were playing ayo, one of them was switching the stones from hole to hole at great speed and Ademola wanted to go home but she said no.

'Don't you? really?'

Abionan confirmed that she didn't and said she had another idea.

'What's that?'

'Let's go for a stroll along the road to Opo Meta.'

'Whatever for?'

'It'll be nicer.'

The man stared at her in distrust.

'Don't you really want to sleep in the house where your mother's buried, eh?'

She laughed:

'Maybe not.'

They were close to each other. Ademola clutched her by the shoulders and pressed himself tightly against her breasts:

'Let's stay in Ketu.

'No.'

She ran off beyond the holy tree and stopped and waited.

The man, who had been watching her as she ran off, calmly started to walk over, caught her up and again clutched her:

'What sort of game's all this?'

She, in all seriousness:

'It's not a game.'

'Don't you really want to sleep in your mother's house?'

'I want to go for a stroll along the road.'

Abionan broke loose again and walked a little way along the street towards the beginning of the road which she travelled every four days, not long before her companions had passed that way, perhaps they would be bathing in the stream by now, she looked round and saw that Ademola was walking up behind her in no hurry, as though forced to accept a woman's whim, when they were together again the last houses in Ketu had already disappeared and he suggested:

'Here will do.'

She looked behind her:

'Too near the houses. Farther on.'

Ademola was baffled:

'You don't really want to do it by the road? do you?'

'Maybe.'

They carried on walking together some way along the now empty road, every so often a house loomed up amid the night with its lights standing out from the gloom, they found a spot that seemed ideal, two stones, one of each side gave shelter, and it was Ademola's turn to go on ahead, he sat down on one of the stones:

'Here?'

'Maybe.'

Abionan sat down on another stone, they remained in silence for a moment, the man seemed to be thinking and she waited for him to start talking:

'What we could do would be to have our own shop in Cotonou.'

She consented to discuss the topic:

'How?'

'Sell what we've got in Ketu.'

She seemed to be pondering what she had heard:

'We've hardly anything. The land which was my mother's is unsaleable. It's where she's buried. The property's at the complex in Ketu is also jointly owned'.

278

She looked on into the night, then she added:

'Apart from that, future men and women in the family will need the land.'

He lifted his eyes to her in distrust, he could hardly see her in the darkness:

'You haven't still got that old idea of having a son to become the king of Ketu?'

He paused:

'Or have you?'

'Perhaps.'

'You're all full of "maybes" and "perhapses" today.'

He approached her, knelt down on the ground and pulled her over to him, Abionan felt him kissing her neck and his hands squeezing her breasts, the man was looking down at the ground as if he was going to lay her on the grass between the two stones, Abionan stepped back and ran down the road calling out from there:

'Come on. It's very near now.'

He got up, walked over and then the girl ran again, he decided to run as well, the couple disturbed the still air of the road from Ketu to Opo Meta and in the distance, Abionan could see the baobab appearing and, farther on, there would be mother's grave with Victor Ajayi's carving and Oya watching over mother, the two stretches were about equal, from where she was up to the baobab and from there on to mother's house, but Ademola caught her up and leant her back against a tree.

'We're going to get very tired.'

'Maybe.'

'Don't give me any more maybes.'

She let herself be hugged but quickly pushed him off:

'The tree's hurting me.'

'We'd better go back to Ketu.'

'Now? It's a long way from here.'

In a twinkling, Abionan got the man off her and stood sad and serious, gazing over to the other side of the road where there was nothing, everything ran through her memory, her child lying on the mat and the sheet strained red, the river Ogun and the canoe descending the river, the market at Ibadan and Adimu making his figures, his hunched back sliding oddly out from his body, the trip to Osholgbo, the river Oshun and the temple, the war at Ejigbo, the man who had robbed them in the festivities at Ijebu-Ode, Mariana, the younger one, reading out the thoughts of the president, the stories of Sousa, the houses in Aduni, the palace, the Water House, Old Mariana talking with her, the journey to Atakpamé, Casimir going off to find the map, the market half way along the road, the river Oya, broad and mighty, the voice of Fatogum telling of what might happen, the tales he related of orishas and kings and Eshu and the Hunter, stories which they said were banned now, the presence of mother and the illness that had no name, the child who was going to be king suddenly dying, the flight down the road with the child in her arms and the baobab patiently waiting for her to arrive, the baobab beneath which she had been born, the strain to dig the grave for her child, her certainty that he would return or would it be mother who would return under the guise of a new son? and the final journey from the moment mother had made her request, then with the lorry driving through the streets of Pobe and through Sakete, stopping in Porto Novo with the fruit stall and the refrigerator, with its strange whiteness, being dragged as if it was an immobile motionless creature, the arrival at the Water House, the dune, mother seeing the sea for the first time with the wedding procession and the boy riding the wave, the clothes of lovely colours everywhere, and mother's voice saying 'I never thought', the journey back and the arrangements made by old Mariana, the celebrations in tribute to the dead woman and the body being carried right into the market, the figure that she had seen Victor Ajayi make little by little for she had kept near him all the time following chip by chip the birth of the figure of Oya which stood today on top of mother's grave, but arising amidst these images was the face of the second Adeniran, not greatly different from the first, but she could see him right before her very eyes, the little boy's face kept coming and fleeing, one day it would be the face of a man and the face of a king, Abionan realised that Ademola had kept back from her and was gazing strangely at her, then the woman smiled, and ran back once again to the road, she reached the baobab, hid behind it and heard the man call out:

'Where are you?'
'Here.'
'Where's here?'
'Behind the baobab.'
She heard his steps, they were hurried and running in the end, she

280

saw him coming, she was leaning against the tree with such a stout trunk that several men together, could not reach round it, Ademola grabbed her hand, looked about and the woman said:

'Here.'

He laid her down where she was born, pulled off her clothes which he threw aside, he opened her legs, all the while Abionan recalled the moments when she squeezed the first Adeniran in her arms before making him the grave, on that ground upon which mother had brought her forth splashing blood on the earth, on the ground where she had buried her son, Adeniran, King of Ketu, and on that ground there would start to exist and start to form the new Adeniran, strong, king of Ketu, her own son, king, king, king of Ketu.

Rio de Janeiro – London – Rio de Janeiro
From 17 August 1978 to 27 July 1980